Contents

1 COMMERCE 4

2 CRIME AND PUNISHMENT 31

3 INTERNATIONAL AFFAIRS 59

4 MILITARY MATTERS 75

5 SCIENCE AND NATURE 95

6 TRANSPORT 106

7 POLITICS AND GOVERNMENT 118

8 PUBLIC LIFE 142

9 ROYALTY 153

10 ARTS, SPORT AND LEISURE 174

1   COMMERCE

 1808   *The last slave trading*

The international slave trade was one of the commercial activities that made Britain a major world power in the 18th century. It had been started, almost casually, by Elizabethan adventurers and explorers in the 16th century. The British slave trade developed into a well-organized and lucrative export business, running primarily from the ports of Liverpool, London and Bristol, before it was abolished by law in 1807.

For British business the trade in human chattel became a means of selling British goods abroad. English cloth and other goods were shipped to the west coast of Africa where they were exchanged for slaves. The slave cargoes were then carried across the Atlantic Ocean, under conditions of great hardship and danger – the infamous 'middle passage' – to be sold in the West Indies and America. The ships returned to their English ports laden with sugar, tobacco and cotton to be manufactured into more cloth for later export.

The perpetrators of this barbarous trade were largely shielded from the sights of their cruel business. The prosperous merchants and their families in Liverpool and Bristol avoided all real contact with this transaction in human misery. All they saw were commercial goods leaving port in their ships, exotic products returning from the West Indies and money accumulating in their banks. About 200 ships, or 'slavers', were involved in the trade, carrying about 50,000 slaves from Africa to the Americas every year.

The first serious attempt by the British government to stop the trade was in 1806 when a law was passed prohibiting the re-export of slaves from British colonies. William Wilberforce was one the campaigners responsible for this law, which stopped slaves in the West Indies from being sold on to plantations in the USA. The primary export of slaves from Africa, however, continued. The anti-slavery campaigner, Charles James Fox, pledged in the House of Commons that 'The African slave trade was contrary to the principles of justice and humanity and would, with all practicable expedition, be abolished.'

A year later the government, led by Lord Grenville, found itself with two pledges to carry out: Catholic emancipation and the abolition of the slave trade, both fiercely opposed by the King and much of the aristocracy. The government pushed Catholic emancipation to one side and chose to address the slavery issue. In the House of Lords a rearguard action was fought by a number of peers. However, positive testimonies for the slave trade from a few slave captains proved too weak. The measure to abolish the trade was passed in both Houses and became law on 25 March 1807.

The slave merchants were allowed a few months' grace. They were given until May to depart from the country on their last trip; and the year's end to cease their trade. The last few months were hectic for British slavers and slaves were crammed even more tightly into the dark holds. But by 1 January 1808 the last legal cargo of human beings

THE GUINNESS BOOK
of
LASTS

CHRISTOPHER SLEE

GUINNESS PUBLISHING

For Liz

HAMPSHIRE COUNTY LIBRARY

RO32. 02 | 0851127835

C003268515

Published in Great Britain by
Guinness Publishing Ltd
33 London Road, Enfield, Middlesex EN2 6DJ

'Guinness' is a registered trademark of
Guinness Publishing Ltd

First published 1994

Copyright © Christopher Slee 1994

All rights reserved. No part of this publication may be reproduced,
stored in a retrieval system or transmitted in any form or by any
means, electronic, mechanical, photocopying, recording or
otherwise, without the prior permission of the publishers and
copyright holder.

ISBN 0–85112–783–5

A catalogue record for this book is available from the
British Library

Designed by Stonecastle Graphics Ltd
Picture Research by Image Select
Typeset by Ace Filmsetting Ltd, Frome, Somerset
Printed and bound in Great Britain by
The Bath Press, Bath

Front cover illustrations clockwise: The dodo,
the burning of the *Hindenburg*, General Custer and Ruth Ellis.

had been landed in the West Indies. The slave trade was dealt another blow that year when the USA also ended the importation of slaves. At the Congress of Vienna in 1814–15 Britain persuaded most other European nations to impose similar bans on their slave traders. In other parts of the world it continued: in Brazil, for instance, the trade continued until the 1850s.

Slavery itself, however, continued, even in British colonies. Total emancipation and freedom for slaves was still only an aspiration for the abolitionists. Illegal slave-trading by British captains and other nations also continued, and it took many more years to disappear.

Britain's naval strength was used to enforce the trading laws and to capture ships carrying the illicit cargoes of slaves from Africa across the Atlantic. But as long as there was a legal basis for slavery somewhere in the world, the high profits to be made ensured that African slave markets would continue to exist. On Zanzibar island, off the east African coast, in what was reputedly the last slave market in Africa, the last slaves were bought and sold in 1873.

The last almanacs tax 1833

A patent of monopoly, granted during the reign of James I (1603–25), allowed only a single publisher in Britain, the Stationers Company, to produce and sell almanacs to the public. These books were issued yearly and contained a curious mixture of astrological jargon and useful statistics. The monopoly was successfully challenged in the 18th century, but a severe tax was placed on each copy which restricted their circulation. The tax was removed in 1833 causing an explosion of different publications of a new and improved kind.

Until 1833, there were only two 'almanacks' available to the British public. Anyone wishing to obtain normal calendar information such as tide charts, phases of the moon or any other similar statistics would have to pay 1s 10d, including 1s 3d tax, to buy a copy of either Moore's or Partridge's almanac. The reader was then hard-pressed to wade through the pages of mumbo jumbo, including 'remarks on the Divisions of the Heavens, with Judgements of the Eclipses and Seasons, handled according to the Rules of the Ptolomean Astrology, with many other things relating to the Truth of Astrology, calculated for the Meridian of London'. They were produced on poor quality paper to keep the cost down and had small circulations. The revenue raised was hardly worth the bother of collecting it.

After the tax was abolished in 1833, over two hundred different new almanacs were published within a few years. Soon there were many millions of copies sold nationwide. They covered every conceivable specialized need. Perhaps the best-known almanac was Whitaker's. Although it was only first published in 1869, it soon developed into an indispensable book for every Victorian household. Other periodicals and newspapers began the tradition of giving away their annual diaries or calendars – with or without advertising – of the type that we know today.

The last slavery in the British Empire

S lavery in its many legal forms, from feudal serfdom to the body-owning slavery on the colonial plantations in the New World, existed in Britain and its overseas Empire for hundreds of years. In 1833, after a long campaign led by William Wilberforce and Thomas Clarkson amongst others, all slaves in the British Empire were freed. The government compensated their owners, in effect 'buying' them to free them. In a famous court case in 1772 it had been ruled that slavery in Britain itself was illegal; nobody could be a slave when actually in the British Isles. For the abolitionists this was just the start of their campaign for full emancipation.

In 1823, with a certain amount of pious hope, the government announced that the colonial authorities in the West Indies should 'reform' the system of slavery. Abolition was still regarded as avoidable and slavery was defended in certain quarters as 'not only expedient for the good of the commonwealth and beneficial for the negro but also sacred, founded on the authority of the Bible'. This cynical argument grew fainter and by the time of the reforming Whig government of the 1830s Wilberforce and his friends found that their time had at last come – public opinion and the arguments of the intelligentsia were behind them.

A plantation owner in the West Indies announces to a group of his slaves that their slavery is at an end. Britain made slave trading illegal in 1808 and granted freedom to all slaves in the British Empire, after protracted parliamentary deliberations, in 1834. (ME)

Legislation introduced in Parliament to end slavery included the sum of £20 million to compensate the owners for the loss of their property. It was argued that because the law had sanctioned slavery – indeed encouraged it – it would be unjust to ruin the plantation owners over this matter. The British taxpayer, it turned out, was quite willing to pay the sum as the price of 'negro emancipation'. There were few to oppose the Bill as it proceeded through Parliament, and on 28 August 1833 the King gave it his royal assent despite his own personal opposition. Wilberforce had died a month before, but he died knowing that his great cause had succeeded. The law came into effect a year later on 1 August 1834.

A complicated system of transferring slaves to a temporary bonded apprentice scheme was part of the Act. Some colonies accepted the spirit of the Act and by-passed the apprenticeships to give their slaves full freedom at once. Other colonies, in a different spirit, treated the apprenticed negroes even more harshly than before. Whatever the variations, by 1 August 1838 all slavery in the Empire was abolished. The one exception was Mauritius in the Indian Ocean, where the authorities had to be prodded into action by the British government. Despite the discontentment of the plantation owners in the West Indies, the economic disaster that they had predicted was avoided. Their trading, on the whole, continued to flourish.

One of the outcomes of the emancipation was the 'Great Trek' in South Africa. The Dutch settlers, unhappy with British rule anyway, operated a very different system of slavery. Their black native slaves, despite their lowly status, were treated almost as household servants. The monetary compensation offered was considered inadequate and the Dutch farmers voted with their feet. Over the next few years they moved out of the Cape Colony, in great ox wagon convoys, to settle in Natal on the east coast and across the Orange and Vaal rivers.

The last of the stone bottle tax   <1834>

Tax reforms often produce unexpected consequences. Until the early part of the 19th century the British government levied a duty on all earthenware bottles and jars. By the 1830s the total income from this tax was a trivial £4,000 a year and it had become uneconomical even to collect it. Although an economic argument does not always ensure the reform of a tax, it did in this case. The tax was abolished in 1834, a move which led to a rapid expansion of the stone bottle industry. The unforeseen result was a huge increase in the production and sale of ginger beer – sold in stone bottles – the most popular 'soft' drink of the century.

The last Irish tithes

At the beginning of the 19th century the Church of England still required tithes, or tenths of the produce of the land, to be paid to it. Tithe payments to the Church of England, with a history going back several centuries, applied to all members of the agricultural community, whether Free Church or Anglican, and – particularly provocatively in Ireland – to all Catholics.

In every parish, a tenth of all the harvest was due to be paid to the local priest. Every tenth part of the grain and corn was stored in tithe barns to be disposed of as the Church saw fit. Some members of the clergy were more rigorous than others in enforcing the tenant farmers to come forward with their due. But, however applied, the tithe system – hitting only certain parts of the community and supporting only the one established Church – was an obvious anomaly that had to be dealt with. Unrest in the countryside, amongst farming communities as well as mill workers, hastened the demise of this outdated system of taxation.

Opposition to the tithes was best organized and, of course, most justified in Ireland. Daniel O'Connell, an Irish Catholic politician who had entered Parliament in 1829 after Catholic emancipation, was at the forefront of the campaign. The Irish 'tithe wars', as they became known, consisted of widespread resistance to paying the tax. Tithe collectors were beaten up and sometimes murdered. Curfews were imposed all over Ireland and the military had to be called out to retain law and order.

When Lord Melbourne became prime minister in 1835 O'Connell struck a deal with him and in 1838 a law was passed which replaced the tithes with a rent charge for the land, payable by the landowner. This satisfied the strong grievances held by the Irish and immediately alleviated the problem.

A similar solution to the tithe problem had been applied to the rest of the United Kingdom two years earlier. Payments in kind were abolished, but the tenants were still responsible for making the payment. They had to wait until 1891 for the landlord to be made responsible. In 1936 the rent charges were phased out completely.

The last private lighthouse

Today all British lighthouses, vital beacons for all navigators around the British Isles, are controlled by Trinity House, an ancient guild specially incorporated to do the job. But this was not always so. Many lighthouses used to be run for private profit. The last of these to be transferred from private hands to Trinity House was the Skerries lighthouse, in 1841.

Lighthouses have a long history, going back to ancient times in the Mediterranean area. In Britain they date at least from Roman times; but the first record of a 'Letter Patent', under the authority of the Great Seal of State, was made in the 13th century. The 'Letter' granted the right to set up and operate a lighthouse, the funding for which was to come from a tax imposed upon all ships entering or leaving the nearby harbour.

By the 16th century Trinity House had been established, and one of its prime functions was to operate the lighthouses required for mariners to navigate the waters around the coast. The first Trinity House lighthouse was at Lowestoft, but it did not have a monopoly on the business. Privately run lighthouses began around the same time. Some of these were held under licence from Trinity House and some were licensed directly from the State, either in perpetuity or under a renewable licence scheme.

The main source of finance for the lighthouses, whether Trinity House or private, was the dues collected by commissioners who visited harbours with the appropriate

The Skerries lighthouse in north Wales, the last private lighthouse in the British Isles. In 1841 it cost the government nearly half a million pounds to bring it into the national ownership of Trinity House.

letters of authority to collect money from the ships' captains – usually around 1d per ton – after entering harbour. This had to be paid before a ship's cargo could be registered at the Custom House. Similarly, before leaving harbour, the dues had to be paid again before clearance could be obtained.

Gradually the system was perfected, usually for the benefit of the operators of the lighthouses. Foreign shipping was charged double the fees that British ship owners had to pay. In 1819 the fees to foreign ships were reduced to those for British ships. Even so, full compensation was paid by the government to the private lighthouse owners.

As lighthouses became more and more profitable, Trinity House ploughed their profits back into the organization and into charitable and philanthropic commitments. The private lighthouse owners had no such worries. Abuses abounded and despite paying large commissions to their collectors their profits soared. In the 1830s, the 14 privately run lighthouses received as much income as all of the 55 lighthouses in the hands of Trinity House.

In 1843, a select committee of Parliament was set up to look into the matter and an Act of Parliament was passed which 'vested all lighthouses of England and Wales in the corporation of Trinity House and gave power to the corporation to purchase all lighthouses remaining in private hands'. This purchase was to include a very generous allowance as compensation to the owners for loss of income.

Gradually Trinity House negotiated the licences, whether permanent or renewable, from the private lighthouse operators. The one which held out the longest and was thus the last to be taken over by Trinity House was the Skerries lighthouse on the northwestern tip of Anglesey in Wales. It had been built in 1717 and initially had been a failure, as far as revenue-earning prospects were concerned. But with the explosive growth of the shipping business in nearby Liverpool, it began to develop as a very profitable operation later in the century. By the beginning of the 19th century it was bringing in over £12,000 per annum for its owner. Originally it had a coal-fired light (burning some 80 tons of coal a year), but in 1804 it was converted to oil and its tower was extended.

The proprietor of the Skerries was Morgan Jones. He fought long and hard to retain his privileges of ownership, claiming that an Act of Parliament gave him the rights over the Skerries forever. He turned down offers from Trinity House for £260,000, £350,000 and £400,000 without ever naming his price. Eventually the matter went to court to be settled by jury after Jones's death. At Beaumaris, under the High Sheriff, on 26 July 1841 Jones's executors settled for the enormous sum of £444,984 11s 3d, which was declared to be the purchase of 22 years of a net income of £20,042 per annum, a phenomenal sum in those days. It was the last such purchase by Trinity House and by far the largest.

Trinity House continues to serve the mariners around Britain today. The Skerries lighthouse in Anglesey is also still operating. Gleaming white with a broad red band, it was modernized in 1963 and is open to the public.

The last years before income tax

U p until the mid-19th century the entire British population was free from income tax. A temporary income tax was first introduced in 1798 at a then shocking 2.5 per cent (sixpence in the pound), by Prime Minister Pitt to pay for the war against France. At the conclusion of the war it was removed, its *raison d'être* having disappeared. But, as Benjamin Franklin had observed some years earlier, 'in this world nothing can be said to be certain except death and taxes', and, sure enough, in 1842 Britain's last income tax-free days came to an end.

Sir Robert Peel, with his free trade ideas, had set about rationalizing the taxation system. These policies reduced the money for the Exchequer from indirect taxes, such as customs duties, but increased it with direct taxes such as income tax. When reintroduced, income tax applied only to those earning more than £150 a year – a considerable and comfortable income in those days. It was set at 7d in the pound (less than 3 per cent). At first it was for a limited period of three years, but it subsequently proved impossible to abolish. Many Chancellors of the Exchequer have tried – Gladstone reduced it to 2d – but it is still with us and has increased considerably over the years.

The last fur trappers' rendezvous

 1842

The fur trappers of the American mid-west were tough, hard-living men capable of surviving in the harshest conditions. They had to be solitary creatures, going for months, sometimes years, without meeting another human being. Every year the trappers attempted to meet at a 'rendezvous', where, at a pre-arranged spot, they would exchange their furs with the traders and the agents of the big fur-trading companies. Their business over with, they would set to with their fellow trappers in a wild orgy of violent celebrations lasting many days. The trappers' huge capacity for endurance in the most rugged conditions was matched only by their equally hard roistering when they returned to the fringes of civilization.

In the early 1840s fashions changed in Europe, and the demand for fur, mainly beaver, declined rapidly. The annual rendezvous disappeared equally quickly. The Rocky Mountain Fur Company came to their last rendezvous in 1838, and the summer of the following year saw the last attendance at a mountain rendezvous by the American Fur Company. In 1840, on the Green River, a rendezvous was held with much of the trading, drinking and other excitements of past years. Finally, in August 1842, near the fort being built by the indomitable Jim Bridger on the Black Fork of the Green River, the very last open-air rendezvous and annual trappers' fair was held. By all accounts it was a quiet affair compared with the heyday of the 1830s.

The preference for silk for top hats in Europe brought about the abrupt demise of an annual outdoor jamboree in frontier America. For the fur trading that survived, permanent trading forts soon took the place of the mountain valley rendezvous and it was to these that the trappers continued to come to exchange their hard won pelts for money and supplies.

The last of the Corn Laws

1846

Imposed by the British government in 1815, the Corn Laws taxed imported wheat and corn and maintained an artificially high price for the staple of the working classes – bread. For some they were an iniquitous attack on the poor, preventing them from eating cheaply, depriving them of their very bread; for others they were an essential bastion to protect the country from economic collapse, maintaining the proper balance of agriculture and prices. Following one of the biggest political campaigns in the first half of the 19th century, which included rioting and public meetings around the country, the Corn Laws were repealed in 1846.

At the end of the Napoleonic Wars, foreign imports of corn started to flood the British market. The country's farming was in ruins after some twenty years of national conflict. In order to protect the farming interests of the politically powerful landowners, the government imposed high duties on all imported corn through the Corn Laws. Essentially, these laws prohibited the import of cheap foreign corn when the price of domestic corn was high; it allowed imports only when the home price was low. These rules were modified later to allow imports to enter the country at any time so long as high duties were paid. All this resulted in a comfortably inflated price for all home producers of corn and a high price was demanded from everyone when they bought their bread.

The town dwellers, the manufacturers and traders, were bitterly opposed to the laws which had financial repercussions for their own businesses. With cheaper bread, the factory owners could get away with lower wages to their workers; with cheaper foreign grain the ship owners could make more money by bringing their ships home from trips abroad with holds full of corn. All was not well with the farmers either, despite the price protection they enjoyed. They soon realized that with the high price of bread, the sales of their other food products slumped. During the early 19th century the unpopularity of the Corn Laws was only matched by the unpopularity of increased mechanization in agriculture and consequent job losses. Together they were the main causes of growing social unrest in the countryside.

In 1838 the Anti-Corn Law League was founded. Two of its brightest stars were Richard Cobden and John Bright, both at various times Members of Parliament. They used many successful campaigning methods that would be recognized and admired today. Creating what is now called a 'pressure group', they lobbied Members of Parliament, held public meetings and, from 1840, used the penny post to send campaigning leaflets to many voters all around the country.

In 1845 famine dealt Ireland a vicious blow. The potato crop failed and over the next five years over three quarters of a million Irish peasants died in the harshest of conditions. Despite deep resistance from members of his own party, the Conservative prime minister, Sir Robert Peel, decided to act. He had no alternative, and the Corn Laws were repealed by Parliament on 26 May 1846. Cheaper bread followed; it was a victory both for the 'free traders' and for the workers.

Cheaper bread was not the only result of the repeal of the Corn Laws. The issue split the Tory Party. Peel's followers, known as 'Peelites', comprised the free-trade advocates including Gladstone. They eventually joined with the Whigs to form the new Liberal Party, while the Tory Party continued under the leadership of the 'protectionists' Lord Stanley and Disraeli. Agricultural interests were also deeply affected in the long term. Many farms moved from arable to sheep farming to try to maintain their income. Sheep farming required fewer workers and so rural poverty increased. Imports of cheap American wheat followed in the 1870s and an increasing number of the agricultural population moved to the towns and cities looking for work.

The last of the window tax

One of the more infamous taxes devised by the British government was the window tax. It was first introduced in 1696 and lasted with varying degrees of strictness for over 150 years until the rationalization of taxation in the middle of the 19th century. Obviously a tax which was levied on house owners and depended on the number of windows in a building led to some strange architecture. It was common practice to stop-up windows to avoid paying at least some of the taxes. Some buildings were designed and built with false window spaces to preserve the correct proportions. More important, for the poorer classes, was the fact that smaller houses had so few window spaces that the health of its occupants suffered.

The tax reached its peak during the Napoleonic Wars. The government, ever on the look-out for ways of increasing revenue to pay for the wars, had increased window tax for a building with up to six windows to 8s a year. Owners of buildings with more than six windows had to pay proportionally more.

Window tax was finally abolished on 24 July 1851. Income tax was by then already a major source of funds for the government's coffers and it was an appropriate time to get rid of such an incongruous tax. Just a couple of months earlier the Great Exhibition had been opened in the Crystal Palace, in London's Hyde Park. The sheer acreage of its glass windows was a suitable monument to the new age of freedom in fenestration! False windows, often painted to resemble the real thing, can still be seen in some 18th-century buildings today – a strange legacy of a past taxation system.

The last Sheffield Plate

1855

In the 18th century one Thomas Boulsover, working in Sheffield, discovered and developed a method of making silver plate. A copper ingot, sandwiched between two ingots of silver, was heated and rolled flat. The resulting sheets were used in much the same way as solid silver to make high quality decorative silverware, but obviously at a much cheaper price. Sheffield Plate, as it came to be called, was manufactured in enormous quantities as a cheap alternative to silver until the middle of the 19th century when it was superseded by electroplate.

At first Sheffield Plate was used to imitate, as closely as possible, the solid silver articles it was replacing. This imitation often went as far as the silver marks themselves – the markings used were designed to look very similar to sterling silver hallmarks. Later manufacturers of Sheffield Plate became more innovative, and the designers began to come up with their own unique styles. In 1784 the silver manufacturers in Sheffield managed to get authority to register the marks they were using. Hundreds did so and the last one registered was in 1836. Indeed manufacturers within a hundred miles of Sheffield had to register their marks at the Sheffield Silver Assay Office. This included, much to their chagrin, all of Birmingham's Sheffield Plate factories.

In 1840 Birmingham had its revenge. The Elkington Company in Birmingham invented and patented a process for electroplating silver onto copper. This process was much cheaper than Sheffield Plate and could be applied to otherwise completely finished items, usually mass-produced. The new electroplated nickel silver, EPNS, very rapidly replaced Sheffield Plate, and by 1855 the Sheffield Plate industry was virtually dead, limited for a few further years to the manufacture of buttons, belt buckles and a few coach lamps.

Today Sheffield Plate is avidly sought after by collectors. Though originally a substitute for the 'real thing', it has a high intrinsic value as most items were made by highly skilled craftsmen. Forgeries abound – a sure sign of collectability. Ironically, electroplated silverware, purporting to be Sheffield Plate, is the commonest type of fake.

1861 *The last of the 'taxes on knowledge'*

The fight for the freedom of the British press was partly a battle against the taxes imposed on it. In addition to some draconian laws on libel and sedition, the newspaper proprietors in the 18th and 19th centuries had to contend with several different taxes. Most of them were intended to curtail circulation and thereby control criticism of the government, rather than raise money. The availability of newspapers to the poorer classes was thus severely limited. High cover prices, equivalent in some cases to more than a day's wages, ensured that the open discussion of political writing was the preserve of the rich. Early trade unionism was severely restricted in its influence by the high tax on its journals. The most notorious of these taxes, the newspaper stamp duty, was, after a long, hard campaign, eventually abolished in 1855, opening the way for a rapid and vigorous expansion of the national press.

The first newspaper tax was introduced in Britain in 1712 specifically to control the flow of information to the public. The Industrial Revolution brought a stimulation of intellectual discussion and a thirst for information. In the early part of the 19th century details on the war with France were eagerly sought after and provided by popular journalism.

All newspapers had to be licensed and each copy was printed with a small red stamp in its corner which signified that the publication was acceptable to the authorities and that the licence duty had been paid. By the end of the Napoleonic Wars in 1815 this duty was 4d per copy sold. It was extended to include magazines which previously had been left untouched. In addition to this tax, any advertisements were also subject to a tax of 3s 6d and the paper itself was taxed at 3d for every pound weight. Each publishing enterprise was then also liable to 10 per cent income tax. No newspapers could be legally produced and sold for under 7d. Despite this, in 1815 there were six daily newspapers with circulation figures ranging from several hundred to several thousand in London alone. The industry became highly developed in spite of the restrictions, but only the wealthy could afford them. The practice of renting newspapers for a few hours was commonplace and many regular readers combined together to buy them.

Many legitimate proprietors were not shy in declaring their opposition to the taxation. The *Examiner*, a weekly periodical, carried a banner on its cover explaining its price, 'Paper and Print 3½d; Taxes on Knowledge 3½d; price 7d'. Many different ways of avoiding the payment of the duty were devised. Many 'unstamped' periodicals sprang up, avoiding the duty. Being cheaper they became available to most of the population. Some unstamped papers achieved circulation figures of 30,000 or 40,000 copies, equalling and surpassing some of the legal stamped press. (The daily circulation of the famous 'Thunderer' – *The Times* – was around 40,000 in 1850.) The *Poor Man's Guardian* was a celebrated case. Established in 1831 by a Mr Hetherington to protest and uphold 'this grand bulwark of all our rights, this key to all our liberties, the freedom of the press', it boldly described itself on the front page as a 'Weekly newspaper for the People. Published contrary to law.'

Extraordinary measures were taken to prevent the authorities intervening. The newspaper's offices in the Strand in London were continually watched by the police. Dummy parcels were despatched from the front door to occupy the police whilst the real copies were collected from the back. Hetherington himself often had to enter and leave the premises disguised as a Quaker. He spent several terms in prison but eventually won an important court case in 1834 which established that the law as it stood did not apply to his paper.

In 1836 the stamp duty was considerably reduced, from 4d to 1d. The government realized that it was impossible to banish completely all illegal publications and it was felt that a greatly reduced tax (with free postage thrown in) might encourage acceptance of the law. The fight for the complete removal of the taxes went on. The Newspaper Stamp Abolition Committee was formed in 1849 by the Chartist Movement. Prominent campaigners of the day, including Cobden, Bright and Collett among others, formed an Association for the Repeal of the Taxes on Knowledge.

The last bastions began to crumble. In 1853 the advertisement tax was abolished. The redoubt itself fell in June 1855 when the stamp duty was repealed. Finally, the very last outpost, the iniquitous duty on the actual paper used, was removed in 1861 by Gladstone after a last flurry of resistance from the House of Lords. It had been a long fight but the result was cheap national newspapers. The first penny paper was the *Daily Telegraph*, formed in the year of stamp duty abolition. The *Manchester Guardian*, the *Yorkshire Post* and the *Birmingham Post* soon followed. A fundamental right for the British people to cheap information was established.

The last of the East India Company ⟨1874⟩

The British East India Company was established in 1600 and built up a huge commercial trading empire in the East. Its power was real and extensive; its influence prodigious. For most of its existence it was free from all interference from government and acquired powers and duties synonymous with the mightiest of colonial powers. The Company's final demise did not come until the latter part of the 19th century.

Although it traded throughout the Far East, India was the Company's jewel in the crown – in more ways than one. The East India Company was a vast and extensive administrative, military and civil empire as well as a trading framework. It had its own civil service, its own armies and its own traders. At the peak of its power this 'Trading Company' ruled with absolute and actual power over one-fifth of the world's population. In India it was known as 'John Company'.

The Company was not always scrupulous in its dealings and such independence and prestige was not fully approved by the government which was overseeing an expanding British Empire in all parts of the globe. At the end of the 18th century an Act of Parliament began to restrict and control, to some extent, the activities of the Company. Its 24 directors (elected by the shareholders) controlled the day-to-day administration and the strictly commercial and trading activities. There was, however, another system of control – a secret inner committee of three directors who were in direct contact with the government. It was this triumvirate which controlled all political matters. In 1834 the Company lost its monopoly of the far eastern and Chinese trade, and became an increasingly administrative body, with fewer and fewer direct commercial functions.

The trauma of the Indian Mutiny in 1857 was certainly instrumental in impelling the government to put an end to the Company's independence. After the Mutiny, the British government stepped in and swept aside the Company. On 2 August 1858 all the powers that the Company held were transferred to the Crown. British control in India, although arguably by today's standards flawed in principle, was to expand and develop into one of the most comprehensive examples of colonial government ever seen. But the British East India Company lingered on. Its smaller outposts were still spread throughout the Far East.

On 1 April 1867 the Straits Settlements, made up of Penang, Singapore and Malacca, were handed over by East India Company officials to the British authorities to become a Crown Colony. They were the Company's last possessions. Its business was finally over, and it was finally wound up in 1874. The greatest, perhaps the most powerful 'multi-national' company ever, faded away almost unnoticed.

1875 *The last chimney sweep boys*

The employment of children as chimney sweeps was one of the most iniquitous exploitations of children in the years up to and into the 19th century. Young boys, small enough to scramble up even the narrowest and most complex of flues, were sent up the chimneys to clean them. These 'climbing boys', as they were known, were cheaper and easier to employ than any of the mechanical devices available. Their employment in Britain finally ceased in 1875 after a long campaign, a number of Acts of Parliament and many unnecessary deaths and injuries.

A chimney sweep buys a child from his mother. Young boys, the smaller the better, were taken on as 'climbing boys' to scramble up chimneys at the behest of their masters. The practice was abolished in 1875 after many deaths and injuries. (ME)

The champion of the climbing boys was Lord Shaftesbury, ardent reformer and publicist of many of the social problems of the day. Employment legislation of 1840 had supposedly outlawed the use of young boys to climb chimneys, but enforcement had proved almost impossible. Although philanthropists and organizations attempted to observe and report the abuse, it was necessary to have an eye-witness account of a boy actually entering or leaving a chimney before the local magistrates would act – not the sort of evidence that was easy to obtain. A further Children's Employment Act was passed in 1864 but, again, it failed to define who was to enforce it.

Occasionally notorious cases did come to court, usually because the climbing boy in question had been found dead – often trapped and suffocated in a difficult chimney. Sometimes boys were even burned to death when a fire was lit beneath them. In 1872 a seven-year-old boy died in a chimney and his master was convicted and sentenced to six months' hard labour. The case was publicized by Shaftesbury and shocked the country and government. Three years later Parliament finally produced legislation which would work. All chimney sweeps would, from now on, require licences to carry out their trade. These licences were issued by the local police and renewed annually. Offending sweeps were deprived of their licences and livelihood. The law of the land had at last taken on the responsibility to protect the nation's children.

The last of the Metropolitan Board of Works ⟨1889⟩

The Metropolitan Board of Works was set up in London to oversee the development of London in the vigorous middle years of the 19th century. During that period London was growing rapidly; it required roads, bridges, parks and, more than anything else, sewers. Despite huge financial corruption at the highest levels of the Board it fulfilled its duty, creating much of grand 'Victorian' central London that is visible, and invisible, today. In 1889 a royal commission finally exposed its corruption and it was abolished in disgrace.

Joseph Bazalgette had been appointed Chief Engineer of the Metropolitan Board of Works when it was created in 1855 as London's first Metropolitan authority. His task was to tackle the capital city's enormous physical problems using London ratepayers' money. This he certainly did to good effect. Sewerage was taken off the streets and buried under them. Over eighty miles of vital sewers were laid, making London tolerable to live in again. With the rapid increase in population it had become an unwholesome noxious mess. If the London sewers were Bazalgette's most important contribution to London's well-being, the Victoria Embankment of the River Thames was perhaps his most visible. The Albert and Chelsea embankments followed. Many of the bridges over the River Thames were improved and re-designed and new ones were constructed at Putney and Battersea.

Whilst all this progressive civil engineering was being carried out, behind the scenes a more invidious kind of engineering was under way – corruption. The officers of the Board had been busy taking bribes on a large scale. Graft became a way of life within the board, all contractors were expected to pay huge percentages before a contract was awarded. Many humble officers seemed to be able to afford extravagantly expensive lifestyles. Something was clearly wrong.

By the 1880s it was publicly known that even if the streets of London had been cleared of noxious odours the Metropolitan Board of Works itself stank. It was commonly called the Board of Perks. A royal commission set up by Randolph Churchill named some of those responsible. No-one was prosecuted, but some of the most obviously guilty fled abroad. On 21 March 1889, much to the relief of the government and the London ratepayers, the Metropolitan Board of Works disappeared, its responsibilities taken over by the newly created London County Council.

Today the publicity surrounding the demise of the Metropolitan Board of Works is still remembered by enough people to serve as a warning. The scandal contributed to the rigorous approach adopted to prevent financial misdemeanours in local government today.

The last penny post

One of the Post Office's proudest achievements of the 19th century was the introduction of the universal penny post in 1840. Along with it came the world's first self-adhesive stamp, the famous 'Penny Black'. The cost of delivering a letter to anywhere in the British Isles was set at the standard cost of one penny (one old penny, 1d) and it was paid in advance, by the sender. Previously the recipient of letters had been responsible for payment.

The penny post lasted more than a lifetime – nearly eighty years. It became a symbol of Victorian stability and reliability. It ended, like many Victorian age traditions, during the First World War, in June 1918. The pressure of the war on the economy was irresistible and inflation was causing many prices to rise. The cost of a letter went up to one and a half pence, 1½d. The common 1d red stamp was supplanted by the 1½d brown stamp on normal letters. Postcards, which had been graced with the green halfpenny stamp, would now have to have the 1d red. Over the next 75 years, the cost of sending a letter through the post was to rise 60-fold, to the equivalent of 60 old pence, five shillings or 25 (new) pence, by the end of 1993.

The last of the Crystal Palace

The Great Exhibition, set up in Hyde Park, London, for 1851, was a high point in Victorian culture, a showcase for the arts, commerce and industry. It was the first of the great international public trade fairs that were soon to become quite commonplace. Prince Albert, Queen Victoria's husband, was the driving force behind the 'Great Exhibition of the Works of Industry of all Nations', as it was properly called. The Exhibition was held in the specially constructed building, designed by Joseph Paxton, and was very soon nicknamed the 'Crystal Palace' by *Punch* magazine. It was opened by the Queen in May 1851 and closed, at its Hyde Park venue, later the same year on 9 October. In 1852 central London saw the last of the Crystal Palace as it was dismantled to be re-erected later in south London.

In many ways the Great Exhibition, with its huge iron and glass building looking like an overgrown 'Victorian' conservatory, epitomized the Victorian age in a way that no other single event did (with the possible exception of the Queen's Diamond Jubilee many years, nearly a lifetime, later in 1897). The actual Exhibition at Hyde Park lasted for only a few months. During that time 6 million people visited it. Many of these visitors were ordinary working-class folk who travelled to London for the first time especially to visit it, paying the shilling (5p) entrance fee to gaze with wonder at the building and the exhibits from all over the country and the world. There were massive machines, boiler houses and steam engines to examine; there were paintings and sculpture to try to understand and textiles and ornaments of tremendous variety to marvel at. Above all there were hundreds of the most ingenious inventions that the age could devise.

When the Exhibition closed it had made a large profit, over a quarter of a million pounds, some of which went to purchase the land on which the Victoria and Albert Museum would eventually be built. There was much debate on the fate of the Crystal Palace. Some wanted it as a permanent centre for the arts, many others, including the government, did not. But it was the gentry who won the day. They had seen their 'Rotten Row' in Hyde Park – the centre for daily horse riding and general socializing during the 'Season' – blocked for many months. The Crystal Palace had to go. A company was formed, by a Mr Leech, which bought the structure, had it dismantled (it was, after all, the first large prefabricated building) and re-erected on 300 acres of purchased land in Sydenham, Kent.

Around 40,000 spectators gathered on 10 June 1854 to watch the Queen, accompanied by the Prince Consort, officially open it for the second time. Much larger and grander than it was in its Hyde Park incarnation, the Crystal Palace contained a museum of the different architectural styles of the ages. It was, however, intended as a concert hall and a permanent 'Exhibition Centre', again the first of its kind anywhere. It became a legend, contributing to industry and public culture, and gave its nickname to a part of London, a motor-racing circuit and a football team. The Crystal Palace was destroyed by fire on the night of 30 November 1936.

The last rationing

1958

In order to avoid serious shortages during the two world wars of the 20th century, Britain imposed various systems of rationing of essential food. The rationing during the First World War was introduced at the beginning of 1918 and was limited first to sugar, then later applied to meat, butter, bacon and margarine. The last First World War rationing was abolished on 29 November 1920.

At the outbreak of the Second World War, rationing plans were dusted off and introduced on 8 January 1940. At first they included the basic foodstuffs that had been limited during the First World War, but over the next two years more and more commodities were brought under control. Tea, jam, milk and eggs were rationed and were followed by tinned meat and biscuits. Personal items such as sweets and chocolate were also soon added to the list as were commodities such as coal, petrol and clothing.

Rationing did not finish at the end of the war; on the contrary, some of it was intensified. By 1947, rationing was at its peak, and it had expanded to include bread and

Women workers preparing ration books at the Food Executive Office in London just after the outbreak of the Second World War. Rationing was phased out in the early 1950s, but supplies of coal remained restricted until 1958. (Hulton)

even potatoes. From 1948, however, stocks began to improve and gradually all food became freely available off the ration. The last food rationing, for some meat products, ended in July 1954; coal rationing, the last, ended in 1958. The Suez crisis of 1956 caused an unwelcome return of petrol rationing, introduced at the end of 1956. It was withdrawn finally on 14 May 1957.

The last mounted post boys ◇ 1961 ◇

Before the introduction of mail coaches in the 18th century Britain's mail was carried from town to town by horse riders. As the mail coaches and then the railways and roads spread throughout the country, the use of post boys diminished. The last use of postmen on horseback, for delivery purposes, was in the Outer Hebrides. This service was replaced by mail van in 1961 when causeways between the more remote islands were constructed.

The last cigarette commercials on TV ◇ 1965 ◇

When commercial TV opened in Britain in 1955, Gibbs SR toothpaste shot to fame as being the subject of the first advertisement to be shown to the eager viewers. Cigarette 'adverts' were quick to follow and soon became one of the mainstays of revenue for the commercial TV network. In 1965, in response to the strong and effective anti-smoking lobby, the government announced that TV advertising of cigarettes would be banned. The last commercials were broadcast throughout the stations of the commercial TV network on the evening of 31 July 1965. Pipe tobacco and cigars were deemed to be much safer, and their commercials were to continue for another 25 years.

The last of the private libraries ◇ 1966 ◇

Privately run mobile libraries were started in the 19th century to satisfy a demand for novels that the public libraries seemed unable to understand. Mudie, an author and publisher, started his 'circulating library' in 1842 in London. He had a huge influence on the publication of novels, buying many thousands of copies of some of the more popular books for his library. Boxes of his books would arrive at arranged sites in shops and halls to be eagerly snapped up by his customers. Mudie's library lasted until 1937, but by then there were many rivals providing the service. The two largest were W. H. Smith and Boots, which had created their own libraries in their stores throughout the country.

As the paperback book revolution grew, and as the public libraries recognized and sanctioned the demand for instant fiction, the private libraries faded. W. H. Smiths closed their collections in 1961 and Boots finally cleared out their libraries in 1966. A handful of private libraries remained for a few more years but the age of the public municipal libraries had firmly arrived.

The last single-tier post 1968

The price structure for sending letters through the post used to be very simple. There were variations of course, postcards were cheaper than letters, printed matter was cheaper still and then there were parcels. But letters were simple, one standard stamp for a letter.

The last of the single-tier letter rate was swept away in September 1968. In came the new two-tier system, first class and second class. The Post Office took the opportunity to raise their prices at the same time: from 4d to 5d for a first-class letter. The second-class service stayed the same as the old service, 4d. The cost of postcards went up to 4d although no-one could quite work out whether they received the first-class speedy, next-day delivery or the slower second-class one.

The first-class service was supposed to deliver the next day – or at least 94 per cent of it, the Post Office claimed. Second-class was delivered the day after, or near to it anyway. Rumours abounded of sacks of second-class mail being deliberately left untouched for 24 hours but of course vigorous denials were issued.

The last high-speed pick-ups 1971

The Post Office became involved with the railways at a very early stage of their development in Britain. Sorting carriages were introduced as early as 1838, running regularly between Birmingham and Liverpool. Trials were conducted that same year, using equipment for collecting and putting down bags of mail from moving trains. Travelling post offices, as the sorting carriages became known, and automatic exchange apparatus became commonplace along the main lines of Britain. Express trains could deliver and collect mail to stations along their routes at high speed. In the postwar years, road transport became more and more important to the Post Office. Use of the automatic exchange apparatus on the railways was gradually withdrawn. The last known use of such equipment was in October 1971, on the line near Penrith in Cumbria.

The last BBC radio licences 1971

The first licences for receiving wireless broadcasts were issued in 1922. They cost 10 shillings a year and entitled the owner of a wireless to listen to the BBC's National Programme. A few regional variations were added over the years before 1939.

In 1946 the listener could receive three programmes: the Home Service, the Light Programme and the Third Programme. For these, the cost of the licence rose to £1, and a combined radio and television licence was introduced at £2. In 1965 the radio-only licence was raised to £1 5s (£1.25). Owners of cars with built-in radios were required to purchase additional licences for each set. By the 1970s by far the largest part of the BBC's income was from television licences. Most television owners also possessed radios so the system was rationalized by abolishing the radio-only licences (including those for cars) in 1971. Only television owners are now required to purchase receiving licences.

Newspapers: a few last editions

Newspaper	Established	Last Edition
Manchester Guardian moved to Fleet Street, as the Guardian	1821	1959
Morning Chronicle	1769	1862
Morning Post started by John Bell and was amalgamated with Daily Telegraph	1772	1937
Morning Herald	1780	1869
Evening News taken over by the Evening Standard	1905	1980
Evening Standard became the New Evening Standard and then the Standard	1860	1980
London Star incorporated with the Evening News	1888	1960
Sketch amalgamated with the Mail	1909	1971
Daily Herald Renamed the Sun	1911	1964
News Chronicle Formed from merger of the Daily News and the Daily Chronicle incorporated in the Daily Mail	1930	1960
Sunday Citizen founded as Reynolds Weekly Newspaper	1850	1967
Sunday Graphic Formed as the Sunday Herald	1915	1960
Weekly Dispatch became the Sunday Dispatch which closed in 1961	1801	1928
The Children's Newspaper published by the Northcliffe Press (Daily Mail)	1919	1965

PROFILE CUTTING
We can Supply all Shapes and Sizes of Plates up to
14 INCHES THICK
DUNLOP & RANKEN
LEEDS

THE GUARDIAN

No. 35,198 ✩✩✩✩ Manchester, Monday August 31, 1959 Price 3d

OFFICE FURNITURE
Are you comfortable?
See the wide range in stock
J. HUNTER, HEIGHWAY & CO., LTD.
St. Mary's Parsonage
MANCHESTER 3

ATOMIC QUESTIONS AT CHEQUERS

Lord Plowden joins in the week-end talks

LIMITS OF "BRIEFINGS"

BY OUR PARLIAMENTARY STAFF

Mr Eisenhower and Mr Macmillan in the Chequers week-end have practised golf shots, they have eaten grouse sent specially by the Queen from Balmoral, they have attended matins in the local church, they have paid a lightning visit to Oxford (while the rest of the company played croquet on the lawn), and they have talked over the future of mankind.

It was this last item which was given only a ghost of a mention in the press briefings which have been laid on with great ingenuity and even greater expense for the many hundreds of correspondents from all over the world.

It emerged, however, that defence and disarmament had been discussed—and that Lord Plowden, chairman of the Atomic Energy Authority, had taken part in some of yesterday's meetings.

The briefings held in a huge hired marquee on the lawn opposite 10 Carlton House Terrace have been a triumph of organisation. Mr James Hagerty, the President's press secretary, and Mr Harold Evans, the Prime Minister's press relations adviser, have determinedly plied to and fro from the front lawn at Chequers in their helicopter. Even their greatest enemies could not fail to admit their determination to give value for money. Not only has every menu for every meal been recited in full down to the Charentais melon and the Balmoral toast, but the full wine lists have been given with Riesling Rauenthaler Pfaffenberg's '53 and the rest spelt out with pedantic precision.

Change of film

The gathering was told yesterday lunch-time that on Saturday night the President and the Prime Minister saw the film "Tiger Bay" instead of what Mr Macmillan had described as a "medieval Western"—"Richard III." It does not say much for the attentiveness of anyone present that the question was not asked there and then why the change was made. But at the evening briefing the omission was repaired.

The reason why the party saw "Tiger Bay" and not "Richard III," said Mr Hagerty with great solemnity, was that the President has seen "Richard III." The reason why "Tiger Bay" was shown instead was that he had not seen "Tiger Bay."

Not that Mr Hagerty's technique has always been quite so primitive. At one point during yesterday evening's briefing he showed some subtlety in reading into Mr Eisenhower's and Mr Macmillan's drive to Oxford an inner, more significant meaning. It was not just the drive that mattered, so he told us. It was the fact that for once the President and Prime Minister were completely alone that really mattered. What they actually talked about must, of course, remain the closest secret, but the conversation, Mr Hagerty hinted, was on something rather more important than the scenery and the beautiful weather.

This was not the first drive that Mr Macmillan and Mr Eisenhower had taken together on their meetings. At Camp David, for example, they had gone for a similar drive and on other occasions too. The important thing was the personal conversation.

Press questions

Then, having given his wink to the blind horse Mr Hagerty sat back to enjoy the occasion. Unfortunately he was not allowed to. It was the political correspondent of the "Daily Herald" who broke the happy atmosphere and he was soon followed by others. Were any of these briefings to be taken seriously, asked the "Daily Herald." Were they meant to provide any information at all about the talks?

The answer to that was simple, said Mr Hagerty. The "two principals engaged in the talks" would themselves give their informal comments when they appeared on television. Did this mean, asked a foreign correspondent, that only television would get these comments? The press, he was told (such is the miracle of television), would get them at the same time.

At this point the diplomatic correspondent of the "Daily Mirror" rose with great dignity to say that "this is supposed to be a serious meeting" and with that every journalist present could agree.

Unavoidably Mr Evans was not present at this particular briefing (even a helicopter was not fast enough to bring him back from Chequers after the return from Oxford) but Mr Peter Hope, the Foreign Office spokesman, stepped in. His Foreign Service phlegm matched Mr Hagerty's doggedness. There was not a great deal coming out during the conversations, he admitted. After all they were private, and no one could expect to get as much on the talks as on the visit to church or to Oxford. He carefully hid any awareness of how monumental was his understatement.

Private meeting

But sandwiched inconspicuously amid all the triviality were one or two facts about the talks. Yesterday morning for about an hour before they went to church the Prime Minister and President as well as Mr Selwyn Lloyd and Mr Herter had a private meeting. It was held not in the long gallery at Chequers, where most of the talks are being held, but in a smaller room. There was no one present besides the four principals, and Mr Hagerty and Mr Hope had been instructed to say nothing at all about what took place.

Then after lunch the Prime Minister and President met for 45 minutes and discussed first defence matters and then the problem of nuclear tests. With them were (besides Mr Herter and Mr Lloyd), Mr Gates and Mr Irwin on the American side and on the British side Lord Plowden, Sir Richard Powell, Sir Patrick Deane, and Sir Norman Brook. On nuclear tests Mr Hope was able to say that there is a broad identity of view on what should be done next.

To-day the Prime Minister and the President will possibly have a brief talk before they go to St Paul's. It will have to be very brief as they leave Chequers at 9 a.m. On the other hand, by Mr Hagerty's ruling, the car-ride to London will provide the most fruitful opportunity for serious discussion of all.

Before lunch they will separate and after lunch Mr Eisenhower will receive a visit from the Spanish Foreign Minister. The President and Prime Minister will then meet for their television broadcast from 10 Downing Street.

[Dr Adenauer's letter to Mr Khrushchev, page 7]

SIR WINSTON BACK FROM NICE

Sees wife in hospital

Sir Winston Churchill arrived back in London yesterday afternoon from Nice aboard an Air France Caravelle jet air liner. After posing briefly for photographers he drove to East Grinstead Hospital where Lady

President Eisenhower leaving Ellesborough Church, Buckinghamshire, accompanied by the rector, the Rev. C. N. White, after morning service yesterday. Mr Macmillan can be seen behind them

Mr Eisenhower thanks the rector for sermon

PRAYER FOR SUCCESS OF TALKS

President Eisenhower and Mr Macmillan paid an unexpected visit to Oxford during an extensive afternoon drive from Chequers yesterday. They were warmly cheered all along the route.

Earlier, the President and the Prime Minister broke off their talks to attend morning service at the Church of St Peter and St Paul at Ellesborough, just outside the Chequers estate. Mr Macmillan read both the Lessons and the congregation offered a one-minute silent prayer for "God's righteous blessing" on the week-end discussions.

The rector, the Rev. C. N. White, said in his sermon:

"I bid you, in the name of Christ, to consider the significance of this occasion, which will be indelibly impressed upon our minds because two of the greatest men in the world have broken off their conference for a while in order to turn to God."

Signed visitor's book

On his way out of the church the President signed the new visitors' book just inside the porch. His is the first signature in it—but unfortunately his pen "ran" and his name is preceded by a blot.

Then the rector took the president's arm and led him to the north side of the church, where for two or three minutes they stood admiring the view. The President said to the rector: "Thank you a lot for your sermon."

There was cheering and waving from the crowd as the two statesmen drove back to Chequers. After a luncheon party attended by a number of British and American officials, in addition to those staying at Chequers, they continued their talks.

The President arrived at Chequers from Balmoral early on Saturday afternoon. The Duke of Edinburgh went to Dyce airport to bid him farewell.

Before the President left Balmoral the Queen and he posed together for photographs on the lawns of the castle. They lined up with the Duke of Edinburgh, the Prince of Wales, Princess Anne, and members of the President's party, then strolled over the lawns for a full ten minutes allowing eight photographers to "shoot" at will.

President Eisenhower turned to Princess Anne while one of the photographs was being taken, patted her head and asked her: "Are you going to learn to cook?" The Queen, laughing heartily, told the President: "I'll send you some samples." To which the President responded: "If you don't I will be bombarding you with letters."

After shaking hands with the Queen and the members of the Royal Family the President stepped into his car. The Queen with Princess Margaret and the Royal children were still waving when the car disappeared out of sight down the drive.

SURPRISE CALL AT OXFORD

Welcome by two college servants

By our Oxford Correspondent

When the Prime Minister and the President drove from Chequers to Oxford yesterday afternoon it fell to two college servants to greet them. Their visit was so unexpected that at the two colleges they visited, Christ Church and Magdalen, there was no member of the governing body on hand to welcome them.

Mr Macmillan, who is an old Balliol ... hower. Then they went into the Cathedral and into the dining-hall. There were few people about, but a small group of Americans spotted their President and by the time Mr Macmillan and Mr Eisenhower had left Tom Gate there was a small crowd to cheer them.

At Magdalen

The official cars went quickly down High Street to the main entrance to Magdalen College where

Indian troops missing

FRONTIER RETREAT

NEW DELHI, AUGUST 30.

Indian troops are pushing north through the jungles of the North-east Frontier area to search for 38 men who abandoned the Longju outpost to Chinese forces on Wednesday. This was stated by official sources here to-night.

The last message from the outpost, then almost surrounded, said the men were withdrawing under heavy Chinese fire, but since then nothing has been heard. As anxiety about their fate grew here to-night, press reports of further fighting on the frontier were denied by the Indian Ministry of Defence.

The Indian Communist party, commenting for the first time on Communist Chinese incursions on Indian territory, said to-day that the "territorial integrity of our people must be safeguarded."

Expressing concern over the "unfortunate" border incidents, the party's national council claimed that India's northern frontier had not been clearly demarcated, and said that the absence of any formal agreement between the two countries in this matter was "liable to give rise to confusion and misunderstanding."

The statement alleged that "enemies of freedom and peace are exploiting these unfortunate occurrences," and called for a peaceful settlement by negotiation.

Earlier to-day, at a public meeting, Congress leaders accused China of jeopardising India's security by violating her territory. They called for measures against Indian Communists who, they alleged, were working against India as Chinese agents.

"Firm measures"

An even stronger stand has been taken by the Praja Socialists, the main Opposition party. The national executive to-night called on the Government to take "firm measures" to make the Chinese "vacate occupied areas of our country." A resolution accused the Chinese of "ruthlessly destroying Tibet" and then turning "against their friend India," in breach of the five principles of coexistence.

The resolution said that the incidents on the northern borders, stretching from the North-east Frontier Agency to Ladakh, seemed to follow a long deliberated plan of action. "China evidently hopes that once she succeeds in breaking the morale of the Indian people, the defences of countries in South and South-east Asia would be greatly undermined."—Reuter and Associated Press.

Spinsters murdered: police issue man's description

A man, aged about 35 or 40, about 5ft. to 5ft. 5in. tall, with receding brown hair, is being sought by detectives investigating the murder of two elderly spinsters whose bodies were found after a fire in their flat at Chesham Court, Trinity Road, Balham, London, on Saturday night.

The women, Miss Elizabeth Ivatt, aged about 80, a bedridden invalid, and her companion, Miss Phyllis Squires, aged about 70, had both been battered about the head. Their bodies were found in a bedroom when firemen were called to a fire at the flat.

Police think that the man they seek, who was seen running from the front of the flats before the fire was found, might be able to help with inquiries. They say he called at the women's flat at about 3 p.m. on August 18 to inquire about an advertisement for a companion. His description has been

Spending more on leisure

LABOUR'S POLICY DOCUMENT

By our Labour Correspondent

Proposals for the arts, sport, the preservation of the countryside, and the revision of "out-of-date laws" which affect the use of leisure are contained in the Labour party's policy document, "Leisure for Living," published yesterday.

It is a more diffuse document than most of those issued from Transport House in the past four years, and in the arts and law revision sections particularly, definite commitments are less in evidence than broad expositions of the party's attitude. It is nice to know, for example, that the corporate taste of the National Executive appreciates the Old Vic but abhors the design for the English Electric Company's building in the Strand, but it would be even nicer to know when they think a National Theatre building can be erected.

"Practical postscript"

To any hard-headed Socialist who has found the coruscations of Mr Tom Driberg's prose style and artistic views and prejudices too much for him, however, the "practical postscript" should bring a measure of relief.

The much larger national expenditure on the arts and sport which Labour proposes would cost the Exchequer less than a penny a week per head of the population, and this would not mean any increase in the level of taxation.

The document proposes that the Arts Council should remain the principal dispenser of public patronage in its field, but should have its annual grant increased by £3 millions or £4 millions, which would cover the capital cost of building and modernisation where it was needed, as well as annual subsidies. The Government should stop doling out funds to the arts on a short-term basis, and should start thinking seriously of a period of at least five years ahead. There is also a pledge that a Labour Government would consider ways and means of encouraging industrial patronage by tax concessions. Other proposals include:

Music: The document appeals to the taxpayer not to begrudge subsidies to opera, ballet, and orchestral music, which must be the chief musical beneficiaries of public funds.

The cinema: A fair chance for the independent producer should be an essential part of the Government's policy for the industry's "rehabilitation."

Television: There is no intention of repealing the Television Act, but evasions of its safeguards by programme companies must be stopped. An independent committee would be appointed to advise on what changes should be made on the expiration of the B.B.C. charter in 1962, and the I.T.A. licence in 1964.

The form of national theatre which is proposed is that a national theatre company at the Old Vic should be linked to a chain of "suitable theatres," some of them apparently new, in English provincial cities, Scotland, and Wales. Regular tours of the main centres outside London should be a statutory obligation, and the company should be large enough to man more than one tour at a time. The prospect of a new building for the National Theatre on the South Bank site is not to be abandoned, but Mr Anthony Greenwood, M.P., the chairman of the working party responsible for the document, told the press conference at which it was launched that the commitment to create a national theatre within five years of the election of a Labour Government did not extend to the building.

A sports council, appointed by the Minister of Education, is proposed, which would receive from a Labour Government an initial sum of not less

[Continued on back page

90 YOUTHS IN RIOT

Break-out from school

By our Luton Correspondent

More than eighty youths yesterday broke windows and furniture at an approved school at Carlton, near Bedford, before breaking out for the second time in 48 hours.

When a Home Office inspector, Mr R. C. Hadley, arrived at the school at Carlton, near Bedford, to investigate a break-out on Saturday the boys demanded an immediate inquiry into charges of cruelty and lack of privileges. Mr Hadley asked for ten minutes to decide. At this some of the boys marched out in a body and went down the hill from the school. There they tried to overturn a contractors' wagon while others flung staves at road-mending vehicles.

Back at the school Mr Hadley announced that it would take weeks for a full inquiry to be held. The youths, aged 15 to 19, then smashed windows in dormitories, the engineering shop, and staff houses. Others dragged tractors from a shed and one boy was nearly killed as he slipped under a wheel.

Furniture wrecked

There was broken glass everywhere and a great deal of furniture was wrecked. Boys scrambled over the roofs, provisions were stolen from the school kitchen. The police arrived and asked for permission to go in and round the boys up, but permission was refused.

The governors decided instead to hold a conference at the cottage of an American author, Mr Talcott Williams, who lives near by and to whom the boys had taken their complaints on Saturday. The police withdrew, saying they were powerless to help. At 6 30 p.m. the boys broke into the store containing their civilian clothes, hurriedly changed out of their khaki suits, and made off across the football field.

Staff evacuated

By this time the staff and their families in six cottages had been evacuated, and the only man left in the school was the deputy headmaster, Mr William Dickinson. A police spokesman said: "We will keep a look-out for the lads and we have cars in the area, but with nearly ninety on the run what can we do about it?"

Only one remained behind after the others had gone. "The Home Office man told us it was against regulations to give mass punishment, and that they could only punish individuals," he said. "We took this to mean there would be victimisation. The boys were in an ugly mood ready for anything and anyone."

One of the boys who broke out said: "We could burn the place to the ground. We want better conditions. At the moment they treat us like animals. There is far too much caning and some blokes are kept here too long. My mates who went to Borstal are better off than I am."

WEEK-END REST ON ISLAND

Break for Princess

BRISBANE, AUGUST 30.

A barefooted Princess Alexandra was soaked to the skin as she skimmed over choppy waters off the North Queensland coast in a catamaran to-day during a break in her Australian tour. The Princess, who is spending the week-end at tropical Lindeman Island on the Great Barrier Reef, reached almost 20 knots and then asked to sail more open waters. But the skipper decided not to because of the rough sea—Reuter.

AVIA
OLYMPIC
FOR ALL SPORTS WEAR
Elegant and extra flat sports models from the Avia range of

One of the first editions of the *Guardian* newspaper. The *Manchester Guardian*, founded in 1821, became Britain's most famous provincial newspaper and finally dropped 'Manchester' from its title in August 1959. Within a year it was being printed in London as well as in Manchester. (British Library)

COINAGE

The last of the Tower Mint

1810

Coins of the realm were first made at a London mint in the year 825. When the Normans built the Tower of London, the Tower Mint was charged with manufacturing much of England's coinage and medals. In about 1300 this was established on a formal footing and lasted until 1810, when the Mint outgrew its premises at the Tower and was moved to buildings nearby.

The main part of the Royal Mint at the Tower was a huge room, between the inner and outer walls, in which many workers were employed in a foundry and rolling mills, turning out the sovereign's coinage. Bars of gold and silver were melted down to produce the coins that were to lubricate Britain's financial machine for over five centuries. The Royal Mint had overall control of the design of the coinage and, for much of its time at the Tower, produced all of the coinage.

But it was not only the manufacture of coins that established the Royal Mint as an important financial institution. Before banks were commonplace, the merchants of London would store their money at the Tower Mint. However, during the Civil War Charles I appropriated all the spare cash there to help with his war effort. Thereafter the commercial firms in London decided that London's goldsmiths were more trustworthy as the guardians of their money – and they paid interest too.

For much of its time at the Tower the Royal Mint employed some of the finest jewellery craftsmen and engravers in the country. Charles II, after the Restoration, brought with him John Rotier, a Frenchman who became responsible for some of the best coinage ever produced at the Tower. The dramatic improvements in the portraiture can be seen on the coinage of that time. His famous design for 'Britannia', still seen on today's coins, was based on one of the King's mistresses, the beautiful Frances Stuart, Duchess of Richmond. The office of master of the mint was an honorary position, once held with some distinction by Sir Isaac Newton. The post was abolished in 1870, the position now being nominally held by the Chancellor of the Exchequer.

The Royal Mint along with the menagerie and the armoury were firm 'tourist' attractions by the end of the 18th century. Thousands of Londoners were greatly intrigued by the Mint and its vast display of visible wealth. But times were changing: the Tower was not a suitable place for a modern factory and the pressure of space made the move inevitable. Premises were found at nearby Little Tower Hill and the end of the Royal Mint at the Tower of London came in 1810. By the 1960s, the Tower Hill premises were also considered unsuitable, and in 1968 the Royal Mint was moved to Llantrisant in Wales. The last of the coin minting at Tower Hill was carried out in 1970.

The last guinea

The golden guinea is a coin which conjures up images of treasure and adventure, gambling and lavish spending. In fact it was the major high-value coin in the currency of the British realm for a large part of the 18th century. Its general issue as a coin had ceased by 1797 but a special minting was made in 1813 to pay the Army, which was fighting in the Peninsular War. This was the last issue of the guinea coin.

The guinea had several different values in its long lifetime. It was first introduced in 1663 and valued at 20 shillings (£1). The gold from which it was made originally came from Guinea in West Africa and its nickname stuck. The first coins even had a small elephant emblem on the obverse below King Charles I's bust, to commemorate the origin of the metal.

At the beginning of William and Mary's reign the guinea was officially valued at 21s 6d. In subsequent years it often reached as much as 30s due to the generally poor state of the other (silver) coinage. By the time of the Napoleonic Wars the value of the guinea had been re-established at 21s. Due to the shortage of bullion, however, guineas were last in general public circulation in 1799. Bank notes and other token money were first issued at this time on a large scale.

In 1813 the very last guinea was minted. On the obverse was a bust of George III by Marchant and the reverse displayed the royal coat-of-arms surrounded by the garter. It was exclusively used to pay the British Army then engaged in fighting in Spain and Portugal. At the same time a half-guinea coin of similar design was also issued. The extreme shortage of silver led to the issue of a third-guinea coin (value 7s) which helped to fill the currency gap. The 1813 guinea has since become known as the 'Military' guinea, and because of its rarity is now highly sought after by collectors. After the Napoleonic Wars, the gold standard was adopted and a complete 'recoinage' began. The guinea was replaced by the gold 20s sovereign. Long after the coin's disappearance, the guinea continues to be used as a unit of currency, mainly in some of the traditional professional services, in exclusive shops and in many auction sales.

 ## The last sovereigns

The sovereign originally had a face value of one pound. With a run on gold and an increase in its price at the start of the Great War, the British government started to reduce the numbers of sovereigns and half sovereigns being minted. By the end of the war they had been replaced with new treasury bank notes of £1 and 10 shillings.

In 1925 Britain returned to the gold standard and the minting of sovereigns for general use was restarted. By the time the gold standard was abolished in 1931, the Royal Mint had issued its last sovereigns for general circulation. The very last sovereigns and half sovereigns for general circulation were minted in South Africa in 1932 and 1926 respectively. British sovereign coins were still traded regularly up until the 1950s in Saudi Arabia at a set amount above their face value. Today sovereigns are still minted, and as legal tender gold bullion coins are worth their weight in gold – about £100.

Guinea coins that are no more

Coin	Last minted	Coin	Last minted
five guinea	1777	half guinea	1813
two guinea	1777	third guinea	1813
guinea	1813	quarter guinea	1762

The last silver threepenny piece

1944

The first silver threepence coin, minted in silver, was issued in 1834 in the reign of William IV (1830–37). In the 1930s complaints about the small size of the coin caused the Royal Mint to issue a new twelve-sided 'nickel brass' threepenny bit in 1937, substantially bigger and heavier than the silver coin. The silver threepenny piece was last minted in 1944.

The last real silver coins

1946

Throughout the First World War, the silver coinage was made from real silver or, to be more precise, '.925 fine' which is 925 parts in 1000 pure silver and 75 parts copper. In 1920 the value of silver had risen too high to sustain this standard. The higher value silver coinage was debased to .500 fine: 50 per cent silver. The half-crowns, florins and shillings were last produced in .925 fine in 1919 and the sixpence and threepenny pieces a few years later. The last silver coins of .500 fine for general circulation were minted in 1946. All so-called 'silver' coins after that date were minted in cupro-nickel. Maundy money and other special commemorative silver money continues to be made from real silver.

The last of the old £sd

1971

When Britain's currency was decimalized in 1971, all the coins of the old pounds, shillings and pence system, £sd, were doomed. The decision to 'go decimal' had been made by the Labour government in 1966. The new decimal currency would be based on the same value for the pound but it would be made up of 100 new pence in place of the old pound of 20 shillings (each shilling worth 12 old pence). A number of the old coins became obsolescent; one old pound equalling one new pound sterling was all very well, but 2.4 old pennies equalling 1 new pence was bound to produce casualties.

The farthing had already gone, in 1960, and the halfpenny (ha'penny) would soon follow, never to contribute to decimalization confusion. However, the old, heavy, half-crown – worth two shillings and sixpence in old currency – would now be worth twelve and a half new pence – probably one of the most awkward coinage values in history. Similarly the old substantial twelve-sided 'brass' threepenny bit, worth three old pennies, would have to go – one and a quarter new pence had no place in the new order. The old sixpenny piece, which was to be worth two and a half new pence, had a temporary reprieve but it too went in the end.

The penny and threepenny piece were to go on 'D-day', decimalization day, 15 February 1971. The half-crown was last used and withdrawn from circulation a year before. Even after 'D-day', some shopkeepers refused to accept defeat and relinquish the 'old money'. Some shops continued to trade with the old coinage, using old cash registers, for several months before bowing to the inevitable.

Old pre-decimal coinage

Coin	Old value	New decimal value	Last minted	Last date in circulation
penny	1d	-	1967	1971
threepenny bit	3d	1.25p	1967	1971
sixpenny piece	6d	2.5p	1967	30 June 1980
shilling	1s	5p	1966	31 Dec 1990
two shilling piece (florin)	2s	10p	1967	30 June 1993
half-crown	2/6	12.5p	1967	1 Jan 1970

The shilling and two shilling coins had several more years' life left with new face values…

5p (old shilling)		5p	1989	31 Dec 1990
10p (two shilling piece or florin)		10p	1989	30 June 1993

The last sixpence

In Britain the public affection with which the sixpence was held knew no bounds, but it had no real place after decimalization in 1971. Originally introduced in the reign of Edward VI, and then made of real silver, the sixpenny coin was small but had a reassuring 'quality' feel. Although the Royal Mint had ceased producing it in 1967, the outcry at its intended abolition brought a half-hearted promise of retention. Sighs of relief were heard, and the coin, now worth 'two and a half new pee', continued in circulation. Some sixpenny coins dated 1970 were minted but were never circulated. Quietly, when no-one was looking, the coin was withdrawn from circulation and ceased to be legal tender in June 1980.

A set of Britain's old pounds, shillings and pence coins specially produced in commemorative sets for 'D-Day', decimalization day, 15 February 1971. The date of 1970 on the coins was unusual, as the last minting for circulation purposes of most of these coins had been several years earlier. (IS)

The last five shilling crown

◇ 1981 ◇

The crown coin, worth five shillings, which had been in circulation for several hundred years, had nearly disappeared from general circulation by the 1920s. Crowns, however, were re-introduced in 1929. They were intended to be bought and given as Christmas presents although some made their way into general circulation, and they were issued regularly until 1936.

The last crown to be issued with a nominal value of 25 pence, the old five shilling coin, was the commemorative crown issued for the wedding of the Prince and Princess of Wales in 1981. The next commemorative crown to be issued, for the 90th birthday of HM the Queen Mother in 1990, was set at a nominal value of £5.

The last new penny

◇ 1983 ◇

The word 'new' in front of the 'penny' or 'pence' appeared on the new decimal coinage until 1982. The last 'new' pence coins, 10p, 1p and ½p, were minted in 1981. The last 'new' pence 5p was minted in 1980. The new halfpenny was a short-lived coin. Introduced on 'D-day', decimalization day, in 1971, it lasted twelve years before inflation took its toll and made it virtually worthless. It was last minted for general circulation in 1983, and in 1984 issued in commemorative sets only. At the end of that year it was withdrawn from use.

1993

The last florin

The florin, the old two shilling piece, was the last of the old pre-decimal coinage in circulation. Along with the original-style new 10 pence coins of the same size and weight, it ceased to be legal tender on 1 July 1993 and rapidly disappeared from public gaze.

The florin was first minted in 1849. Interestingly, it was introduced on a trial basis as a preliminary to early attempts at decimalization, having a value of one tenth of a pound. It was even nearly called a centum, but the name was dropped in favour of an imported 'gothic'-sounding word to avoid confusion with the lesser 'cent' from the USA. Originally minted in silver, the florin ended its days, like all other modern 'silver' coinage, made of cupro-nickel, an alloy of 75 per cent copper and 25 per cent nickel.

In 1887 a double florin, worth four shillings, was introduced as a continuing experiment towards decimalization. It was sometimes known as the 'barmaid's grief' as it was easily confused with the crown coin worth another shilling more. The double florin was never a popular coin and minting ceased in 1890.

The old two shilling piece was last officially called a 'florin' in 1936 with the last of the George V currency. In 1937 with the George VI coinage, the word 'florin' was omitted and the new coin was enscribed with the words 'two shillings'. When the currency was decimalized in 1971, the two shilling piece carried on in circulation. New coins of the same size and weight were minted, first as 'ten new pence' and then in 1981, simply as 'ten pence'. The 'florin', or two shilling piece, or old size ten (new) pence piece was last minted in 1989 and was replaced with the smaller and much lighter ten pence coin (along with its half-sized companion the new 5p coin).

Its demise in 1993 lightened the purses and pockets of the nation, but deprived the nation of its final reminder of the old pounds, shillings and pence. In theory, old shillings dating from 1816 and old florins dating from 1849 could have been used as legal tender until well after decimalization. The likelihood of finding such old silver coins in one's small change was small. However, their real silver content had made them collector's items many years before.

'Copper' coins that are no more

Coin	Value (old currency)	Last minted	Coin	Value (old currency)	Last minted
quarter farthing	$\frac{1}{16}$d	1853	third farthing	$\frac{1}{12}$d	1913
half farthing	$\frac{1}{8}$d	1856	farthing	$\frac{1}{4}$d	1956
three halfpence	1$\frac{1}{2}$d	1862	halfpenny	$\frac{1}{2}$d	1967
groat*	4d	1888	two pence (old currency)	2d	1797

*The groat, a coin worth four pennies, is still minted as Maundy Money. The reigning sovereign gives it, with other coins, to pensioners at the annual Maundy service, but it is never issued for general circulation.

CRIME AND PUNISHMENT 2

The last royal execution

1685

The last 'royal' to suffer the ultimate penalty, for treason, was James, the Duke of Monmouth, the first-born of Charles II's many illegitimate sons. Proximity by blood to an unpopular reigning sovereign was always a dangerous condition. Any aspirations to the throne were often quickly snuffed out by a royal execution.

The Duke of Monmouth took his treasonous plans too far, his rebellion against his uncle, James II, was crushed at Sedgemoor in 1685 and his pleas for mercy were not granted. His execution was carried out by the original bungling executioner, Jack Ketch. Ketch swung his blunt axe at the Duke's neck several times before his assistants had to step in to finish the job with their knives.

The last criminal witches in Britain

1712

Witchcraft, the application of supposed magical or supernatural powers to bring about an evil outcome, has usually been treated with vigorous persecution by the authorities. Belief in the existence of witchcraft was encouraged by the Church. Superstitions about witches and their connections with Satan abounded. The most commonly exposed 'witches' were generally lonely old women who were the least able members of the community to defend themselves, both physically and in courts of law.

Witchcraft was a recognized crime in Britain for a relatively short period, from 1542 until 1736 when the witchcraft act was repealed and removed from the statute books. This action formally abolished the death penalty for witchcraft but parliament at the time was unable to resist the retention of a penalty of one year's imprisonment for 'telling fortunes or pretending to locate stolen or lost property'.

In most of Europe, including Scotland, during the years when witchcraft was a crime punishable by death, the execution was by burning, in England the penalty was mere hanging. King James VI of Scotland, later to become James I of England, was thoroughly engrossed in the increasing hysteria against supposed witches. In the late 16th and early 17th centuries thousands of unfortunate women were 'detected', brought to trial and executed.

The most absurd accusations were made against women; even quite normal behaviour was interpreted in the most preposterous way to prove witchery. In the middle of the 17th century one of the most ardent searchers of witches was the Witch Finder

General, Matthew Hopkins. He travelled extensively to unearth witches and his enthusiastic questioning was responsible for the deaths of hundreds of women whose only crime would have been some slight eccentricity of behaviour. Towards the end of the century rational behaviour gradually returned to most of Britain and witch hunting died away.

The last execution of witches in Britain took place in 1682. Three women, the sisters Temperance and Mary Lloyd along with Susannah Edwards, were hanged at Exeter on 18 August 1682 after being found guilty of witchcraft and sentenced to death by Judge Sir Francis North.

The last person to be found guilty of witchcraft in Britain was Jane Wenham in Hertford. One of her crimes was to be seen and heard conversing familiarly with the family cat. She was convicted of 'bewitching Matthew Gilston and Anne Thorpe' in 1712 but was reprieved later. The last woman to be charged formally with being a witch was Jane Clerk of Great Wigton a few years later, but she was found innocent.

Intermittent mob hysteria against supposed witches continued. The behaviour of the authorities, however, improved. In 1751 an angry mob at Tring in Hertfordshire lynched Ruth Osborn for alleged witchcraft, but the ringleaders were arrested, convicted and hanged for murder. As late as 1863 a man suspected of being a witch was drowned by a mob in Essex.

The last witch to be executed in Europe was Anna Maria Schwägel who was beheaded in Germany. She was a pathetic deranged creature who, having been seduced and abandoned by her lover, confessed to having carnal relations with the Devil. The Prince Abbott of Kempten, Honorius, duly approved her execution and she was put to death on 11 April 1775. The burning of convicted witches in Europe had ended in 1749 when Sister Maria Raenata, also of Germany, was beheaded first then her body burned at a huge ceremony at Marienburg.

◁ 1747 ▷ *The last head on the block*

The removal of someone's head with an axe was a method of execution reserved for the nobility. Tower Hill, next to the Tower of London, was a favourite site for such events. Crowds of many thousands assembled to watch their betters die, usually for the crime of treason. The '45 Jacobite rebellion ended at the Battle of Culloden in 1746. Among the many Jacobites captured by the English army was the old Scottish lord, Simon Fraser, Lord Lovat, found hiding in the hollow of a tree. He was brought to England and duly tried. He was found guilty of treason and sentenced to death by beheading.

Lovat was 80 years old when he went to the block on Tower Hill. On the day of his execution, 9 April 1747, two other Scottish rebel lords had gone to their deaths, the Lords Kilmarnock and Balmerino. Lovat was to be the last that day and, as it turned out, the last ever in Britain to lose his head in execution. He was extremely fat, with a very broad neck to match and there was some doubt as to the axeman's ability to remove the head with one blow. Lovat died bravely and the axe was swung so hard that it took the old head from its body and was buried in the block to a depth of two inches.

In 1760 when Earl Ferrers was found guilty of common murder he petitioned to be beheaded at the Tower as had many a noble lord before him. His request was denied and he was hanged ignominiously at Tyburn.

The tools of the torture trade presented for public viewing in the Tower of London during the 19th century. They included various leg-irons and thumb screws as well as the executioner's block used to behead Lord Lovat in 1747. (AR)

The last hanging at Tyburn Tree

Tyburn was the site for many of the executions in the London area. Its site, close to where Marble Arch now stands, is today commemorated by a short stretch of road called Tyburn Way. For hundreds of years it was a place of public death and excoriation. Originally the malefactors were hanged from one of the trees in what was the open countryside some two miles from the city walls. The tree, 'Tyburn Tree', was eventually replaced with a gallows, renewed from time to time as required. In the 16th century a special purpose-built gallows was erected at the site. It consisted of three vertical posts arranged in a triangle across the tops of which were the beams for hanging. It was called the Triple Tree or, still, the Tyburn Tree.

By the middle of the 18th century the passing traffic had increased to such an extent that the much used Triple Tree was causing an obstruction to the free flow of people and horse-drawn vehicles. In 1759 it was removed to be replaced by a portable gallows that was brought out on 'hanging days'. With time the area around Tyburn became a fashionable residential area. The obstruction to traffic and complaints from the locals about the rowdy behaviour of the spectators at the regular hangings eventually prompted the authorities to end hangings at Tyburn.

John Austen was the last to meet his end on the Tyburn Tree on 7 November 1783. The street outside Newgate prison, in the heart of London, became the site for most of the subsequent public executions in the London area. The city of York also had an execution spot called Tyburn for most of the 18th century. The gallows outside the city walls were last used in 1801.

1789 *The last execution by burning*

If witches were never judicially burned to death in England, there were other categories of crime that specified burning at the stake. A woman who murdered her husband, a crime legally regarded as 'petty treason', could expect flames and smoke as her last sight on earth as could women convicted of 'coining' or forgery.

A woman called Murphy was one of a gang of coiners convicted in London in 1789. She was burned to death, presided over by the public executioner of the time, William Brunskill. Her male colleagues in crime were simply hanged. The law was changed the following year and Murphy thus became the last person in Britain to die a fiery judicial death.

1809 *The last of the ducking stool*

The ducking stool and ducking pond were curious methods of punishment used from the 17th century, mainly for women. It was employed for the fairly trivial offences of 'quarrelling' and 'gossiping' but sometimes for blatant dishonesty; the excessive watering down of beer was a common example. It seldom, however, resulted in lasting damage to the victim. The culprit was tied to a stool or chair which was attached to the end of a long beam. The beam was positioned, see-saw fashion, close to the edge of a pond. Controlled from the bank by a village official and some stout lads, the offender would be dipped into the water. The use of ducking stools (sometimes called 'cucking' stools) ceased completely in the early 19th century.

The last recorded instance of someone being 'officially' ducked in a ducking stool was in 1809 at Leominster when Jenny Pipes was paraded around the town on the stool and then ducked off Thenwater Bridge. Eight years later officials of that same town – obviously fanatical supporters of this particular method of punishment – were unable to carry out a similar sentence on Sarah Leeke as the water was not deep enough.

Many towns and villages had ducking ponds and the associated apparatus of a ducking stool. It was an alternative to stocks and, although the justice was rough, it was cheap and quick – and even provided some enjoyment to the public. Today, at the site of Westminster's own ducking pond, exuberant revellers still take soakings, usually voluntarily, in London's Trafalgar Square fountains.

The last execution of escaped convicts

1810

A sentence of 'transportation for life' meant what it said at the beginning of the 19th century. It was a capital offence for a convict who managed to escape from one of the penal colonies and return to Britain. Those few who made it back to the home country were hanged if caught by the authorities. Although this penalty was officially abolished in 1834, the last illegally returned convict was hanged in 1810. However, the transportation of convicts to penal colonies carried on for many more years.

In his book *Great Expectations* (1861), Charles Dickens gives Magwitch, the illegally returned convict, a literal fear of death on being caught. Dickens used true artistic licence to exaggerate his fear as the law had already been changed by the time it was published. Despite the abolition of capital punishment for unlawfully returning from transportation, the distance from Australia made it very difficult to return, even for those who had their full 'ticket-of-leave' to do so. Most freed convicts settled in the Antipodes and formed an important element of the make-up of the Australian nation.

The last prime minister to be assassinated

1812

Political assassinations are not unknown in Britain, but the last time a British prime minister was murdered – in 1812 – was also the first time. Spencer Perceval was appointed prime minister in 1809 to lead the Tory government. Despite the grave political problems of the time (Britain was still at war with France) he was popular. On 11 May he was walking in the crowded Lobby of the House of Commons which was then, as now, open to the public. He was approached by a man who pulled out a pistol and shot him at close range. Perceval collapsed and died immediately. Amidst the shouting and confusion, the assassin quietly walked over to a bench and sat down. When the crowd realized that he was the murderer he quietly surrendered his weapon and declared, 'I submit myself to Justice.'

Justice for the assassin, John Bellingham, was indecently swift. At his trial the following Friday, he confessed that he had acted alone. He had planned his crime meticulously. For several days he had reconnoitred the Parliament buildings carefully making sure he knew the identity of the

Popular in his day, Prime Minister Spencer Perceval was able and young enough to have been one of Britain's great leaders if he had not been fatally shot in the lobby of the House of Commons in 1812. (Hulton)

prime minister. He had bought a pair of pistols specially for the job, had practised with them and had a special pocket sewn into his jacket to conceal them.

He had no grievance against Spencer Perceval personally but claimed to have 'shot the prime minister, not the man'. He had been interned in Russia for four years during a business transaction and had become desperate to claim redress and compensation. All other ways had failed and he had come to the conclusion that by killing the prime minister, the government would be forced to take notice. He fatally miscalculated. By Friday evening he had been convicted and sentenced. On the Monday morning he was hanged in front of huge jeering crowds.

Perceval today is remembered usually only for his unexpected end. In a democracy, even that of Britain in 1812, life is expected to go on much as before after the death of its Leader. Lord Liverpool thus became prime minister, a position he held for 15 tumultuous and significant years, for Britain and Europe, until he was forced to resign in 1827 after a stroke. Who knows where the course of history would have flowed had not John Bellingham in the House of Commons Lobby cut down the young and certainly gifted prime minister Perceval?

The last beheading

Even after the end of 'hanging, drawing and quartering' by the 19th century it was customary for traitors to be hanged and then beheaded. This gruesome act was last inflicted, in Britain, in 1820 when members of the Cato Street Conspiracy were beheaded for their part in trying to kill members of the Cabinet and overthrow the government.

The years after 1815 were years of great unrest and distress for large parts of the population. Arthur Thistlewood was an active campaigner who had led the riots at Spa Fields in 1816. He had already spent a year in jail for libelling the Prince Regent and for issuing a challenge to a government minister, Lord Sidmouth. He was a vigorous and colourful character, slightly irrational but, by the standards of his day, a sincere advocate of reform. In 1819 he devised plans to assassinate the key members of Lord Liverpool's Tory Cabinet. However, one of the members of his gang, Edwards, was a government agent. Acting as an *agent provocateur*, he had actively encouraged Thistlewood, and the authorities knew all about the conspiracy from the beginning.

Information reached Thistlewood and his fellows that members of the Cabinet were due to meet at a dinner in Grosvenor Square in February 1820. They decided that it was the most convenient moment to strike. The plan was to rush in, slay all those present, and then, with the assistance of the mob which they expected to rise in their favour, storm the Tower and the Bank of England and set up a provisional government of their own. It was a particularly harebrained scheme and would have stood little chance of succeeding even if the authorities had been unaware of the plan.

At their final rendezvous in Cato Street the conspirators were interrupted by the Bow Street Runners. In the ensuing struggle nine of the gang were arrested. Thistlewood killed one of the Runners by stabbing him in the chest and, with thirteen others, made his escape. He was arrested the next day at a friend's house in Moorfields, betrayed by the agent Edwards. Three of the gang were sentenced to transportation but the five ringleaders, including Thistlewood, were sentenced to die traitors' deaths.

On 1 May 1820, outside Newgate Prison, the five conspirators were hanged to death. Their bodies were then cut down to be beheaded by a masked executioner. For some reason the axe specially prepared for the purpose was not employed. Instead, a large surgeon's knife was used to cut off the heads. The anonymous person employed to carry out the beheading was an experienced body snatcher who normally made his living cutting out the teeth from bodies to sell for dentures. One by one the heads were sliced off and handed to the hangman, Jemmy Botting. One by one he held them aloft and cried 'Behold a Traitor!' to the customary roars of approval from the thousands of spectators.

The last highwayman

The 18th century was the heyday of the highwayman in Britain. Travelling on horseback, the highwayman was usually an elusive thief who carried himself with a dash of bravado and glamour. The image of a masked horseman carrying a pair of pistols crying out, 'stand and deliver' was a fair description of hundreds of the gentlemen of the road who robbed the rich on their travels across the wilder parts of Britain.

The last recorded highwayman was George Cutterman who plied his trade in North Yorkshire. He was responsible for scores of robberies in the area, usually from travellers on the Great North Road. A reward of 200 guineas was offered for his capture, and law officers finally tracked him down in 1824. His normal occupation was the landlord of the King's Head public house at Kirklington. On his way to York for questioning and trial, Cutterman leapt from the top of the coach that was transporting him. He made good his escape and was never seen again.

The last mantraps 1827

The illicit killing of game for food was once the subject of a very severe set of game laws in Britain. A capital offence in the 18th century, armed poaching was still punished with transportation in the 1820s. The court magistrates who enforced these laws were very often the same landowners on whose land the poaching was discovered. Shooting game, even with the landowner's permission, could still be a serious offence. Only 'esquires' or gentlemen of senior rank, and their eldest sons, could legally use a shotgun to shoot for sport.

One of the more vicious methods of deterring the poacher was the use of mantraps. These were similar in principle to a mousetrap. Chained in place on the ground, hidden in the undergrowth, a large pair of metal jaws with jagged interlocking teeth was held open, waiting for its victim. The jaws were spring-loaded and anyone stepping onto the metal plate between them was immediately clamped in a fierce grip. The serrated jaws caused broken limbs and permanent injury. To the dismay of the rich landowners who suffered from poaching, Robert Peel's law reforms made the use of mantraps illegal and they were last used legally in Britain in 1827.

1832 — *The last of the body snatchers*

Great advances were being made in the study of medicine at the beginning of the 19th century. To achieve this, the surgeons needed a large supply of human bodies to dissect and on which to demonstrate their theories. These were supplied by body snatchers. The fresh corpses were usually dug up from recent graves and sold by the body snatchers, or 'resurrectionists' as they were called, to the medical schools. The bodies of many executed criminals went the same way. The practice of body snatching died out in 1832 when a more reliable supply of bodies from the poor houses was provided by Act of Parliament.

On their deathbeds, paupers did not fear the unmarked grave that was to be their lot but the almost certain journey for their corpses, after burial, to the dissection tables in nearby schools of anatomy. Those with wealth could go to their deaths in peace, knowing that their graves would be protected and defended, at least for the first few weeks. After that the growing putrefaction of the corpse was its best and lasting protection. It was quite legal to take recently buried bodies as, according to law, the bodies were not actually owned by anyone. The shrouds, coffins and any clothing, however, was personal property and could not be taken. At the dead of night the body snatchers would approach the graveyards looking for signs of freshly dug graves. With wooden shovels to deaden the noise, the grave would be dug up, the body removed and the grave refilled. The fresher and younger the corpse the more it could be sold for. A corpse with its full set of teeth was also highly prized as they could be removed and sold separately for use as dentures by the rich.

William Burke, one of the last of the 'body snatchers', is hanged in front of huge crowds in Edinburgh in 1829. He had been convicted of murdering a number of people to supply bodies for scientific dissection. In keeping with his trade, his body was donated to the local school of anatomy. (ME)

Burke and Hare were perhaps the most infamous of the body snatchers, if not quite the last. Unfortunately for their victims, and ultimately for themselves, they by-passed that part of the process which involved digging up the graves of the naturally departed. Impatient and greedy, they took to strangling the poorer clients in Hare's lodging house and selling the bodies to Dr Knox, a famous Edinburgh surgeon. They were eventually apprehended in 1829. Hare turned king's evidence to get off scot-free, but Burke was hanged and, in a most appropriate and fitting end, his body ended up under the dissectionist's knife.

It became quite common in the early part of the 19th century for murderers to attempt to sell the victim's body to anatomists. It had a neatness that could hardly be denied: there was no body left as evidence but there was money from the medical school. Which came first, the intention to sell the body or the murder itself, was often in doubt. Probably the last person to be convicted for murdering to obtain a body to sell was Eliza Ross, a 38-year-old wife and mother in London. She was found guilty of murdering an old woman, Catherine Walsh, and disposing of the body by selling it to a London hospital. She was hanged and her own body given to the Royal College of Surgeons.

The medical profession, however, was severely tainted by body snatching. So, to protect their reputation, rather than the feelings and susceptibilities of the poor, the Cadaver Act was passed in 1832 which gave legal access to any unclaimed corpses of paupers from the poor houses and jails. Once again, however, it was the poor who suffered, but it did stop body snatching and brought midnight peace once again to the graveyards. With the new and assured supply of cadavers, the study of anatomy thrived and developed. Its progress led to the success of detailed and complicated internal surgical operations in the 1850s and 1860s, which in turn did so much to establish the high reputation of British surgeons that endures to this day.

The last gibbeting

1832

In the days when the capture and conviction of vicious criminals was even less certain than today, those who were caught received particularly brutal and savage punishment. Even after death, a convicted highwayman was not left in peace. Gibbeting, the hanging of the body 'in chains' in full public view, was considered a useful deterrent to other would-be 'gentlemen of the road'.

Gibbets were the gallows from which the bodies of the dead villains were suspended. They were usually positioned by the sides of the roads where many of the crimes of murder and robbery were committed. A metal cage, usually in the shape of the human form, was locked around the body to secure most of it from souvenir hunters and to prevent its premature disintegration. Often the corpse was tarred to prevent it from decaying too quickly.

Permanent gibbets, with their grisly displays, were common, especially on Hounslow Heath to the west of London, an area that suffered from a disconcerting wave of highway robberies and murder in the early part of the 19th century. The gibbets were useful landmarks and even appeared on maps. Despite the hideous sights and smells of decomposing bodies, many of the travelling public treated them as commonplace, as a reassuring sign of civilization, of law and order and, perhaps, even of safety.

The last recorded instance of gibbeting in England occurred in 1832. James Cook, a bookbinder, had waylaid a Mr Paas to rob him. He beat him to death and then took the body home where he cut it into pieces and burned it to try to hide the evidence. He was apprehended, convicted, executed and hanged in chains at Aylestone in Leicestershire on a 33-ft high gibbet.

Two years later the practice of gibbeting was abolished by law, to the relief of many, but to the dismay, no doubt, of some. The legislation was pushed through by William Ewart, a Member of Parliament and active abolitionist.

The last footpads

Footpads, the unmounted version of the more glamorous highwayman, and the forerunners of today's muggers, continued well into the 19th century. The last footpad was convicted in 1837. The traveller, Mr Isaac Benjamin, was robbed of jewellery and other valuables on the road near Iver in Buckinghamshire on 20 October 1837. Of the two footpads who were accused, Gowlatt and Johnson, Gowlatt was found to be innocent. Johnson, however, was found guilty of highway robbery, the last recorded case in Britain.

The last of the Bow Street Runners

The policing of Britain's capital has always been a controversial role, sometimes achieved with honesty and vitality, sometimes less so. Magistrates and constables existed in plenty but justice was rough and their effectiveness usually patchy. By the beginning of the 19th century London had a number of official and semi-official groups for keeping law and order. Among the best known were the Bow Street Runners.

The Bow Street Runners, the first attempt at a regular London police force, had been created in 1750 by the writer Henry Fielding who was also a magistrate at Bow Street. At first the force was a small group of detectives pitted against the criminal gangs of London. Later, developed by Henry's brother John, they were enlarged, and in 1805 a mounted patrol group was added to guard the public from the expanding activities of highwaymen in a 20-mile radius around the city.

The Runners gained a reputation for determination and incorruptibility. The criminals feared and respected them, as a highwayman's song of the period exclaims:

> I went to London one fine day
> With my sweet love to see the play,
> Where Fielding's gang did me pursue
> And I was ta'en by that cursed crew.

They continued to play a useful role in and around London for some years after the Metropolitan Police was created by Robert Peel in 1829. They were a curious mixture of a service – half private, half public – sometimes earning good money working for wealthy clients who required their specialized services. In 1836 the horse patrols joined with Metropolitan Police to form the nucleus of the mounted branch. The foot patrols eventually disappeared in 1839, fully absorbed into the Metropolitan Police. Today the memory of the Bow Street Runners lingers on. Bow Street Magistrates Court is still in use, dispensing justice for a large part of central London.

The last of the wreckers ◇ 1842 ◇

For centuries the dangers to ships' crews in coastal waters was increased by the possibility of being lured onto the rocks, wrecked and then robbed by the lawless inhabitants of the wilder coastal regions. Wrecking was considered a legitimate perk for those living near the shore. The last known instance of deliberate wrecking on British shorelines was in 1842 when the ship *William Wilberforce* foundered on the North Devon coast.

Tradition has it that on stormy nights wreckers would carry lanterns up to cliff tops to entice storm-battered ships to head for them in the belief that they were entering a friendly harbour. A lantern tied to the tail of a donkey led along a cliff-top path would appear to a ship at sea as the riding light of a ship safely at anchor. The captain would head for this apparition, and before he could realize his mistake found himself wrecked on the rocks.

The wreckers were not usually outlaw bands of desperate cut-throats but local inhabitants who indulged in this brutal behaviour to supplement their income. Nevertheless they were prepared to murder an entire ship's crew as they stumbled ashore. Making their way through the surf to the ship, the wreckers would bludgeon any surviving crew members who got in their way, and carry off the cargo and any valuable fittings they could find. Any sailors left in distress were left to the mercy of the tides and weather.

In 1842 the *William Wilberforce*, a Canadian-built brig of 167 tons, was heading for Ilfracombe in North Devon. She never made it. The ship was lured ashore at Lee, a small harbour a few miles from Ilfracombe, on the night of 23 October 1842. During a night of raging seas and very high winds, the captain and his crew of five seamen were drowned. The locals knowingly put the incident down to wreckers.

The instances of proven deliberate wrecking were always rare. Any mysterious wreck – especially when a ship was lost with all hands – would be attributed, sometimes unfairly, to wreckers. As the forces of law and order spread to the more remote coasts, especially to prevent smuggling, instances of wrecking became rarer.

Strangely, the *William Wilberforce* was not a total wreck. She was bought by a local ship repairer who had her refloated and towed off the rocks. Seaworthy again within a few months, she made many more successful voyages carrying timber to America and the Mediterranean. She eventually foundered and was wrecked off Portugal in 1856.

The last prison hulks

Prison hulks were the hulls of de-commissioned Royal Navy ships-of-the-line. They were first used as temporary prisons in 1776. Positioned on the downstream banks of the River Thames and other major estuaries, they each held hundreds of prisoners. In the close dark spaces of the old rotting ships' hulls, the occupants were confined in conditions of great depravity. Discipline was difficult to enforce by the authorities, and disease and vice of every kind were commonplace. As the land-based jail-building programme got under way, the need for the hulks diminished, and their use was finally discontinued in 1857.

The use of hulks was, at first, a temporary measure. But like so many temporary measures it became permanent out of necessity. They were originally intended to hold convicts before they were transported. Transportation to the American colonies had to be stopped during the American War of Independence (1776–83), and when the war was over a new destination had to be found. Those convicts marking time before their sentences were held on board the hulks to await events. Ten years later some were still waiting and life on the hulks had become a way of life.

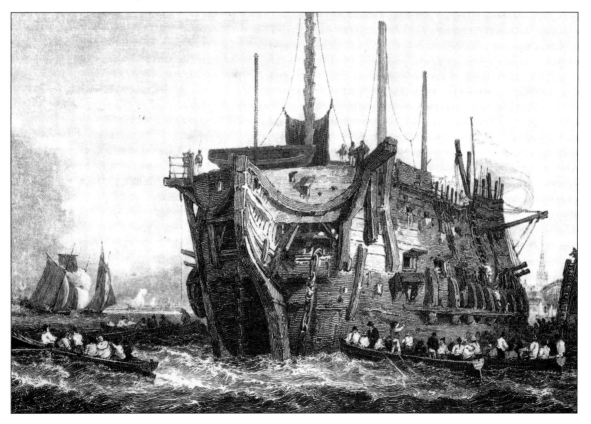

The rotting glory of a Royal Navy ship-of-the-line used as a prison hulk at Deptford on the River Thames in the 1820s. Prison hulks, originally a temporary measure while the American colonies were in revolt, were last used as prisons in 1857. (AR)

Gradually over the years incarceration in the hulks became the sentence in itself. The convenience and cheapness of a floating prison, however unsavoury the conditions on board, was too hard to resist for any government with a need to save money. Usually the sentences included hard labour and gangs of prisoners were marched ashore daily to carry out back-breaking labour in a local public works project. The sad old decaying warships, their rigging and masts removed, were a grim sight on the river banks of the major ports of England. The convict gangs who were imprisoned on board every night were a stark reminder to the passer-by of the inadequacies of the jail system.

By 1842 the prison population of the hulks had peaked at over 3,000. The main hulks of *Justitia*, *Leviathan*, *Stirling Castle*, *Warrior* and *York* each had more than 500 prisoners aboard. But reformers were active. A vast prison-building programme was in hand and by 1840 the need for the hulks was declining. The last was abandoned by the prison service in 1857 and broken up for scrap. 'Hulks' or at least their equivalent have been used since then. In the 1970s, in Belfast Lough, Northern Ireland, internment prisoners were held temporarily on various ships until more permanent prisons ashore could be found for them. There are also plans, currently being considered by the British government, for permanent floating prisons.

The last county to create its police force ◇ 1862 ◇

Many counties in England and Wales had their own police forces, under local government control, by the end of the 1840s. There were, however, some which were still operating a system of local part-time parish constables. An Act of Parliament in 1856 forced all counties and boroughs, which had not already done so, to form their own police force. In order to obtain a grant of money from central government they had to submit to central inspections. The last county to achieve a fully operational police force was Rutlandshire in 1862.

The County and Borough Police Act introduced by Palmerston when he was Home Secretary was much opposed by mayors and borough corporations from all over the country who thought the whole idea 'centralised and tyrannical'. Nevertheless the Act forced all boroughs and counties to establish fully manned and disciplined forces. Certain standards of discipline and minimum and maximum numbers of constables per head of population were set down.

Rutlandshire had first ventured into the world of running its own police in 1848 when it set up a force consisting of one chief constable and just one constable to look after the entire – admittedly tiny – county of 12,000 people. The complete legislation, as originally planned in 1854, would have forced small counties such as Rutland to combine with others. That particular clause of the Bill, however, did not appear when the Act was eventually passed in 1856, so Rutlandshire remained on her own. It took a further six years before the county was finally satisfactorily inspected and judged as possessing an efficient force.

The Rutlandshire police force lasted some 90 years until 1951 when it was combined, in name as well as in fact, with the neighbouring Leicestershire force. In 1974, following the reorganization of local government boundaries, Rutlandshire itself, Britain's smallest county, was absorbed into Leicestershire and the name disappeared.

The last pillories and stocks

Public pillories, wooden frames in which petty criminals could be locked, were once widely used throughout Britain. The public humiliation was the essence of the punishment, which was last officially used in Britain in 1837. There were pillories and stocks erected in many public places. Every ward in London, for instance, had its stocks to deal with 'vagabonds and other petty offenders' at the end of the 16th century. The writer Daniel Defoe was one of the pillory's more famous victims early in the 18th century when he suffered a spell in the pillory for publishing a libellous essay.

In the pillory the hapless offenders were clamped by their necks and arms while they were left standing; in the stocks they were secured by their legs and sometimes their necks. In this position, they were at the mercy of the passing crowd. Sometimes the treatment they received was a mild affair. Missiles such as rotten fruit and perhaps a few nastier items of refuse were thrown at the victims but they came to no real harm. On other occasions the mob was stirred to cruelty, sometimes prompted by anger at the crime but in some cases by a sense of malicious fun. In these instances, those in the pillory could be seriously injured. In line with many other civil and legal reforms of the 1830s the use of the pillory was abolished by statute in 1837. The stocks lingered on, especially in the market squares and village greens and were never actually officially banned. The last recorded instance of their use for punishment was in Rugby in 1865.

The last transportation

The transportation of convicts to the wilder, more distant outposts of the world was first introduced by the British authorities in the early 1600s, primarily to the colonies of the New World. After American independence (1783), distant Australia was used instead. Transportation eventually ceased after growing public protest in the 1860s.

In the 17th century, Virginia colonists were only too happy to buy the rights to convict labour so that they could run their plantations cheaply. But the use of this convenient dumping ground for criminals ended in the 1770s after American independence. The British government was forced to find a new destination for its convicts. Africa had been ruled out on health grounds, and for strategic reasons the newly discovered continent of Australia was chosen. In 1787 the first fleet of convicts and soldiers set sail from England to found the penal colony at Botany Bay in New South Wales and the Australian colonies were born.

The treatment of criminals was a brutal, callous business in the 18th century. Transportation was considered a very useful solution to a tricky problem: it removed what was considered the 'criminal classes' from the homeland and put them to useful work but also punished them. The convicts – men, women and children – were transported, often for no more than the trivial theft of a few loaves of bread. In a form of semi-slavery, they lived out their sentences in a bleak, savage and hostile territory. At the end of their terms of punishment they were usually granted their 'ticket-of-leave' which forced them, under a continuing strict discipline, to live out the rest of their lives in Australia. Very few were permitted to return to Britain again.

As more and more free emigrants settled in Australia and as the iniquities of the system of bonded labour became widely known – in Britain as well as in Australia – pressure for the abolition of transportation grew. The last remaining penal colony in the antipodes was Western Australia. It was almost wholly supported by the convict system and needed a thousand new convicts a year just to keep going. Most of the rest of Australia, the burgeoning eastern colonies which had already rejected convict labour, was adamant that transportation must stop. Finally, in 1865, Palmerston's Government in Britain agreed that the system would end.

In 1867 the last group of convicts to be transported set sail from Britain. Among the 451 prisoners were some 60 Fenian agitators from Ireland. They arrived at Fremantle in Western Australia on 10 January 1868 to begin their peculiarly harsh sentences. In the short term the end of transportation was disastrous for Western Australia. But those colonies that put their reliance on bonded labour firmly behind them soon developed and grew. Britain's shiploads of convicts to Australia, numbering 160,000 persons over 80 years, must surely be one of the most questionable legacies ever bequeathed on one country by another.

The last public hanging   ◇ 1868 ◇

The spectacle of the public execution of a convicted criminal was an awful, but relatively common, sight in all parts of Britain for many centuries. The last such occasion was in 1868, outside Newgate Prison in London. Michael Barrett was a Fenian, an Irish patriot, who had planted a bomb outside Clerkenwell prison walls in an attempt to free two of his compatriots from the prison. When it exploded it killed four passers-by and wounded many others. Barrett went to his public death knowing that he would be the last to do so. Legislation for all future executions to be carried out inside prison walls had already passed through Parliament but was not due to receive royal assent until three days later.

The campaign for the reform of the law on all aspects of capital punishment had started many years earlier. At the turn of the 19th century there were over 150 crimes which attracted the death penalty. These ranged from the minor offences of robbery of goods worth more than 5s, sheep stealing and picking pockets to murder and high treason. Boys of less than ten years of age were hanged for stealing trivial amounts of food needed to keep them alive. By the middle of the century only four capital offences remained, but public hangings were still drawing huge crowds. Apart from the moral condemnation of this public spectacle, the problems of maintaining law and order at these events was enormous. Thousands of people from all sections of society would pack themselves in front of the prison, as close as possible to the temporary scaffold.

It was said that on an execution morning one saw faces that were never seen save round a gallows or a great fire. The crowds usually started to gather many hours before the event. The heaving masses of people fell easy prey to pickpockets and many other thieves and criminals. Riots often occurred and it was quite usual for members of the crowd to be crushed to death. At the set time the criminals were led out from the prison, up onto the scaffold and, to yells of excitement and howls of execration from the crowd, dropped to their death.

William Ewart, a Member of Parliament and an active abolitionist, was responsible for persuading Parliament to set up a select committee on capital punishment. One of the outcomes of this investigation was the measure, introduced in 1868 by Hibbert, that removed probably the most hideous aspect of capital punishment, the huge crowds who watched the hangings for entertainment.

On Tuesday 26 May 1868, however, the new law was too late to save Michael Barrett from public humiliation. He was 27 years old and despite several appeals against his conviction (he claimed he had been in Glasgow at the time of the crime), his sentence was upheld. He had no known relatives or friends present to see him die.

At 8 am he was brought out of the side door of Newgate to mount the black gallows which had been dragged into position a few hours earlier. The crowd of nearly 40,000, many of whom had been waiting all night, immediately went quiet. Barrett, wearing a short red jacket and grey striped trousers, quietly submitted to his hands and legs being tied and went to his death with a serene dignity that put the crowd to shame. His body was cut down an hour later and the crowd was, with great difficulty, dispersed by the police. The last woman to be hanged in public, the murderess Frances Kidder, had dropped to her death less than two months before at Maidstone amid similar scenes of public curiosity.

The Times recorded Barrett's death and the next day pontificated: 'London yesterday witnessed the last of those hideous spectacles familiar enough to the hard eyes of our predecessors but more and more repulsive to the taste of these days. We have

A small well-behaved crowd, held back by a few gendarmes, witness the last public guillotining in France. Murderer Eugene Weidman was executed on 16 June 1939 outside the prison in Versailles. (Popperfoto)

only to think of the horror with which we all now instinctively regard the barbarous punishments inflicted lately down in our history and we may conceive what posterity will think of capital executions before a motley crowd of vulgar and often brutal spectators,'

Few people at the time utterly condemned capital punishment itself. Those who had hoped that the new Act against public execution would herald the abolition of the death penalty were to be disappointed. It took nearly another hundred years before the last person was executed in Britain. Notorious Newgate, however, was pulled down in 1903, to be replaced by the Central Criminal Court, the Old Bailey.

The last public hangman   ◇ 1874 ◇

Public executioners were both scorned and applauded by the general public, depending on the crimes involved and their own performance in consigning criminals to oblivion. A botched execution, resulting in a twitching, gasping body, half alive for longer than even the cruel public could endorse would bring forth howls of derision. A neatly conducted quick death would result in a sigh from the crowd. One of the first publicly recognized executioners was Jack Ketch who was notoriously incompetent and almost universally hated by the public. Long after his death in 1686 anonymous hangmen were given the soubriquet of 'Jack Ketch'.

The last executioner in Britain to carry out his work in public was William Calcraft who hanged Michael Barrett outside Newgate on 26 May 1868. A quiet and respectable man, Calcraft was married with two sons who bred rabbits as a hobby. He was first appointed hangman for the London area in 1829 earning a weekly wage of a guinea with an extra guinea for every hanging. He had various jobs before his appointment, notably as a cobbler and bootmaker, but also earned extra money for the occasional flogging at Newgate. As a hangman he made a comfortable living although he was often in debt. He was also Britain's last executioner to be salaried – after him the job was strictly part time.

After the end of public executions in 1868 the job of hangman instantly became a more secret one, much to the relief of Calcraft who was tiring of the robust treatment he received from the public. Calcraft retired in 1874 and died five years later at the age of 79.

The last flogging of soldiers and sailors   ◇ 1881 ◇

The harsh conditions in both the British Army and Navy in the 19th century are well documented. By today's standards, military and naval punishments for undisciplined behaviour were brutal. A mutinous sailor could receive a 'flogging round the fleet' and a soldier who had deserted could be tied to a wheel and given 1,000 lashes; they were violent solutions in violent times. After a century of increasing public concern and the gradual introduction of more humane conditions of service, the last flogging of a British soldier took place in 1881.

In the Royal Navy, flogging members of the crew as a punishment was commonplace. Captains were urged to restrict the number of lashes with the cat-o'-nine-tails on a seaman's bare back to no more than a dozen. This order was usually ignored and floggings of three or four dozen strokes were often the rule rather than the exception. The offender was made to strip to the waist and was then lashed by his arms and feet to a grating or ladder. All hands were ordered on deck to witness the grim punishment while a company of Royal Marines stood by to maintain discipline.

The 'cat' was a multiple whip made of many leather thongs with knotted ends, and it was not uncommon to have lead shot attached to cause deeper cuts. There were many opportunities for sadism amongst the all-powerful captains as well as the boatswain's mates who swung the cat. Some captains would give summary punishments, without trial, to members of their crew for relatively trivial offences such as 'sullenness' and perceived 'slowness' to react to orders. Others used it sparingly, but even as late as the 1850s many ships witnessed a flogging at least once a week, even in peacetime.

In the Army punishment was even more severe. Desertion – what today might be termed AWOL, 'absent without leave' – was rewarded by hundreds of lashes to the offender's bare back. The victim was usually spreadeagled and tied to a triangular wooden frame. Traditionally, a drummer administered the blows supervised by the drum major, with the regimental doctor standing by to prevent a fatality. Offending soldiers were often maimed for life; many had to be discharged from service to almost certain penury and beggary in civilian life.

In the Navy the maximum number of permissible lashes for any flogging was reduced to 48 in 1866. A few years later, in 1871, it was suspended in peacetime and in 1879 officially abolished. The soldiers in the Army had to suffer a few more years. In 1868, driven by the reforming zeal of Cardwell, the Secretary for War, the Army abolished flogging altogether in peacetime. Out too went the barbaric practice of branding or tattooing for desertion. Wartime floggings continued, however, and the last recorded official flogging took place in 1881. In 1900 flogging in all the armed services was abolished even in wartime. The new century brought in an age, which lasted until the First World War, of a highly trained, professional Army with very respectable conditions of service and more humane punishments.

The last scaffold reprieve

Old stories of last minute reprieves for condemned prisoners on the scaffold are legend. Gallows protocol had it that if the hangman was unable to execute his victim after three attempts, the prisoner was allowed to live. The last occasion of such a reprieve was at Exeter jail in February 1885. John Lee escaped the hangman's noose and lived to tell his tale to many a fellow prisoner and astonished journalists for years after.

Not many criminals who have been condemned to die survive to describe the awful experience of mounting the scaffold – but there were a few. An inefficient executioner, chopping a head off with an axe, had very little option but to carry on if the first blow did not achieve its intended swift purpose. With a hanging, if the rope broke, the scaffold collapsed or the trap door failed to open, a second or even third attempt could be carried out or abandoned altogether. In the rough and ready days of hangings, when some hangmen were not as professional as others, hangings were often botched. It became a tradition that if the victim survived three attempts at being hanged, he would be reprieved. On some occasions he was granted his freedom but more often he had his sentence commuted to life imprisonment.

In November 1884 John Lee was a servant in Babbacombe, Devon when his employer, a Miss Keyse, was savagely beaten to death. Lee, protesting his innocence all the while, was convicted of her murder and condemned to death in February 1885. On the day appointed for his execution he was bound and blindfolded by the hangman, James Berry, and led out from his cell. The hanging was to take place in the coach house. Instead of a scaffold there was a pit in the floor, some 11 feet deep, covered by trap doors and operated by a lever.

Lee was positioned over the doors, the noose about his neck. He was calm and dignified. Asked if he had anything to say, he replied, 'No – drop away!' He held his breath, clenched his teeth and prepared to die. Berry pulled the lever and, to gasps of astonishment from the prison officials, nothing happened. Berry kept pulling – but still nothing. Lee had the noose removed from his neck and was led away into the next room while the trap doors were tested. They seemed to work well, with no-one on them. Lee was brought back and again prepared to meet his maker. Again the executioner tugged at the lever and once again the trap doors refused to drop away. The officials decided to postpone the execution again, but Lee – perhaps with a traditional reprieve in mind – insisted on a third attempt. The lever was pulled but again to no avail.

The prison chaplain could bear it no longer and decided to leave. An execution had to be witnessed by the chaplain and without him the proceedings had to be stopped anyway. Lee was led away to his cell to wait the whole day in dreadful uncertainty. Late that evening the governor visited him. The message was that he was to live. He was officially reprieved and had his sentence commuted to a life term. There were no more such reprieves; the prison authorities learned their lesson from the incident at Exeter and built their scaffolds with more care. John Lee spent 23 years in jail, before walking out a free man.

Jack the Ripper's last victim   ◇ 1888 ◇

The Whitechapel Murderer, or 'Jack the Ripper' as he called himself in his taunting letters to the police, was responsible for a series of horrifying murders in the east end of London. They shocked everyone, even those who were used to the daily routine of criminal violence in Victorian cities. His victims were all women and the bodies were all brutally, disgustingly disfigured. He was never caught and certainly went to his death, by whatever means, unidentified as the cause of one of the greatest criminal legends ever. His last victim, Marie Jeanette Kelly, met her end in November 1888. She was the most severely mutilated of all.

The name of Jack the Ripper is synonymous with the most vile of criminals, the unpredictable, unbalanced, unhinged and, above all, unidentified multi-murderer. In the summer and autumn of 1888 the public waited with bated breath for news of the next victim. As each mutilated body was found, tension within the police force grew amid increasingly shrill public demands that they find the perpetrator of such ghastly crimes.

In the maze of the overcrowded east end of London in the 1880s, the police were seemingly helpless in their attempts to track down, identify and arrest the Ripper. Many suggestions as to the Ripper's identity were made but the Ripper was never identified and never caught. Many murders were attributed to him (or her, as some have even claimed), but it is now commonly believed that he was only definitely responsible for the murder of five women.

The first of the Ripper's victims was found in Whitechapel, in the east end of London. All the subsequent murders were thus initially referred to as the 'Whitechapel' murders even though the last four took place in Spitalfields to the north of Whitechapel. After his second victim was discovered the murderer wrote a mocking letter to the police and signed himself 'Jack the Ripper'. Thus the name was born, to haunt the police and public and remind them forever of the fallibility of crime detection.

Spitalfields was an area of closely packed houses, frequented by the lowest criminals and dregs of Victorian metropolitan society. Prostitutes plied their trade here and it was exclusively among them that the Ripper selected his unfortunate victims. Marie Jeanette Kelly was a 25-year-old Irish prostitute who lived in Dorset Street. Like all prostitutes in the area she was disturbed and frightened by the Ripper affair and was actually planning to leave London for a while until he had been caught. On the evening of 8 November, after many hours of drinking and plying her trade, Marie Kelly picked up her last customer. The next morning, 9 November, she was found horribly murdered, mutilated, disembowelled and partially dismembered, almost beyond recognition.

Three days later the Metropolitan Police Commissioner, Sir Charles Warren, admitting the failure of his force, resigned. Kelly proved to be the last of the Ripper's victims, although this was not realized at the time and many subsequent murders were initially attributed to him. The Ripper's file was kept open, officially, until 1892. Since then hundreds of books have been written on the subject, many of them claiming to reveal the true identity of the Ripper. Many thousands of documents and photographs have come to light, but there has yet to be a convincing, conclusive story which encompasses the full facts and lays bare the truth of Jack the Ripper.

 ## The last of the treadwheel

The Victorian penal system was an area of thoughtful experimentation in which some genuine attempts to reform convicts were combined with some extraordinarily futile corrective measures. One of the weirder machines found in most prisons, used for the infliction of hard labour on prisoners, was the treadwheel. Work in a Victorian prison was monotonous and hard. In some cases it was also originally intended to be corrective, but the work was usually of the most fruitless kind. If picking oakum, unravelling bits of old rope for use as a caulking material, was the convict's most useful activity, his most useless must surely have been the time he spent on the treadwheel.

The treadwheel was a large iron frame like an elongated water-wheel, with steps placed around the circumference. A gang of prisoners was required to walk the steps, turning the wheel in pointless motion for hours at a time. The prisoners held onto a wooden cross-piece to keep the gang in unison, and each prisoner was set a certain

One of the early treadwheels at Brixton Prison in 1835. A hard session on the wheel was intended to bring discipline to a tedious prison regime. Gladstone eventually recommended their abolition and they were last used in 1898. (AR)

calculated theoretical 'height' to climb in a period of about six hours each day. An average daily height of 10,000 feet was expected. The very young and the very old were excused this exercise, but it was not the physical exertion that was disheartening but its futility.

The treadwheel was invented by Mr (later Sir) William Cubitt of Ipswich at the request of the Brixton prison governor in 1817 who despaired of finding some hard labour for his convicts. In some prisons there were attempts to use the power generated to good effect, to grind wheat for prison consumption, to power saws or to pump water to storage tanks. At one stage some prison authorities, in anticipation perhaps of a more modern, 'cost-effective' age, actually tried to sell the power generated by their prisoners by offering the rotating axle projecting from their prison walls to entrepreneurs.

In the 1870s more and more wheels were built as the easiest method of occupying the prisoners, but their acceptability was soon to fade. The Gladstone Commission on Prison Reform report of 1895 recommended among other things, the abolition of the treadwheel regime. In Scotland the prison governors had already banished the dreaded machine, and the use of treadwheels as routine hard labour was finally stopped in 1898. They remained unused in many prisons for some years. The huge 'Victorian' contraptions became monuments to a society which was often long on inventiveness and ingenuity but short on humanity and commonsense.

Hard labour was also provided in some prisons in the form of the crank. This was a hand crank set to be turned by a force of about 12 pounds. Hard-labour prisoners were required to turn it 10,000 times a day. It was abolished at the same time as the treadwheel.

The last trial in the House of Lords

The House of Lords, the upper chamber of the British Parliament, regularly tried and sentenced its own members who were charged with criminal offences. Trials held in Parliament – whatever the offence – were understandably given a dramatic twist unrivalled in any other court of law. Such proceedings were rare and were followed with great eagerness by the public. The last House of Lords trial took place on 18 July 1901 when the Earl Russell was tried for bigamy.

John Francis Stanley, Earl Russell, married his first wife Mabel in 1890. He soon discovered she was only after his money and that she was tragically unbalanced. He refused to settle any money on her and spent the next ten years defending himself from her malicious attacks. After meeting Mollie, his second wife-to-be, he travelled with her to the USA. In Nevada he obtained a legal divorce from Mabel and then – also quite legally – married Mollie. However, his divorce was not recognized as legal in Britain although his second marriage was.

On his return to Britain, he was arrested and found guilty of bigamy under British Law at the Old Bailey in London. It was never made clear why, if the American marriage was recognized, the American divorce was not. After being found guilty, it was pointed out that as Russell was a peer of the realm the case would have to go to the House of Lords for sentencing. The trial, to decide the appropriate sentence by the Lords, cost £30,000. It was a public sensation and resulted in a stinging three months' prison term for the Earl. Despite the salacious interest of the public, they were outraged by the severity of the sentence for what was certainly a minor technical offence.

The reputation of the House of Lords suffered greatly in public esteem for its spurious sentence against one of its own. Whilst still in prison Russell obtained his real, legal divorce from his first wife and, ten years later, received a free pardon and full public rehabilitation. An Act of Parliament in 1948 removed forever the obligation for the House of Lords to try its own members.

 ## The last prisoner in the Tower

Rudolph Hess was Germany's deputy Führer at the beginning of the Second World War. In one of the strangest episodes of the war, he flew alone to Britain on a so-called 'peace mission'. Hitler disowned him and no known deals were struck. After being thoroughly interrogated Hess was imprisoned by the British authorities for the remainder of the war. For some of this period Hess was imprisoned in the Tower of London, the last prisoner of any importance to be incarcerated there.

After the war Hess was sent back to Germany to stand trial at Nuremburg for war crimes. He was convicted and spent the remainder of his long life at Spandau Prison in Berlin in solitary confinement. He was also the last prisoner at Spandau. After he died in 1987 – in suspicious circumstances – the prison was completely demolished to prevent the possibility of it becoming a Nazi shrine.

Hitler's deputy, Rudolph Hess, eats a prison meal during the Nuremberg Trials in 1945. Imprisoned in Britain during the war, Hess was the Tower of London's last major prisoner. After being convicted of war crimes he spent over forty years in Spandau Prison in Berlin. (Popperfoto)

The last hanging of a traitor

Postwar Britain and much of Europe became fertile ground for spying. Many British citizens and others were caught and convicted for selling state secrets to the Soviet Union during the Cold War from the 1950s right through to the 1990s. However, despite the gravity of many of their offences none were executed even though the death penalty for treason remained on the statute books.

The last person to be executed for treason was sentenced before the Cold War. During the Second World War William Joyce, an Irish-American with a shady pre-war background in the British Union of Fascists, turned up in Germany. Broadcasting propaganda for the Germans, he quickly became known to his avid British audience as 'Lord Haw-Haw' from his nasal intonation. His most famous opening lines of 'Jairmany Calling, Jairmany Calling' teased and amused many in wartime Britain.

At the end of the war he was captured and tried at the Old Bailey. Despite his American citizenship he was convicted of treason. Before the war he had once falsely tried to claim British citizenship. That was enough for the court and for the British public who were in an unforgiving mood in the grim postwar winter of 1945. There was no reprieve and Joyce went to his death, bravely and still defiant at Wandsworth Prison on 3 January 1946.

Two days later a Private Schurch of the British Army was hanged after being convicted of treachery at a court martial. He too had been a pre-war fascist and had deliberately offered his services to the enemy after being captured in North Africa. On his death the British government felt that enough token traitors' lives had been taken.

The last of the 'First Division' in prison

The prison system in Britain has undergone many changes over the years. Until quite recently a remnant of the class system remained formally in the prison system with its three divisions. The first division was reserved for a superior type of convict from the upper classes who was able to hire fellow prisoners as servants, have meals brought in and generally disport himself with a degree of superiority. Second division prisoners were also afforded privileges whilst the majority of the prisoners, third divisioners, suffered the usual rigours of jail unalloyed by the comforts that money could buy. In 1948 all such distinctions were abolished along with the punishment of hard labour.

The last woman executed

In 1955 Ruth Ellis became the last woman to be executed in Britain. She had fatally shot her lover, racing-car driver David Blakely. Despite the claim that it was a crime of passion, she was convicted of murder at her trial on 21 June and sentenced to death. She was hanged at Holloway prison, London, at 9.00 am on 13 July by Albert Pierrepoint,

Britain's executioner from 1932 to 1955. She was one of his last 'clients'.

Ellis's trial and subsequent execution caused huge public disquiet. In the days after her conviction many thousands of signatures were collected from the public appealing for clemency. The Home Secretary eventually decided that the 'Law must take its course' and refused a reprieve. In 1958 66-year-old Mary Wilson was convicted of murdering two of her three husbands. Her death sentence was commuted to life imprisonment. Her case and that of Ruth Ellis were instrumental in bringing hanging to an end in 1964.

The last executions ◁ 1964 ▷

The last executions to take place in Britain were in 1964. Two men, Gwynne Owen Evans and Peter Anthony Allen, had been found guilty of murder while carrying out a theft. They killed John West, a van driver at Whitehaven in Cumbria, and were sentenced to death. There was no reprieve. In two different prisons, Strangeways in Manchester and Walton in Liverpool, Evans and Allen were hanged to death at 8.00 am on 13 August 1964. It was a quiet affair compared with the last public execution in 1868 outside the walls of Newgate in London. Outside the gates of both prisons were the usual regular campaigners for the abolition of the death penalty but there was very little fuss. Nobody knew that they were to be the last executions in Britain.

In December Parliament agreed to abolish capital punishment for an experimental period of five years. At the end of the period, on 18 December 1969, Parliament confirmed its decision and decided to abolish the death penalty for murder completely. The restoration of the death penalty remains on the political agenda and has been debated in the House of Commons from time to time. Hanging is still retained as a punishment for treason and for piracy, but has not been used since that day in 1964 when Evans and Allen dropped to their deaths.

The last political prisoners ◁ 1975 ▷

In 1971, at the height of the troubles in Northern Ireland, the Northern Ireland government introduced internment without trial in an attempt to stop the violence. Under the Special Powers Act suspected members of terrorist organizations – mainly the IRA but also other republican groups and later, protestant 'loyalist' groups – were rounded up and imprisoned at the Long Kesh Prison (later renamed the Maze) near Lurgan. The internees were kept separate from convicted terrorists and segregated into the different factions. They regarded themselves as either prisoners of war or political prisoners. For the British government, who took over direct rule in Northern Ireland the following year, it was a political 'own goal'. International condemnation was widespread, and the sense of injustice only fuelled the violence. The imprisoning of new suspects continued but with a limited amount of success.

Although new detention orders were made, the total number of detainees was gradually reduced over the next few years, as the authorities judged it was safe to do so. The British Home Secretary, Merlyn Rees, announced on 24 July 1975 that all detainees would be home by Christmas. The last 75 detainees were freed, without charge, on 5 December 1975. The law authorising internment was never used again and was finally dropped on 9 July 1980.

The prison camp at Long Kesh near Lurgan used to hold Northern Ireland's internees in 1971. Inside the prison, which resembled a prisoner-of-war camp, the inmates who considered themselves innocent political prisoners were granted various privileges. The last of the internees were released in time to be home by Christmas, 1975. (Topham)

The last judicial corporal punishment

The Isle of Man is often remembered as the last place in Britain to retain laws that allowed judicial corporal punishment. The island specialized in 'birching', a punishment handed out to young offenders in the 14 to 21 age group for violent crime. The 'birch' was a bundle of birch rods tied together with leather straps. Under medical supervision, the offender was held down while a police sergeant administered a number of strokes on his back from the birch. Offenders under 14 years could be sentenced to a caning.

The last birching was carried out in 1976 on a young Irishman in Douglas who had been convicted of assault. In 1979 the European Court of Human Rights condemned the use of the birch as 'cruel and unusual' and encouraged its removal from the statute books. In 1981 another young tourist on the island was convicted of assault and in the last judgement of its kind he was sentenced to four strokes of the birch. The birching was never carried out and punishment was reduced to a fine on appeal. Finally in March 1993 the Tynwald, the Isle of Man's parliament, agreed, under pressure from the United Kingdom government, to abolish the punishment.

The last death sentence — 1992

The last death sentence to be pronounced in Britain was in Douglas, the capital of the Isle of Man, on 10 July 1992. The Isle of Man was the last place in Britain to retain the death penalty (for murder), although the few death sentences since 1964 have been commuted to life sentences by Royal Prerogative. In fact the last execution to take place on the island was in the 19th century.

In 1991 Tony Teare was paid £600 to kill Corinne Bentley, the victim of a family row. Teare lured her to a remote spot and cut her throat with a modelling knife. She staggered to some nearby farm buildings, fell into a disused silage pit and died. Teare claimed he needed the money to pay off his bank overdraft. In sentencing him after the guilty verdict, Judge Henry Callow said, 'I can only pronounce one sentence: you will be taken to the Isle of Man jail and thence to a place of legal execution and there hanged by the neck until dead.' Tony Teare's execution never took place, he was moved to mainland Britain to serve his life sentence and the penalty was removed from the island's statute books later that year.

The last of the Cold War spies — 1992

With the break up of the Soviet Union and the end of the so-called Cold War in 1990, the emotive term 'Soviet Spy' seems about to be consigned to the history books. In November 1993 Michael Smith was convicted at the Old Bailey of spying for the Soviet Union and for Russia in what could be the last trial of its kind in Britain. Michael Smith was an electronics engineer who had been recruited as a Soviet spy years earlier by Victor Oshchenko, a KGB agent working at the Soviet Embassy in London in the 1970s. Smith subsequently worked on classified defence projects at two important defence products companies, EMI and GEC. It is believed that he passed on defence secrets over many years, making him one of the most damaging spies ever to western interests.

When Victor Oshchenko defected to the West on 20 July 1992, Michael Smith's fate was sealed. His name was one of the first that Oshchenko revealed. Smith was arrested on 8 August and his complex trial a year later lasted nine weeks. He was convicted of three charges of spying and Mr Justice Blofeld had no hesitation in sentencing Britain's last Cold War spy to 25 years' imprisonment. Oshchenko provided other names of Russian spies in other western countries, but they have yet to stand trial.

Previous to Michael Smith, the last Briton to be convicted of spying for the Soviet Union was Michael Bettaney. He started work for MI5 at the age of 25 and was eventually assigned to Soviet counter espionage. He became disillusioned, however, and in 1983, on his own initiative, contacted the Soviets and began to pass them secrets. Bettaney was, like most agents, a loner but was generally affable and agreeable to his colleagues. His treachery was soon discovered, and in 1985 he was convicted and sentenced to 23 years' imprisonment.

Oleg Gordievsky was a Soviet agent working in London for the KGB. He was also a secret agent for the West. It is assumed that it was he who exposed Bettaney as a Soviet spy, probably in 1983. In 1985 Gordievsky was forced to flee to the West to avoid discovery by the Soviets. He named many Soviet agents in Britain and, it is thought, many more minor British agents. The alleged Soviet spies, 31 of them, were expelled from the UK in the last major public expulsion of its type. This action was reciprocated by the expulsion of 31 British staff from the embassy in Moscow. Some of the British agents named by Gordievsky fled abroad, others, 'fringe agents', stayed and were left to sweat it out; no proceedings have yet been taken against them.

 1994   # *The last gallows*

A lthough Britain has abolished the death penalty for murder and other grave crimes, the punishment of death by hanging is still theoretically available to the courts for the punishment of convicted traitors. Britain's last remaining gallows are inside Wandsworth Prison. The south London jail, situated close to the River Thames, has a foreign, fortress-like appearance with its square towers and construction of dull dirty brick. The Wandsworth gallows – a beam across a trap door – has seen many a condemned man take his last step and swing to his death. When all other gallows were dismantled after the abolition of capital punishment for murder, Wandsworth's mechanism for judicial death was retained. In theory at least it could still be used and is checked regularly.

INTERNATIONAL AFFAIRS

3

The last pagan Roman Emperor ◆ *363* ◆

The Roman Empire adopted Christianity at the instigation of the Emperor Constantine in 313. He issued the Edict of Toleration at Milan which allowed religious freedom throughout the Empire. In 312 he gained control of the Empire in the west from his rival Maxentius in battle at the Milvian bridge. Before the battle he had a vision which told him to bid his army of Gauls to fight under the sign of the cross. They did so and completely routed Maxentius' troops, most of them drowning in the River Tiber. Constantine placed great significance on the symbol of the cross in his victory and made Christianity the state religion in 324. He was formally baptized into the Christian faith on his deathbed in 337.

Most subsequent Roman Emperors followed him by becoming Christian and supporting Christianity as the official religion for the Empire; the last not to do so was Julian, Flavius Claudius Julianus, Constantine's nephew. As a boy Julian had become

---

The Decline and Fall of the Roman Empire

313 Edict of Toleration issued at Milan. Emperor Constantine allows freedom of worship and Christianity becomes the Roman Empire's religion.

330 Establishment of the 'New Rome' – Constantinople – by the Emperor Constantine.

363 Death of Julian, the last non-Christian Emperor.

391 Paganism proscribed throughout the Empire.

394 Battle of River Frigidus. The defeat of the last pagan to aspire to be Roman Emperor.

395 Death of Theodosius, the last sole Emperor able to unite the east and the west of the Roman Empire. His two young sons, Arcadius and Honorius, become Emperors in the east and west respectively.

410 The Romans withdraw their last legions from Britain.

410 The Visigoths, led by Alaric, capture and occupy Rome.

438 The Roman Empires, one in the east and the other in the west, begin to separate constitutionally.

476 The last Emperor in the west, Romulus Augustulus, is deposed by Gothic ruler Odoacer.

1453 The last Byzantine Emperor, Constantine XI, dies fighting as Byzantium falls to the Ottomans.

utterly embittered with Christianity after the massacre of his family during a series a vicious court intrigues, on the orders of his Christian cousin the Emperor Constantius. After briefly studying Greek philosophy, he embraced paganism before serving very successfully as a soldier for the Empire. When his cousin died in 361 he was acclaimed Augustus, Emperor of the Roman world, and nicknamed 'the Apostate' for his adoption of paganism.

As Emperor he was tolerant of other religions, allowing Christians and Jews full freedom to worship as they chose although he stripped the Church of many of its established state privileges. He devoted a considerable proportion of his short reign to the restoration of the dignity of the old pagan state religion, which worshipped the ancient gods.

The statue of the goddess Victory in the Curia, the Senate House, at Rome was highly symbolic in the old pagan culture of the Empire. The senators on entering the building were expected to make an offering of incense to the goddess. Christians had ignored the ritual for many years and the statue had been removed in 357 on the orders of the Emperor Constantius. Along with many similar gestures throughout the Empire, Julian had the statue replaced in the Curia as soon as he became Emperor.

His moves to push back the spread of the Christian faith did not prove popular. He spent a year at Antioch and in 363 he set out with his army on an expedition of conquest into Persia. He was killed by an unlucky spear in a retreat from an enemy cavalry force. When he died the Constantine dynasty died with him and he was succeeded by an elected Emperor, Jovian, a pious soldier. Although he too died within months, Jovian declared for the Christian faith and the Empire never faltered towards paganism again.

The last pagan pretender

In 388 Theodosius I, the Emperor in the east, defeated and killed the rebel leader Maximus who had deposed his young brother-in-law Valentinian II from the throne of Emperor in the west. Theodosius then left Valentinian in what he thought to be the capable hands of Arbogastes, a Frankish general. Valentinian was young and inexperienced. He quarrelled with Arbogastes and was later discovered strangled to death in 392. Arbogastes was not willing to take the throne himself but instead proclaimed an unknown pagan rhetoric teacher, Eugenius, as the new Emperor.

Theodosius took nearly two years to decide how and when to re-conquer the western Empire and punish Arbogastes. In 394 he moved his troops into battle near the River Frigidus in Italy's northern plains, but the eastern army's first encounter with the Gauls of Eugenius and Arbogastes nearly ended in disaster. They retreated in some disarray. During the night, however, some of the Gauls deserted to Theodosius' army. On the following morning, Theodosius was confident of victory; he was helped by a turn in the weather which blew a gale into the faces of his enemies. Theodosius' confidence was well founded and during his defeat of the Gauls Eugenius was captured. Begging for mercy at Theodosius' feet, Eugenius was decapitated for his pains. He was the last pagan to be acclaimed Roman Emperor. The real cause of the Western Emperor's troubles, Arbogastes, escaped capture but took his own life by falling on his sword a few days later.

The last of the united Roman Empire ⟨ 395 ⟩

The Emperor Diocletian was the first to realize that the Roman Empire was too large to be ruled by one man. He introduced an idea to help share the burden of governing the hugely spread and diverse Empire. When he came to the imperial throne in 284 he appointed Maximian his Caesar, his heir. In 286 Diocletian introduced an innovation which had significant consequences for hundreds of years. Maximian was named by Diocletian as another Augustus, or Emperor. There were now two Emperors, Maximian who was broadly responsible for the western part of the Empire, and Diocletian, who was responsible for the eastern part. In 293 Diocletian and Maximian appointed two heirs, or Caesars, one for the east and one for the west. The Empire was not actually divided constitutionally at this stage; Diocletian remained the senior of the two Augusti. Later it became the practice for one Augustus to live in the east, at Constantinople, with the other remaining in Italy, usually at Ravenna.

The 'tetrarchy' (rule of four) was intended to be a permanent institution, but when Diocletian retired in 305, civil war erupted between his various heirs. Constantine, son of Maximian's Caesar, was victorious in the west in 312, and in 324 defeated the Eastern Emperor. He thus reunited the Empire under his sole rule which lasted until his death in 337.

There were several other sole emperors. The last sole emperor who could claim to rule over a united Empire was Theodosius. After Valentinian II's death at the hands of Arbogastes, Theodosius continued to rule alone without the help of another Emperor until his own death at Milan in 395. He was succeeded by his two young sons, Arcadius, who became Emperor in the east, and Honorius, who became Emperor in the west. Until its final collapse, the Roman Empire was always then divided between east and west.

The head of Theodosius I, 'The Great', on one of his coins. He was the last sole emperor to rule over the complete Roman Empire. On his death in 395, he was succeeded by two emperors, one in the east and one in the west. (AKG)

Last of the Romans in Britain ⟨ 410 ⟩

The Roman occupation of Britain began in 55 BC when Julius Caesar first led his troops across the Channel. A further Roman invasion in AD 43, instigated by the Emperor Claudius, was followed by the Roman occupation of much of Britain. As part of the Roman Empire, Britannia lasted until the early 5th century. In 410 Honorius, the Western Emperor, began the withdrawal of Roman troops and told the Britons to be prepared to defend themselves. The withdrawal from Britain was intended as a temporary arrangement as the soldiers were required to repel German invaders elsewhere in the Empire. But they never returned and the Roman-style civilization began a slow decline. A British leader, Vortigern, fought hard against the invasions of the

Germanic peoples from across the Channel, Picts from the north and Irish from the west, but without lasting success. Not until the Norman Conquest six centuries later was Britain to experience unity and universal firm rule again.

The last Roman Emperor in the west

The fall of Rome to the Visigoths in 410 was not the end of the Empire in the west. The sack of Rome by Alaric and his army only lasted three days and in fact was a symbolic demise of the city rather than an actual and final fall to barbarian invaders. Rome by then was no longer the capital of Empire anyway as the Emperors in the west resided at Milan or Ravenna in the north of Italy. The final act in the story of the Empire in the west was played out some 60 years later. Julius Nepos was the penultimate ruler of the Empire in the west. In 475 he fled Italy, and the throne, after a coup led by Odoacer, the German commander of the Imperial Guard in Rome. Romulus, the son of Orestes, one of the high-ranking court officials, was selected and proclaimed Emperor. Fittingly for the last Emperor he was ineffectual and harmless.

Romulus Augustulus – literally 'little Emperor' – was ousted in 476 when Odoacer and his Germanic mercenaries stormed and took the city of Pavia. During the seizure of power, Orestes, the Emperor's father was slain. Odoacer considered the young Emperor of so little consequence that he was allowed to abdicate and his life was spared. Odoacer became the first barbarian King of Italy, and the young Romulus Augustulus, the last Roman Emperor in the west, was sent to live out his days at a villa in Campania on a pension of 6,000 gold solidi.

The last crusade to the Holy Land

The last proper Crusade to the Holy Land was the so-called 'Seventh' Crusade, led by King Louis, 'the Pious', of France in 1248. Louis was a brave and saintly man but was unable to overcome the overwhelming forces of the Saracens. In 1249 his Crusade came to brutal and bloody end in the Nile delta region when his army was surrounded and massacred by the Saracens at the Battle of Mansourah. In the retreat the Christian army was annihilated and King Louis himself was captured and only released after a ransom payment of 800,000 gold pieces. Louis was later to die in the hot North African sun in 1270 during the siege at Carthage. By this time the rest of the Christian Kings of Europe were too occupied with their own affairs to do more than dream of the fading glories of the Crusades against the Saracen forces in the Eastern Mediterranean.

The last serious attempt on another Crusade to the Holy Land was nearly 200 years later, in 1464. The senile Pope Pius II managed to get a small force together in the port of Ancona. However, enthusiasm amongst the army was already low and deteriorating fast when Pius died on 14 August before embarkation. The last remnants of Europe's crusading zeal died with him.

The last King of Jerusalem
1291

The Christian Kingdom of Jerusalem was founded by the Crusaders to hold the Holy Land – the lands on the eastern shores of the Mediterranean – safe for Christendom. It was nominally part of the Byzantine Empire but its rulers acknowledged the Pope as its head. King Guy was expelled from Jerusalem after being defeated by Saladin at the Horns of Hattin in 1187, and he and his family retreated to Cyprus. A new dynasty was founded on the island which supplied some of the kings of Jerusalem for the next 100 years.

The last King of Jerusalem, Henry II of Cyprus, was crowned in 1286 even though the kingdom by then excluded Jerusalem and simply consisted of a narrow strip of land along the coast. Acre was the last city in Eastern Christendom to hold out against the Saracens. It was besieged and fell in May 1291 amid scenes of dreadful slaughter. All Christians, barring a handful who managed to escape by sea, were put to the sword. It was also the swan-song for the two orders of priestly Knights, the Templars and the Hospitallers. Deadly rivals for nearly two centuries, the Templars and Hospitallers found themselves fighting side by side at Acre against the common foe. In the end they too were slaughtered almost to a man in their last battle. It was the end of all serious Christian ambitions to control the Eastern Mediterranean.

The last Knights Templars
1314

The Knights Templars were members of a powerful priestly order of Crusader knights originally established to protect the Holy Lands from the Saracens. By the 14th century they had been expelled from most of the Eastern Mediterranean but were still strongly entrenched in many parts of Europe. In France the Knights were hated for their arrogance and particularly feared for their power and influence. King Philip IV, 'the Fair', initiated moves which were to lead to the Templars' extinction. With the backing of the Pope, Clement V, Philip confiscated the lands and wealth of the Templars throughout Europe in 1308. The Templar Knights were arrested and put on trial for heresy. By 1311 most had been convicted and thrown into prison. Their leader, the Grand Master Jacques de Molay, was eventually burned at the stake in Paris in 1314. The Templars' bitter rivals, the Hospitallers, however, lived on. They survived to become the Knights of Malta and then the Knights of the Order of St John.

The last Crusader battle
1396

The battles fought by the Crusaders against the Saracens and the Turks were vicious and cruel on both sides. The last battle in the cause of the Crusaders was fought in Europe. King Sigismund of Hungary led an army against the newly emerging Turks under the Ottoman Sultan, Bayezit I. The Christian army was slaughtered at Nicopolis on the Danube in 1396. Of those Christians who survived the battle, over 3,000 were beheaded; only those lords and princes who could drum up the enormous ransom demands survived. Christendom understood the message and any thoughts of continuing a Holy War against Islam died on the banks of the Danube.

◁ 1453 ▷ *The last Byzantine Emperor*

The siege of Constantinople and its eventual destruction by the 100,000-strong army of the Ottoman Turks were the last acts in the story of the once mighty Roman Empire. At its end in 1453, the capital city of the Empire for over a thousand years was not the city it had been in its prime. The Roman Empire, still named after the city hundreds of miles away across the Mediterranean, had shrunk to not much more than the city of Constantinople itself. The once busy markets and teeming streets were all but deserted. A garrison of only 7,000 was on hand to keep the Muslim army at bay. The city walls, which until then had never been breached, stood massive and waiting for Ottoman Sultan Mehmed's attack.

Constantine XI was Emperor of a small, fast-disappearing Empire. He had succeeded to the throne on his brother's death in 1448 at the age of 44. Now in 1453 he waited for the end with the rest of the city's occupants. He had finally succumbed

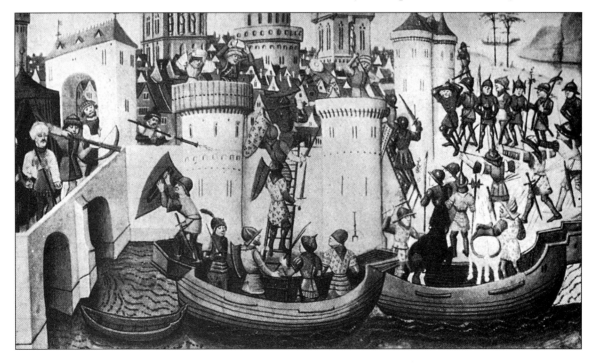

The conquest of Constantinople in 1453 by the Ottoman Turks marked the end of the 'Roman' Byzantine Empire. Its last emperor, Constantine XI Palaeologus Dragases, died bravely fighting as the city fell. (Popperfoto)

to the Church in Rome and had agreed the union of the Greek church with that of Rome in exchange for military assistance against the Turks. The help came but not in large enough numbers.

The siege lasted for seven weeks, the walls were never successfully breached despite the best efforts from some of the largest and most powerful cannons in the world. In the early hours of the morning of 29 May 1453, a small group of Turks found one of the sally ports in the walls with a less than adequate guard. They forced an entry and the city was doomed. The Emperor, in the thick of the fighting, flung himself at the massed enemy soldiers. He was hacked to death and his body was never recovered.

The last Christian service to be held in the city's most famous church, the Cathedral of St Sophia built by the Emperor Justinian 900 years before, was interrupted by the Turkish troops as they overwhelmed the doors and burst in. It was the last day of Constantinople and the Empire.

England's last possession in France

From the moment that the Norman Duke, William the Conqueror, won the English crown at the Battle of Hastings, English kings and queens have held land in France. Through a mixture of marriage and military conquest, control of French territory was an everyday concern for most English sovereigns. Large tracts of lands stretching from Gascony in the south to Calais in the north were ruled by English kings. In some instances they paid homage to the French throne for their possessions, but in other cases they fought bitter wars with French kings to claim their inheritances and conquests. Some of the fiercest fighting was carried out during the Hundred Years War when England actually claimed the French throne. All this came to an end in 1563 when Elizabeth I finally lost the last English outpost at Le Havre.

Several years earlier, in 1558, Calais was lost to the French. Elizabeth's sister, Queen Mary, grieved for its loss, claiming just before she died that 'when I am dead and opened you will find Calais lying on my heart'. Le Havre was seized by the English in a deal with the French Huguenots as a bargaining tool to regain Calais. However, when the French civil war ended early in 1563, the Huguenots withdrew their co-operation and support and left the English to defend Le Havre on their own. The garrison commander, the Earl of Warwick – brother to Queen Elizabeth's favourite, Robert Dudley – was forced to surrender at the end of July 1563 after months of siege.

The last Moors in Spain 1609

In 711 the Muslim Arabs of North Africa crossed the Straits of Gibraltar and conquered Spain. By the year 732, just one hundred years after the death of the Prophet Muhammad, prayers were being said in mosques all along the north coast of Africa and throughout all Spain. The Europeans called the Muslim invaders Moors, probably after Morocco, the land by which they entered Europe. Their occupation of

Spain was to last for nearly 800 years. From the mid-11th century the small Christian Kingdoms of northern Spain, principally Castile and Aragon, began to regain territory from the Moors. By 1492 the *Reconquista* (reconquest) was almost complete. That year the last Moors – living in Granada – surrendered to the forces of Ferdinand and Isabella of Aragon and Castile. The King and Queen entered the Alhambra Palace to preside over the abdication of the last Moorish ruler, Muhammad Abu-Abdullah.

The Moors left their mark on many parts of Spain. The architecture and art of Moorish Spain is unique and much of it still survives today. The Alhambra Palace and fortress – much admired today as an architectural gem – was the last Moorish stronghold to fall to the Christian Spaniards. After the capture of Granada, the few Moors remaining in Spain sought refuge in the mountains of the Spanish Alpujarras region. In these remote villages they survived until 1609 when the last few were driven into exile across the sea in North Africa.

The last of the Hanseatic League

The Hanseatic League was a powerful group of cities and commercial traders which dominated trade in northern Europe from the middle of the 13th century until the 17th century. Its aims were to secure their trade by controlling navigation, pilots and lighthouses and protecting its ships from pirates. The Hansa, as it was also known, even had its own parliament or Diet. At one stage the League took over and ruled the state of Denmark to protect its members. With the onset of extended voyaging and trading, especially with the New World from the 1500s, the influence of – and necessity for – the Hanseatic league faded. The Diet last met in 1669.

The last Holy Roman Emperor

On Christmas Day in the year 800 a new Emperor in the west was crowned by Pope Leo III at St Peter's Church in Rome. Charles the Great, King of the Franks, had swept into Italy with his troops to support the Pope against the rebellious people of Rome. In the ceremony he was grandly named Carolus Augustus, Emperor of the Romans. In an imaginative attempt to unite Christian Europe, he revived the idea of the Roman Empire and established the Holy Roman Empire.

This largely symbolic position of Christian Emperor was more often than not filled by the Kings of the Frankish or Germanic peoples. The possession of the Emperor's crown was not hereditary until hundreds of years later when Charles V of Spain was elected in preference to Francis I of France. The founder of the Habsburg dynasty, Charles, was elected Holy Roman Emperor in 1520. Thereafter the crown stayed with the Habsburgs. Charles V's successor as Emperor, in the late 18th and early 19th centuries, was Francis I of Austria, Francis II of the Holy Roman Empire.

After the defeats at the hands of Napoleon at Ulm and Austerlitz, Austria was forced to concede a separate peace at Pressburg. Napoleon took Berlin and formed the

Confederation of the Rhine. This forced Francis II to renounce the title of Holy Roman Emperor and Napoleon duly announced that the Empire was abolished. The Holy Roman Empire had lasted a thousand years, twice as long as its inspiration, the western Roman Empire.

Britain's last battle with the USA ◇ 1815 ◇

In 1812 the United States of America declared war on the United Kingdom. Two and a half years later the war was brought to an inconclusive end. The final engagement of the war, the Battle of New Orleans, proved to be the last armed conflict between the two countries. The British troops, led by the ill-fated Sir Edward Pakenham who died in the battle, were defeated by the Americans ably led by Andrew Jackson, a future US president.

The war was essentially over the USA's right to neutrality and maritime rights during the Anglo-French Wars. American trade with Europe was blockaded and constantly interfered with by the British. There were also other more emotive issues such as American sailors being press-ganged into service with the Royal Navy. Napoleon, who was keen to foment hostilities between the two countries to help his own cause, was

The Battle of New Orleans, scene of the last battle between Britain and the USA, in January 1815. The British redcoats were defeated by the Americans who were led by General Jackson, later to become the 7th President of the USA. The British General, Pakenham, was killed in the battle. (ME)

also involved. In the end, the war was too late to help the French and, just as the British government were about to lift the blockade, the USA lost patience and declared war.

Most of the fighting took place on the Canadian border. The USA greatly outnumbered the British and Canadian colonial forces and made some headway. Considering their numbers and short lines of communications, however, they made little long-term progress. The British troops enjoyed some success such as the capture of Washington, where they burned the presidential mansion. (On rebuilding the mansion the Americans painted it white, to hide the scars of violence and ever since it has been called the White House.) At sea the Royal Navy understandably had the best of it.

At the end of 1814 the British decided to move a contingent to the south, to attack the Americans at the mouth of the Mississippi River. General Pakenham landed his troops and supplies, complete with heavy cannons, and they made their way up the river bank towards New Orleans. Hostilities began in December at Bonaventura when the British opened up with their surprisingly well-placed guns. After much initial confusion the Americans managed to bring their own artillery into action and drive off the attackers, forcing them to abandon their guns. A new plan was devised by Pakenham which involved capturing the Americans' guns to turn them on themselves. Cutting a section of canal to bring in new supplies also figured prominently in the preparations.

The final assault from the British battalions came in the new year on 8 January. Pakenham's men, now reinforced and about 8,000 strong, were soon thrown into confusion. The defences prepared by Jackson were almost unassailable and the redcoats had very little chance of success. Assault equipment was found to be missing and the attack on the enemy artillery was so long delayed as to be useless. The American sharpshooters, firing from cover, picked off the officers, one by one. Pakenham himself was killed along with 290 others. Another 1,262 were wounded and 484 went missing. The Americans suffered only a handful of casualties and the British limped back to their ships under the command of General Lambert. While moving his depleted forces along the coast, Lambert captured Fort Mobile in Alabama on 11 February thus regaining some of his pride if not the initiative.

By the time the Battle of New Orleans had been fought the war was in any case over. The news of the Treaty of Ghent concluding the hostilities was signed the previous year on 24 December. News travelled slowly, so an unnecessary battle, in an even more unnecessary war, was fought out ignominiously for the British forces in the swamps of Louisiana. The battle, whilst it had no effect on the outcome of the war, did confirm the Americans' right to that part of their continent. In addition to establishing Jackson's reputation, the battle swept away any international doubts on the ownership of the Mississippi delta area and led to full-scale Americanization of the south west. In Britain the defeat was soon forgotten in the euphoric celebrations of the defeat of Napoleon at the Battle of Waterloo.

The last Anglo-American frontier conflict

There were many conflicts between Britain and the United States of America well after the War of Independence in the 18th century. The longest running dispute was over the frontier territory of Oregon in the extreme north-west of what is now indisputably the USA. Britain's last territorial claim in the USA was settled by treaty in 1846.

Since the early part of the 19th century Oregon had been the centre of considerable diplomatic activity between the two countries. Canadian fur traders had settled there, and in 1818 an agreement was reached that the official border between the British colony of Canada and the USA was to be the 49th parallel. Despite this, a joint occupation of Oregon was agreed for a period of ten years. Nine years later the joint occupation was extended for an indefinite period. During this time Oregon was dominated by the British Hudson's Bay Company at Fort Vancouver on the Columbia River. A few fur traders and missionaries from Canada and Britain moved into the territory in a slow trickle.

In the early 1840s immigration from the USA began to increase. Farmers looking for land came over the Rocky Mountains by way of the 'Oregon Trail'. Initially only a handful braved the hardships of the long journey from the Mississippi, but within a few years settlers were pouring into Oregon in their hundreds. The dangers of the trail have been immortalized in many Hollywood Westerns since, but they were very real. The trail itself was rocky, very ill-defined and criss-crossed by streams, rivers and mountains. The attacks on the wagon trains by Indians were matched by the rigours of disease and wild animals. Those who made it to Oregon, to settle down on their own farms, felt it was all worthwhile.

The few Canadians and Britons in the territory were gradually swamped by the American settlers. By 1843, the first real year of the Oregon Trail, it was clear that Oregon was more American than British or Canadian. American politicians were by this time proclaiming that it was 'America's "Manifest Destiny" to overspread the continent allotted by Providence for the free development of our yearly multiplying millions'. The northern border with Canada soon became an issue again. James Polk, on being elected president in 1844, declared that the USA's title to Oregon was 'clear and unquestionable'. Opinions across the Atlantic were equally firm that it was British but it was really only a matter of time before America's legitimacy was recognized.

Eventually Britain had to compromise and a treaty was signed on 15 June 1846 giving the USA all the territory south of the 49th parallel except for Vancouver Island. All British claims on land south of this line were at an end. Two years later Oregon became a Territory within the United States of America. The Hudson's Bay Company moved out to Vancouver Island and the American immigrants settled down to enjoy their land.

The last British conquests in India ◁ 1849 ▷

The end of the Second Sikh War in 1849 marked the end of the armed British conquest of India. The last battle of that war, at Gujarat, took place on 21 February 1849. The British force, commanded by Lord Gough, defeated the Sikh army decisively and the Punjab was immediately occupied to become part of British India. Until this period the Punjab was a separate independent state. In the 1830s it was ruled by Ranjit Singh. His Sikh army was highly developed and, apart from the British East India Company's sepoy armies, was the most modern and efficient in the sub-continent of

India. On Ranjit Singh's death in 1839, the new Sikh rulers began to look outside their borders for employment for their troops. The first Anglo-Sikh engagement came in 1846. There followed an uneasy period when the Punjab was nominally free, with a boy maharaja on the throne guided by some British advisers.

The Second Sikh war began in 1848, after two British political officers were murdered in Multan, in the south-west of the Punjab. Two inconclusive battles, one at Ramnagar and the other at Chillianwallah, left the two opposing armies manoeuvring in heavy rains in January 1849. The British losses at Chillianwallah had the public and politicians at home baying for Gough's blood. A replacement was sent to relieve him of his command. The 80-year-old Duke of Wellington had persuaded the dying Sir Charles Napier, the hero and conqueror of Sind province, to return to India with the memorable words, 'If you don't do, I must.' Before Napier could reach the Punjab, however, the last battle of the war was fought and, to the relief of the British nation, won.

Gough led a force of 25,000 men, both British and Sepoy, equipped with 96 guns. He and his army finally encountered the Sikhs – an army of about 60,000 men and 59 artillery pieces led by Sher Singh and his father Chattar Singh – on grassy plains near Gujarat. Both armies arrayed themselves in classic formations facing each other, guns and infantry at the centre, cavalry on the flanks. Gough's infantry advanced and the Sikh guns opened fire at a great distance. The British artillery replied and soon were tearing great holes in the Sikh ranks. The British infantry and cavalry again advanced and the Sikh lines broke. All their guns were captured and the entire Sikh army, including their commanders, surrendered or were put to flight. The last remnants surrendered to British-led troops on 14 March near the North West Frontier, ending Sikh resistance in the Punjab.

The tactics employed throughout the two Sikh wars were reminiscent of those used at Waterloo, and even earlier. Many of the British soldiers were actual veterans of those campaigns. Gujarat marked the end of the set piece battles on the Indian subcontinent. It was also the last major battle in which the Sepoy troops took part. After the Mutiny in 1857, the East India Company was dismantled and the Indian Army was formed to replace the Company's troops.

Sikh resistance was over, for the moment, and the Punjab was annexed by the British on 7 April. Although defeated in battle, the Sikhs were never really conquered. Their soldiers have served honourably and with great distinction in the Indian Army ever since. Today the Punjab is still part of India, but the spirit of the Sikh nation makes them as independently minded as ever. They present a series of problems to the Indian government at least as difficult as those faced by the British Raj.

◁ 1923 ▷   *The last of the Julian calendar*

The Julian calendar was devised by the Romans in 46 BC and named after its chief supporter, Julius Caesar. It was almost universally adopted in the developed world, and by the middle ages had spread throughout Europe and beyond. Under the Julian system, a year was divided into 365 days (rotations of the earth) and every fourth year was a leap year of 366 days. The leap year, however, was an approximation. The annual error of over 11 minutes, year after year, accumulated and by the 16th century astronomers noticed that the spring equinox, which should have been on 21 March each year, was now on 11 March.

The 19th Ecumenical Council of the Church of Rome, under Pope Gregory, declared that an extra ten days must be added to the date to correct the deviation. For much of Europe the last use of the old Julian calendar was 4 October 1582; the day after that was 15 October 1582 – the ten days had 'disappeared'. The new calendar was named after the Pope and became known as the Gregorian calendar. It altered the calculation of leap years, to avoid future problems, by specifying that century years would only be leap years if divisible by 400 (for example, 1600 and 2000).

Britain and several other countries soldiered on under the Julian system. Lord Chesterfield was a British diplomat who travelled widely in Europe and was aware of the absurdity of a date deviation between different countries. By 1750 he had persuaded the British Parliament to come to a decision. The Calendar New Style Act decreed that, for Britain and its colonies, the change to the Gregorian calendar would be made in 1752. By this time a further one day's error had appeared so there were eleven days to catch up.

On Wednesday 2 September 1752 Britain had its last day under the Julian calendar. The following day, Thursday, was the 14 September 1752. The loss of days from the 3rd to the 13th, inclusive, gave rise to riots from the ignorant and (understandably) confused who took to the streets shouting 'Give us back our eleven days!' But the days were gone. Gone too was the new year's day of 25 March for England and Wales. In line with the rest of Europe, the English and Welsh made 1 January the beginning of the year. The Scots had already changed to a new year's day of the 1st of January and celebrated their last 25 March Hogmanay back in 1600. Today the ecclesiastical year still begins on 'Lady Day', 25 March.

There were still some important outposts holding out against the Gregorian calendar. In Russia the calendar remained Julian until after the First World War but not without some confusion in its final years. At the 1908 Olympic Games in London, the Russian Military Rifle team missed their competition slot. They turned up, after the event, bemused and annoyed to learn that their calendar was, by now, 12 days adrift from the rest of the world. After the Russian Revolution, Lenin brought the Soviet Union into line with the rest of the world when he declared that 1 February 1918 would instantly become 14 February. For over 70 years the Soviet Union celebrated the October revolution on 7 November. Greece was the last western country to come into line with the Gregorian calendar, abandoning the Julian calendar in 1923.

The last invasion of British soil ◇ 1940 ◇

The Channel Islands, situated just a few miles off the coast of France, have their own internal government but come under the sovereignty of the United Kingdom. At the beginning the Second World War, after the fall of France to the German forces in 1940, it became obvious that a successful defence of the Islands would be impossible. A token defence would have resulted in large civilian casualties and so a decision was made by the British government in June not to try to resist the inevitable German occupation. Orders were issued to completely demilitarize the Islands, and by 21 June all troops had been evacuated along with most of the children and men of military age.

The Luftwaffe was to play the major part in the capture of the Channel Islands. Prior to their invasion, the Germans gave a show of strength. On 28 June St Peter Port on Guernsey and St Helier on Jersey were bombed and strafed and many building were badly damaged. On Guernsey a line of lorries loaded with tomatoes, mistaken for ammunition trucks, was machine-gunned and several of the drivers were killed. The St Peter Port lifeboat on its way to Jersey was also attacked and its coxswain was killed. In all, the attentions of the Luftwaffe killed 29 people on Guernsey and 9 on Jersey. On the evening of 30 June the Luftwaffe again visited the islands. Pouches containing demands to surrender were dropped on St Peter Port and St Helier. Later an aircraft carrying a party of German officers landed at Guernsey airport to be met by four of the island's police officers. After their meeting with the Bailiff, Guernsey passed into German occupation. The next day, 1 July, Jersey too was occupied in the same way.

The German capture of the Channel Islands was the last successful invasion of British soil. The occupation lasted nearly five years. The Germans spent much of that time heavily fortifying the islands' coastlines, expecting counter invasions from British forces. Apart from a few covert reconnaissance missions, Allied troops never came until the war in Europe was over. On 8 May 1945 Prime Minister Winston Churchill announced in a radio broadcast that 'Our dear Channel Islands will be free today.' Two Royal Navy destroyers were on their way across the Channel to liberate the only part of the British Isles to have been occupied during the Second World War. The following morning, on 9 May, the German occupation forces surrendered without a shot being fired.

◄ 1948 ► *The last links between the UK and Ireland*

In 1922 the Irish Free State was created out of the 26 southern counties of Ireland. The six northern counties had opted to stay within the United Kingdom as the Province of Northern Ireland. Although the violence and conflict would continue, as far as Britain was concerned, this settlement brought to an end more than a century of political debate on Irish Home Rule.

The Irish Free State remained linked to Britain for many years in a number of ways. The Anglo-Irish Treaty of 1921, which set up the Irish Free State, allowed Britain the military and naval use of three ports on the southern coast of Ireland. In 1938 British troops finally moved out of these 'treaty ports' of Berehaven, Lough Swilly and Cobh after talks between Irish President de Valera and British Prime Minister Chamberlain. This was vital to Irish interests as it allowed them to remain neutral during the Second World War.

The colonial links between the two countries lasted until 1949 when John Costello, Eire's premier, decided to take his country out of the British Commonwealth. Southern Ireland, now Eire, declared full republican status and severed all but the normal diplomatic links on Easter Monday, 18 April 1948.

The last state to join the USA

1959

The make-up of the United States of America, across a complete continent and beyond into the oceans, reached its present form in 1959 when Hawaii became the 50th – and so far the last – state to join the Union. The USA grew from the original 13 states which declared independence from Britain in 1776 to the 50 that exist today.

Hawaii, a group of volcanic islands in the middle of the Pacific, had attracted explorers from Europe and America in the 18th century. The indigenous inhabitants generally welcomed their visitors with open arms. By the end of the 19th century, the USA had achieved a colonial dominance over the affairs of the islands, ahead of Britain and France. In 1898 they were formally annexed to the USA and in 1900 achieved Territorial status. After the island's almost front-line participation in the Second World War strong pressure for full statehood gained ground. On 18 March 1959 Hawaii closely followed Alaska (which had achieved statehood in January) into the United States of America.

The last of the Berlin Wall

1989

The Berlin Wall had been erected by the East German authorities in 1961 – at the height of the Cold War – to keep the population of the divided city apart. For 30 years the 96 miles of concrete and barbed wire thwarted attempts by East Germans to defect to the West. The Wall reflected a similar barrier running the complete length of the international frontiers across Europe and Germany itself, and came to symbolize the divisions between East and West for the full period of the Cold War. Its last moments came in 1989 as the icy relations between East and West began to thaw. On the night of 9 November 1989, with the authorities watching but allowing it to happen, the first breach in the Wall was bashed through by excited crowds from both East and West Berlin. It was the culmination of a movement for democratic reform fuelled by a growing economic crisis. Knowing they could not stem the tide of reform, and could not expect

The decaying reinforced concrete of the Berlin Wall symbolized the end of the Cold War between East and West. Fragments of the wall were chipped off as keepsakes by thousands of souvenir hunters. (Gamma)

help from the crumbling Soviet Union, the Communist East German authorities stood by as the Wall collapsed.

The demolition of the Wall was as much about a desire for freedom as a desire for German reunification. The following October, less than a year later, the East German state ceased to exist as East and West Germany were politically united. Today only a few small segments of the Berlin Wall remain as a monument to Germany's divided past.

The last of the Soviet Union

On coming to power in 1985, Mikhail Gorbachev introduced the dual policies of *glasnost* (openness) and *perestroika* (re-structuring). Together these policies began an unstoppable tide of reform across the Soviet Union. Despite his desire for change, Gorbachev himself still believed that the Communist Party could reform itself from within and retain power. But criticism of Communism in the USSR became more open and the idea of a new – capitalist – system gained in popularity. The Baltic Republics – Lithuania, Estonia and Latvia – were the first to declare independence and leave the Soviet Union, and resisted Gorbachev's attempts to force them back.

The continuing economic collapse and fragmentation of the Soviet Union was viewed with horror by members of the Politburo, the Soviet Union's ruling elite, who remembered the days when the Soviet Empire was a respected and feared world power. Their attempt to stop reform and take control led to an abortive coup against Gorbachev in September 1991. However, the newly elected Russian President, Boris Yeltsin, was instrumental in forcing the conspirators to surrender. The crisis precipitated the secession of the remaining republics within the Soviet Union, and in December the USSR was dissolved. On 1 January 1992, the President of the Soviet Union, Mikhail Gorbachev, quietly left office in one of the most peaceful surrenders of Communist power ever seen.

The last of Europe's Communist Dictatorships

When the Soviet Union's iron grip on Eastern Europe began to slip, it was only a matter of time before the Warsaw Pact countries at least gained the freedom to choose alternatives to Communism. Even those countries outside the direct influence of the USSR were affected by the feeling of anti-Communism and succumbed to the pressure for democracy. Albania was the last to go. The Balkan state, isolated by its extreme Stalinist approach to Communism, too severe even for the Soviet Union's approval, was ruled by the dictator Enver Hoxha from 1946 until his death in 1985. Internecine feuding within the government followed his death and an even more severe international isolationist stance was taken. The Communist government was returned to power in the first multi-party elections in 1991, but fell in March the following year when Europe's poorest country took its first faltering steps to freedom.

MILITARY MATTERS   *4*

Naval affairs

The last of the 'fir' frigates

1814

Most of the magnificent square-rigged ships of the line of the Royal Navy were constructed of oak, one of the hardest woods available in the northern hemisphere, and were known as 'wooden walls'. A first-rate ship, carrying 100 guns or more, required over a quarter of a million cubic feet of solid timber, obtained from some 75 acres of mature oak forest.

During the Napoleonic Wars, the Royal Navy found that more and more ships were needed to maintain and expand its influence around the world. In a desperate measure to make up for the shortage of oak, some 50 of the smaller ships of the line, fourth- and fifth-rate frigates, were made of imported softwoods, mainly from Canada. Various softwoods were tried: pitch pine, red pine and yellow pine; all generally (and incorrectly) called 'fir'. These ships had a relatively short life but were cheaper and quicker to build. They plugged a vital gap in the Navy's ship-building programme and became known as the 'fir' frigates, serving with distinction alongside their tougher-hulled sisters. The last of these fir frigates was the *Leander*, commissioned in 1814. She was finally broken up in 1830.

The torpedo worm was the enemy of all ships' hulls. It attacked the wooden planking, burrowing deep into the timber, causing major structural problems. As a measure of protection all hulls were covered in copper sheathing. If this was well fastened and regularly maintained it gave the hardwood hulls many years of service; some ships lasted over a hundred years. The softwoods were not so easily protected. Fixing the copper sheets in place with copper nails was difficult; they worked loose and the ships had to pay regular visits to dockyards to be re-sheathed. In addition the softwoods were especially susceptible to rot. However, at the time ships were expected to take heavy gunfire directly into their hulls from close quarters and the question of whether a hull could last ten, fifteen or even a hundred years was regarded as somewhat academic.

In 1812, just as the war at sea was all but won and the ship shortage seemingly solved, Britain managed to embroil herself in another war, this time with America. Frigates were needed on the USA's eastern seaboard and the construction of what was to be the last batch of softwood frigates began. The *Leander* was one of the last of these ships to be constructed. The keel was laid in June 1813 at Wigram and Green's shipyard on the River Thames at Blackwall. She was constructed in pitch pine and was launched a few months later in November. From Blackwall she was towed round to dry-dock at Greenwich where the copper sheathing was nailed in place.

The *Leander* carried 58 guns, 26 of the 42-pounder carronades and 32 of the long 24-pounders. She had a tonnage of 1,572, was 174 feet long at the water line and had a beam of 45 feet. In February 1814 she sailed with a full crew for the USA, Captain Sir George Ralph Collier in command.

By June she was already in action, capturing a 16-gun American ship, the *Rattlesnake*. Later the *Leander* was involved in a famous action, along with two other Royal Navy ships (both fir frigates), against the USA's *Constitution* off the Cape Verde Islands. In the very short time before the war was over the *Leander* gained a respectable reputation with the Americans and considerable glory for the Royal Navy. In 1815, when the wars with both France and the USA were over, the *Leander* already needed repairs to her hull. In 1816 the ship took part in the bombardment of Algiers and its crew suffered heavy casualties.

The *Leander* was completely re-coppered twice more in the next three years and in 1822 was docked at Portsmouth and taken out of active service. Here she rotted away for several years until in March 1830 she was put out of her misery and 'taken to pieces'. Her destruction was the end of the last fir frigate of the Royal Navy. It is appropriate that the 'Leander' name lived on. The Royal Navy's habit of using its famous ships' names over and over again means that the present-day Leander class frigates have their roots, in name at least, in an inauspicious class of softwood sailing ships constructed in great haste at the beginning of the 19th century.

The last naval fleet action under sail

The Battle of Navarino on 20 October 1827 is notable for two things: the utter confusion during the course of fighting, and the fact that it was the last naval fleet engagement to be fought wholly under sail. On one side were the ships of Britain, France and Russia. They were mediating in the Greek War of Independence, where Turkey and its ally Egypt were engaged in fighting the Greeks.

The fleets of the three Western Allies had joined together in October 1827 to form a squadron under the command of Trafalgar veteran, Vice-Admiral Sir Edward Codrington. He had ten ships-of-the-line, ten frigates, one corvette and some half-dozen schooners at his command. The Egyptian commander, Ibrahim Pasha, had his combined Turkish and Egyptian fleet of well over sixty-five ships anchored in a large semi-circle in Navarino Bay, on the western edge of the Greek Peloponnese peninsula. Two large Turkish shore batteries provided protection. Ibrahim Pasha had agreed that he would not leave the bay until the Turkish Sultan had responded to the Allies' mediation attempt.

Unfortunately a Greek naval division arrived in the nearby Gulf of Patras incensing Ibrahim Pasha. Twice he sent some of his fleet to intercept them. Both times they were turned back by the Allies. On land the Turkish army was busy attacking the Greeks. Codrington decided to intervene directly with a show of force which he hoped would induce Pasha to desist. On 20 October he ordered his squadron to enter the bay and moor alongside the Turkish and Egyptian ships. His flagship *Asia*, 80 guns, in the lead, sailed into position but there was no reaction. The battle began when the British frigate *Dartmouth*, which was sent to warn off some Turkish fireships, was attacked.

The smoke from gunfire gradually obscured all visibility and added to the confusion at the Battle of Navarino in October 1827. The action of the British, French and Russian ships against the combined Turkish and Egyptian forces was the last fleet battle involving traditional sailing ships. (ME)

Gradually, as ship after ship on both sides started to engage its nearest enemy, the bay was engulfed in gunfire and smoke.

The shore batteries opened up on the French ships as the Russian ships, with wind dropping, struggled to reach their positions alongside the enemy. Visibility through the gunsmoke was poor, and most of the ships' crews had great difficulty in seeing their neighbours. However, before moving into the bay, Codrington instructed all his squadron in the words of his old commander Nelson 'If a general action should take place, no captain can be better placed than when his vessel is alongside one of the enemy.' His words were heeded and despite the overwhelming superiority in numbers of Ibrahim Pasha's fleet, the Western Allies' ships and men gave an excellent account of themselves. Many ships caught fire and after about two hours of close quarter fighting, most of the Turkish and Egyptian ships were either ablaze or blown up and sunk.

In his dispatches Codrington wrote of the enemy ships that 'out of a fleet composed of 81 men-of-war, only one frigate and 15 smaller vessels are in a state ever to be again put to sea'. Damage to the Allies' fleet was also quite substantial; most of the British ships and all of the French had to return to home ports for repairs. The Allies' casualties were relatively light: 150 killed and less than 500 wounded. With crews numbering in the hundreds and each subject to cannon and grape shot, musket fire, grenade explosions and vicious wood splinters for several hours, the Allies got off lightly.

The British government were unsure how to react to their victory. None of the countries concerned was actually at war. Codrington was, for a short time, recalled home in disgrace. Navarino was an accident of arms that should never have happened. Britain's navy was regarded as supreme and had seldom been challenged after the defeat of the French in 1815. Throughout most of the 19th century only relatively small naval skirmishes occurred. The Royal Navy had to wait until the Battle of Jutland in the First World War for its next full fleet action. By then the 'wooden walls of England', driven only by sails, had given way to the steam power of the dreadnought battleships.

The last Lord High Admiral

The political chief of the Royal Navy was, for centuries, the First Lord of the Admiralty. The post developed from the older title of the Lord High Admiral, held by Buckingham in James I's day. The use of the title of Lord High Admiral fell into disuse for most of the 18th century, occasionally one or other of the navy chiefs would have it bestowed on him as a mark of honour. Most, however, made do with First Lord of the Admiralty. Then in April 1827, William Duke of Clarence, George IV's younger brother, who had served in the Royal Navy in his younger days, became the last Lord High Admiral.

The Duke of Clarence wanted to take his duties as the First Lord of the Admiralty very seriously, he even went to sea and hoisted his flag, the last First Lord of any description to do so. However, his attempts at establishing an active role for himself were not appreciated. In October he gave his public support to Admiral Codrington who was in disgrace over his high handedness at the Battle of Navarino. The following year he attempted to enquire into the low standards of naval gunnery. Both the government and his brother, the King, stepped in. After a furious series of rows the Duke of Clarence resigned as Lord High Admiral in August 1828. His brother died two years later and the Duke of Clarence ascended the throne as William IV, the 'Sailor King'.

An administrative shake up in the armed forces took place in the 1960s, and the Board of the Admiralty had its last meeting on 26 March 1964. When it was reconstituted as the Admiralty Board of the new Defence Council, the Lord High Admiral rose from the waves in the form of the present sovereign, Queen Elizabeth II. It was in this guise that she was presented to her Royal Navy when she reviewed the Fleet at Spithead on 28 June 1977, the occasion of her Silver Jubilee.

 ## *The last of larboard*

Over many centuries, larboard and starboard were the words used throughout the world's navies, for what landlubbers call left and right. The origins of the words are not certain, but it is probable that starboard is a development of 'steer board', or 'steer side'. It was the side of the ship on which the side rudder would traditionally have been mounted, the right side. The origin of the word larboard is a bit more obscure; the only certainty is that it meant the opposite of starboard, that is, the left.

Occasions for possible confusion between the two similar sounding words are obvious, especially at the height of roaring gale in an emergency. The word 'port', for left, came into use around the 17th century. When docking, a ship with a side-mounted rudder would obviously be manoeuvred with the rudder side away from the quay, the opposite side becoming the 'port' side.

The Royal Navy, however, retained the term larboard until the 19th century when it finally recognized the need to avoid misunderstandings in directions. On 22 November 1844 the Admiralty declared that, 'as the distinction between starboard and port is so much more marked than between starboard and larboard it is their Lordships direction that the word larboard shall no longer be used.' But one can imagine the older salts taking a few more years yet before they uttered their last 'larboard'. Curiously, the next biggest English speaking navy, that of the USA, quickly followed their Lordships' lead when their Navy Department made a similar pronouncement on the demise of 'larboard' on 18 February 1846.

The last of the Royal Navy's semaphore   ◁1847▷

In the early 19th century the Royal Navy had a most ingenious method of rapid communications between its headquarters in London and its coastal and port commanders around southern England. A series of semaphore stations, manned round the clock, connected the Admiralty in Whitehall with its main ports at Portsmouth and Plymouth. In the days when travelling (and therefore communication) times were normally measured in hours or even days, messages on naval business were relayed quickly from station to station. Complicated information travelled hundreds of miles in a matter of minutes. This system served the Navy well throughout most of the wars with France. It continued throughout the 1820s and 1830s and was eventually replaced by electric telegraph in 1847.

The first semaphore stations were positioned around the coast in 1795. An arrangement of balls and flags was hoisted to send limited messages on the weather and other coastal navigation matters. The system was further developed and streamlined, and a line of relay stations from London to Portsmouth opened in 1796. Complicated signalling boards, mounted on masts above the stations, consisted of batteries of shutters which were operated by ropes from below. An observer with a telescope read the signal from the adjacent station. This was repeated by the signaller in his own station for onward transmission. The lines were expanded a few years later to include Plymouth in Devon and Chatham in Kent. A highly sophisticated code system was devised which could cope with all the requirements of the Royal Navy's orders and commands.

When Britannia ruled the waves, semaphore helped speed messages to the ports which could dispatch ships to the farthest corners of the globe. From the moment a plan was devised in Whitehall, a ship could set sail from Plymouth within an hour with full orders to carry out a complicated diplomatic or naval mission. A speeding frigate reaching Plymouth with urgent news from a distant ocean could have its information on an admiral's desk in London within minutes. The system generally was a great success. It was obviously dependent on good visibility and operation at night was usually impossible. On a good day, however, the Royal Navy could send its time signal from the Admiralty's Whitehall headquarters to Plymouth and back again in under three minutes – an almost unbelievable communications achievement for the times.

At the end of the Napoleonic Wars the lines were closed, but in 1822 the line from London to Portsmouth was re-opened with a fully modernized system. Construction of a new line to Plymouth was also started but this was incomplete when abandoned in 1830. The semaphore service maintained a regular uniformed corps of signallers. Over the next two decades they developed a proud tradition of service and performance.

In 1837 Sir Charles Wheatstone patented an 'electric telegraph' which was soon adopted by the railways. In 1844, Samuel Morse in America set up the first public telegraph, between Washington and Baltimore. Its capabilities were astounding and left any mechanical semaphore way behind. Back in England, the Royal Navy was not slow to catch up. On 13 September 1847 the crews at all the semaphore stations received their notices. On the very last day of the year they were paid off and the semaphore closed down. Today some of the stations still exist, curious reminders of an intriguing and truly successful communications system absolutely right for its time.

The last of the press gang

By the end of the 18th century 'impressment' was the most common method of recruitment for the Royal Navy. During the Napoleonic Wars the press gangs would roam the streets of Britain's seaports capturing and taking men forcibly into the Navy. Officially they were supposed to take only trained seamen from the merchant service, but in practice any able-bodied male could be hauled away for indefinite duty in the hard and dangerous world of the Royal Navy's warships. The system lasted until the 1850s when the conditions of service for naval ratings were changed. In 1853 the Navy introduced a system for training and for fixed terms of service; the provision of crews for Her Majesty's ships became the responsibility of the government rather than the local ports or the captains of the ships.

There were many volunteers in the Royal Navy but in time of war this method of manning was never enough. If the captain of a ship required more men to keep his ship properly run he organized a press gang when he reached port. In the busy naval ports this often led to rival press gangs, from different ships, fighting each other for the hapless impressed men. There were few, if any, qualifications necessary; two arms and two legs were the only essentials. No training in naval duties was required and the newly conscripted men soon learned the ropes alongside the old hands on board. Those who could not learn did not last long.

As the numbers of men available for the ships dwindled, especially at the height of the wars with France, the responsibility for pressing was given over to a centrally organized Impress Service. In 1795, the country was divided into areas, each with the responsibility to find a certain quota of likely men. These were usually found in the prisons and the magistrates courts. As life in the Navy was even more vicious than in the Army (the local militia also had a quota to be filled) if there was any choice in the matter the Navy was left with the dregs. In terms of human misery the system was a disaster; as a way of running a successful navy the system, incredibly, seemed to work. Brutal times required brutal solutions and life in the Navy's ships had never been easy.

The tramp of the press gangs on the cobbled back streets of the ports and seaside villages finally faded away in 1853 when the Continuous Service Act provided for the recruitment of young men who were to be trained before they went to sea. A fixed term of service was defined. The older men who had experienced almost indefinite service, 'the Queen's hard bargains' originally from the prisons, died out. The crews were now generally younger, more respectable and certainly more humanely treated. Conscription – along with all the paraphernalia of paperwork that bureaucracy could devise – returned to Britain only in 1916 during the First World War. Ironically, during the war, it was the Royal Navy and not the Army that was considered the 'soft option'.

The last hanging at the yard arm

The grim process of executing a sailor for a capital offence, on board one of the 'old wooden walls of England', was customarily carried out by hanging from the yard arm. The yard arm is the large cross piece on the mast for supporting the mainsail. The ritual of execution began with the hoisting of a yellow flag at the masthead. The condemned man was escorted to the bows of the ship and his head placed in the noose. On the signal, usually the firing of the gun, a party of sailors would heave on the rope and the poor man would swing out and up to the end of the yard. Then, if he was lucky, he would soon black out and lose consciousness. His body would hang there until he had strangled to death.

The last unfortunate to be judicially hanged to death on board ship in the Royal Navy was a Royal Marine. Private Dallinger was convicted of attempted murder, and on 13 July 1860 he was swung up to the yard arm and there strangled to death in front of the full ship's company. Those sailors and marines condemned to death after this date were taken ashore to swing from land-based gallows.

The last of the 'wooden walls'

In 1861 the *Warrior*, the first British warship to be built entirely of iron, was launched. All other warships – until then built of wood – were immediately made obsolete. Old methods and ideas die hard and because it took several years to build a ship-of-the-line, for a few years wooden ships were still brought into service. The last all-wooden, first-rate three-decker to be commissioned into the Royal Navy was the *Victoria*. It was almost identical to the ships that Britain's sailors had been sailing in for the previous 200 years.

Contrary to some accounts that suggest that the Royal Navy was over-cautious and highly resistant to new ideas, the middle of the 19th century was a period of exciting innovations and great change. In the 1850s the ships-of-the-line were sail-driven and made entirely from wood; they fired solid cannon balls through holes in the hull from muzzle-loading guns. By the 1880s the battle fleet consisted of steam-powered, iron-armoured ships firing explosive shells from turreted breech-loaders. For such a transition to have taken place in peacetime, in the largest navy in the world, was a considerable achievement. The transition period lasted several years. Many battleships that were started as wooden sailing ships were converted to ironclads and steam power before launching. Several others were deliberately made of wood to use up the vast supplies of timber in the dockyards and then clad in iron armour plate.

The response to invention and new ideas, of course, came in fits and starts. *The Times* of London saw fit to criticize the efficacy of the obsolete *Victoria* which had her keel laid in 1859. A week before she sailed on her first commission as flagship to the Mediterranean fleet, the newspaper wrote: 'In time of war, the Admiral on board *Victoria* would have to decide between going into port or going to the bottom!' Nevertheless she did sail, all magnificent 250 wooden feet and 3,000 tons of her, with a crew of 680 officers and ratings. It could have pulled alongside any ship-of-the-line from the Napoleonic Wars and not have been out of place. At 3 o'clock in the afternoon of 23

November 1864, the *Victoria* sailed from Spithead for Malta and, with her, the 'wooden walls of England' sailed into history.

The *Victoria* was the first of several Royal Navy ships to be named after Queen Victoria. Fortunately she never saw action as *The Times* was probably correct in its observation about her possible usefulness. She was decommissioned in 1880 and sold for scrap in 1893.

The launching of the *Victoria* at Portsmouth in November 1859 in the presence of most of the senior members of the Royal Family including Queen Victoria and the Prince Consort. Obsolete by the time it sailed on its first voyage, the Victoria was the last three-decker wooden ship to be commissioned into service with the Royal Navy. (Hulton)

1903   *The last Royal Navy ship with a figurehead*

For centuries the prows of fighting ships were adorned with dramatic carved figures. The Royal Navy's ships were no exception; their figureheads often represented some item connected with the ship's name. The carved wooden figureheads were often saved when the ships themselves were broken up in old age; many now have pride of place in naval museums.

HMS *Cadmus*, a sloop for use under sail and steam power, was launched at Sheerness in 1903. On its bow was a figurehead representing Cadmus, King of Thebes. The ship was decommissioned and sold to a buyer in Hong Kong in 1921. It was the last ship in the Royal Navy with a figurehead.

The last grog ration

Grog, every sailor's favourite drink, was issued daily to all those serving aboard Her Majesty's ships. Grog was diluted rum: one part rum to three parts water, known as 'three-waters' (any ship's captain who tried to get away with 'five-waters' risked mutiny). It was introduced to the Royal Navy by Admiral Vernon whose nickname was 'Old Grog' on account of the grogram boat cloak he used to wear. His drink thus became known to sailors everywhere as 'grog'.

Issued twice a day in half pint measures, grog was a major part of life on board ship. To the sailors in the old wooden walls, it made their hard life just a bit more bearable. Drunkenness was an offence serious enough to have the offender clapped in irons in the ship's brig and, to prevent inebriation, rum was never allowed to be issued neat, undiluted. However, with a little ingenuity a sailor could save up his ration from the early part of the day and drink it with the second tot in the evening. With care the pleasure of serious intoxication could be had by any sailor, at least once in every day, and drunkenness was rife.

Grog became more than a comfort, it became a right. Over the years the ceremony of measuring it out and issuing it to all the representatives of the different messes on board was a greatly treasured tradition. The ceremony continued even after the ration was cut from the original one pint in Nelson's day to a more civilized quantity in the late 20th century. That rare thing, the teetotal sailor, could receive a small cash allowance in lieu of their grog. Naval professionalism finally caught up with the grog ration in 1970 and the last daily issue of grog in the Royal Navy was drunk on 30 July.

The last aircraft carrier

The Royal Navy's last fixed-wing conventional aircraft carrier was the *Ark Royal*, which was decommissioned on 21 December 1978. The disbanding of the naval aircraft squadrons, with Phantoms and Buccaneer aircraft, was the end of an era for Royal Naval aviation. The building of the *Ark Royal* was started during the Second World War. Originally intended to be named HMS *Irresistible*, it took until 1950 for the carrier to be launched and it was renamed the *Ark Royal*. It was finally commissioned in 1955.

HMS *Ark Royal* never saw any action. Its last major appearance in public was at the 1977 Silver Jubilee Spithead Fleet Review although in 1978 it made a farewell cruise around the UK. The last naval squadron to fly from the *Ark Royal*'s deck was 892 Squadron equipped with Phantom FG1, general-purpose fighters. The last launch of a Phantom from the deck of the *Ark Royal* was on 27 November 1978. The Squadron disbanded in December and the aircraft were transferred to the Royal Air Force. *Ark Royal* was paid off for disposal, sold for scrap and in 1980 was broken up in Scotland. The Royal Navy still has three Invincible class carriers and from these it still flies aircraft, the STOVL (short take off vertical landing) Sea Harriers, but the role of naval multi-layered air defences with deep strike ability has gone.

THE LAND BATTLE

The last castle sieges

The last time British castles were used for the purpose for which they were originally built – as fortified strongholds withstanding attacks from an enemy – was during the English Civil War in the 17th century. During the war many castles were held, by their owners, in the Royalist cause but they all eventually fell to the Parliamentarian forces, sometimes after years of siege. Corfe Castle in Dorset for instance, the home of the Bankes family, held out against the Roundheads for two years until finally in 1646 one of the family retainers betrayed them and let in the enemy.

Some larger castles and fortified walled towns were occupied by larger formations of the Royalist army. After the King was imprisoned the war drew to a close and the last Cavalier castles surrendered. The last castle siege, that at Colchester in Essex, came to an end in August 1648. The Parliamentarians under Colonel Raisborough had besieged the castle for many months. The Royalists held out inside the walls of the town, much against the wishes of the townsfolk who supported Parliament. The besieging army was eventually reinforced by a 40-gun siege train brought from London by Lord Fairfax. After months of starvation and extreme privation the town's Royalist forces surrendered to Fairfax on 28 August, much to the relief of the Colchester townsfolk. Little mercy was shown. Two of the Royalist leaders, Sir Charles Lucas and Sir George Lisle, were executed, shot beside the walls of the town keep for earlier having broken parole. Many of the other officers were imprisoned and later executed.

In the final months of the war smaller castles such as Deal and Sandown also surrendered, acknowledging the victory of the Parliamentarian forces. At Pontefract in Yorkshire there was one last castle which held out well into the next year. Pontefract Castle was a 13th-century stronghold built on solid rock. It had a strong quatrefoil-shaped keep and had the luxury of its own water supply. It had been one of the premier castles of the middle ages.

During the Civil War, cannon, tunnelling and even bribery had failed to shift the Royalists from Pontefract. But when they learnt of King Charles's execution in January 1648, the occupants admitted their cause was lost, surrendering to the Parliamentarians in March. It was a bitter blow; theirs had been a valiant siege and they had resisted to the end.

Cromwell took his revenge for the Cavaliers' impudence. The Parliamentarian forces were ordered to 'slight' – completely demolish – Pontefract Castle. It was reduced to rubble and even most of the stone was removed from the site. Today a small part of the tower and a fragment of the outer curtain wall survive as a monument to the ending of a bitter civil war and the last castle siege in Britain.

The last battle on English soil

1685

The Duke of Monmouth, the bastard son of Charles II, was living in exile at The Hague in the Low Countries when his father died in 1685. Charles had left no legitimate son as heir, so his brother, James II, a professed Roman Catholic, became King. Monmouth, an experienced soldier, and a Protestant, was soon persuaded to make a bid for the throne. His ill-advised adventure ended just a few weeks later with his defeat in the last battle to be fought on English soil. Monmouth landed with less than 100 men at Lyme Regis in June. His Army soon grew to about 6,000, although it was never properly equipped. After several inconclusive skirmishes with the Royalist Army and local militias, it camped at Bridgwater in early July. Monmouth and his officers were well aware that a decisive victory was needed soon to secure his bid for the throne.

The Royalists were camped at the nearby village of Weston Zoyland with an army of about 3,000 men and cavalry forces under the command of the Earl of Feversham, a Frenchman and the King's close friend. Despite Royalist patrols, Monmouth succeeded in marching his foot soldiers, horsemen and artillery pieces, in silence and in darkness, five miles around the village of Chedzoy which lay between Bridgwater and Feversham's troops. They remained undetected until the very last moment in the early hours of the morning of 6 July 1685. The rebels moved forward and reached a drainage ditch between them and the Royalist camp. Monmouth's forces attacked and inflicted great casualties with their musket fire and eventually their artillery, but their luck soon ran out. Monmouth's men could not be persuaded to cross the ditch and seize the initiative. Feversham held his cavalry back until first light when they crossed the ditch on both flanks; the Royalist infantry followed. Only a few hundred of Monmouth's men left the battlefield in formation. Some 1,300 were dead and many more were wounded.

Little mercy was shown to the prisoners, many were hanged on the spot and many others treated with extraordinary cruelty. So ended the Battle of Sedgemoor, the last pitched battle on English soil. During the trials of the captured rebels – known as the 'Bloody Assizes' – the infamous Judge Jeffreys condemned many hundreds to be put to death. Monmouth was captured a few days after the battle. He pleaded with his uncle for his life, but to no avail. He came to a grisly end on Tower Hill where the incompetent axeman, Jack Ketch, needed seven blows to remove his head.

The last battle on British soil

1746

On a misty September night in 1746, Prince Charles Edward, the 'Young Pretender', boarded a French ship and left Scotland for ever. The '45 Jacobite Rebellion, along with the hopes of restoring the Stuart dynasty, had ended. His bid to oust the Hanoverians from the British throne had failed earlier that year at Culloden, about seven miles east of Inverness. The rebel Jacobite army clashed with the British in the last full scale battle to be fought on British soil. Prince Charles was an arrogant 25-year-old and, unfortunately, no soldier. His army was made up of less than 5,000 tired, hungry and dispirited Scotsmen. The British Army of some 13,000 was commanded by the Duke of Cumberland, George II's younger son.

The cairn on Culloden Moor marking the site of the final defeat of the Jacobites in 1746, which was the last battle on British soil. Bonnie Prince Charlie escaped from the clutches of the British troops to the continent via the Isle of Skye and into legend. (Hulton)

On the morning of the battle, 17 April 1746 the two armies drew up facing each other about 500 yards apart on Drumossie Moor to the south east of Culloden House. The battle of Culloden began with exchanges of artillery fire. The Jacobites were soon outgunned by Cumberland's Royal Artillery and took heavy casualties. Prince Charles ordered his regiments to attack. The right flank of the Highland army charged and for some moments was successful in punching great holes in the British front line. The British regiments held their nerve and at close quarters their return fire wreaked havoc amongst the Scots. Many hundreds were cut down and the attack lost momentum. The Jacobite left flank tried to move forward to assist but was unable to come to grips with the British and they turned and fled. Those Jacobite regiments engaged in the British lines made desperate efforts to continue the fight, but it was too late. The British cavalry methodically made their way through the retreating Highland army and the British Infantry were soon ordered forward to finish it off. Prince Charles retreated from the field and made good his escape. Despite a reward of £30,000 for his capture, he reached safety on the Continent, to die, many years later, in Rome. Cumberland's victory at Culloden, in what was to be the last battle on British soil, and brutal pacification of the Highlands, was received with much relief and rejoicing in London.

◁ 1837 ▷ *The last Martello towers*

Permanent fortifications in the shape of the squat round 'Martello' towers have been prominent landmarks on many parts of the British coastline ever since the Napoleonic Wars. The last one to be built in the British Isles was in Jersey in 1837. The name Martello comes from a typically British corruption of a foreign word. A fortified Mediterranean watch tower at *Mortella Point* in Corsica so impressed some Royal Navy officers and British engineers (sent to capture it), that the design was later copied all around Britain when Napoleon's invasion threat was at its height.

The idea was that a series of 'Corsican' or Martello towers – strategically positioned – would keep a heavily armed naval force at bay for an indefinite period. It was a revolutionary idea for the time as the notion that anything could resist a broadside from a modern 74-gun battleship, the supreme fighting machine of the early 19th century, was hard to imagine. But experience at Mortella Point had proved it. Work began to defend the coastline from the attentions of the over-confident 'Boney' and his 'Army of England' in Boulogne just a few miles across the English Channel.

While at war with France, Britain built nearly 200 towers, mostly around the British coast although some were constructed as far afield as the Cape of Good Hope and North America. The main features of the Martello tower were its thick stone walls and its single entrance well above ground level. The design evolved and changed over the years and was adapted to local materials and conditions. Most were about 40 feet high, and thicker at the base than at the top with a ground level diameter of about 45 feet. The towers were armed with a few relatively light guns and could be manned by a handful of men. They were never used to protect Britain from invasion. The French and Spanish Fleets were destroyed at Trafalgar in 1805 making the towers unnecessary.

After the war with France ended in 1815, Martello building on mainland Britain ceased. A reappraisal of the defences of the Channel Islands, however, in the new era of steam-driven ships, brought about the need for some new fortifications on Jersey. Five were planned and built in the 1830s, the last erected on the east of the island, overlooking the bay of Petit Portelet. It was named *Victoria* in honour of the new young queen who had ascended the throne. Martello building continued further afield, however, the very last being started, but never finished, in Florida in 1873. *Victoria*, along with many of its contemporaries, still stands today. Some towers have been restored and are now permanent memorials of defences that were never used. Like their more recent counterparts, the Second World War 'pillboxes' that are still dotted about the English landscape, the Martellos can still be regarded as part of a very successful deterrent strategy.

The last cavalry Brigade charge ◇1854◇

The last British cavalry charge of brigade strength was at Balaclava during the Crimean War. On 25 October 1854 the 600 officers and men of the Heavy Brigade successfully charged into action under the command of Brigadier General James Scarlett; they routed nearly 3,000 Russian cavalry. The more famous but less successful charge of the Light Brigade followed on the same day.

Misunderstanding his orders, through incompetence and the general fog of war, the Cavalry Commander, Lord Lucan, ordered Lord Cardigan to lead his Light Brigade in a charge against heavily fortified Russian artillery positions. For many in the cavalry it was certain death. Along a narrow valley the brigade galloped furiously at the guns, overran them, and turned to fight their way through them and reach their own lines.

Casualties were high. Of the 673 who rode into the valley of death, 247 were killed and many more seriously wounded. Observing from a distance, the French General Bosquet summed up the incident for generations to come when he said 'C'est magnifique mais ce n'est pas la guerre. C'est de la folie.' The era of large cavalry units had drawn to a bloody end.

 ## The last purchase of Army commissions

One of the great features of the British Army in Victorian times was its overtly aristocratic officer class. Promotion and success for an officer depended on influence and, above all, on money. Until its abolition in 1872, the 'purchase' system allowed gentlemen of the correct social background, quite literally, to buy their commissions and promotions. Purchase of commissions in the Army had a long history dating back to the reign of Edward VI (1547–53), long before the regular army existed. Several attempts had been made to stamp it out and many Royal Commissions had reported on it. This attention seemed only to make it stronger and more entrenched. The Duke of Wellington favoured it, believing, like many others, that it ensured that officers came from the correct part of society.

In the 18th century it had been given official sanction and various restrictions on prices had been imposed. This completely failed to stop corrupt and incompetent officers from attaining high rank, at least up to lieutenant colonel, above which purchase was prohibited. Lord Cardigan was reputed to have paid £20,000 for the colonelcy of his regiment, the 11th Hussars. The price to enter some regiments, at the lowest commissioned rank of ensign, could reach the small fortune of £3,000 or more.

In the Crimean War in the 1850s the Army had proved to be ill-supplied with recruits and equipment and ill-served by its commanders and many untrained, effectively part-time, officers. But reform was slow in coming and it was only in the 1870s that Edward Cardwell, the Secretary of State for War, swept through the Army and set it on a modern footing, much to the consternation of the old soldiers in command at 'Horse Guards' in London.

Amongst the reforms that were eventually passed through Parliament was a centralized, unified High Command, firmly subordinate to the Secretary of State and Parliament. Terms of service for soldiers were reduced and included several years 'in reserve', thus paving the way for an adequate reserve of trained men who could be called up if needed. Pairs of battalions were re-organized into formal regiments: one battalion would be on overseas service while its sister battalion was back at the home depot, recruiting and training for both of them.

The one reform that caused the biggest problem was the 'abolition of purchase'. After a struggle in the House of Commons, Cardwell and Prime Minister Gladstone had to wait for the vested interests in the House of Lords to do their worst. Those Tory peers who had connections with the Army (which was most of them) had their say on the matter. Very few wanted change. Some supported the purchase system because it provided for a cheap form of retirement. Others supported it because it kept out 'the professional man with professional politics'. Yet some thought that the compensation required for existing holders of commissions would cost too much.

Gladstone in the end lost patience. It turned out that parliamentary legislation was not needed anyway. At a stroke he altered *Queens Regulations*, which had provided the official sanction for the purchase system, and declared that from the following year (1872), purchase would end. The Tories and the members of the House of Lords were furious but in the end there was nothing they could do. 'Purchase' ceased to exist on 1 November 1872. The cost of compensation reached around £6 million, a large sum for the price of a fundamental reform.

The thought of buying promotion in today's Army, quite openly, seems ridiculous. As a system it enabled the mediocre to thrive as long as they were wealthy. On occasion it gave way to disaster. Yet paradoxically it was the same system that provided some vital, gallant leadership at some crucial moments in time of war.

Custer's last stand ◇ 1876 ◇

After the American Civil War, the major conflicts that the US Army had to deal with were the Indian Wars in the Mid West. The overwhelming superiority of the US Army compared to the Indians' forces made the outcome inevitable. There were setbacks for the US Army, however, the last of which was the Battle of Little Big Horn in 1876, which came to be known as 'Custer's last stand'.

George Armstrong Custer was a young flamboyant Major General who had served with distinction in the Civil War. In 1876 he was leading the 7th Cavalry Regiment into Dakota Territory to make contact with the Sioux Indians who were refusing to go back to their allotted reservations. When his scouts reported an encampment of Indians ahead in the valley of the Little Big Horn River, Custer decided to act quickly and pressed ahead. His force of 265 troopers came upon a huge force of over 2,500 Indians under the command of Chief Sitting Bull.

The 7th Cavalry had no option but to shoot their horses where they stood and make a stand. Custer was probably the last to die. There were no human survivors although one of the horses, 'Commanche', survived to become famous and die of old age in 1891. The American nation was stunned, it was the most serious defeat ever suffered at the hands of the Indians. It was also their last. The Indians were the ultimate losers, as a much larger US Army force, under General Terry, defeated them in battle soon after and forced them back to their reservation while Chief Sitting Bull fled to Canada.

Chief Sitting Bull led the Sioux braves at the Battle of Little Big Horn in 1876, 'Custer's last stand', but was forced to flee to Canada soon after. Years later he was ignominiously killed in a skirmish just before the Battle of Wounded Knee, the last battle on American soil. (ME)

The last battle on American soil ◇ 1890 ◇

The last battle on American soil was one between the US Cavalry and the tribal Sioux Indians. In 1890 the pride of the Indian nations was trampled into the snow in an ignominious little battle that brought shame on the US Army and the government.

Towards the end of the 1880s a religious cult had developed among many of the Indian reservations. Loosely based on a mixture of the old tribal ancestor worship and Christianity it spread throughout many of the settlements. It became known as the Ghost Dance, and followers believed that one day soon all the dead braves and buffaloes would rise up and rejoin the tribes in their old way of life. Some of the reservations became hotbeds of insurrection. All the inhabitants were hungry, many were starving to death. Encouraged by the Ghost Dance cult, some groups of Indians armed themselves and left the reservations in their search for food and satisfactory living conditions. The US government declared them to be hostile and the Army was given the job of forcing them back.

At the Pine Ridge Reservation in Dakota, on 15 December 1890, Chief Sitting Bull, now returned from exile in Canada, was part of a group of Sioux approached by members of the government-sponsored Indian Police. Resistance was offered and in the ensuing melée, Sitting Bull was killed. The US Army arrived just in time to save the Police from being massacred in retaliation for the chief's murder. The situation grew worse. Chief Big Foot was also on the list of supposed trouble makers to be arrested. Severely ill with pneumonia, he and another group of Sioux Indians were making their way back to the Pine Ridge reservation when they were intercepted by a detachment of US Cavalry on 28 December who escorted them to a camp at nearby Wounded Knee creek. There were 120 men and 230 women and children. The Cavalry commander, Major Whitside, intended to disarm them but as it was now dark he left it until the next morning.

The next day Colonel James Forsyth of the 7th Cavalry (Custer's old Regiment) took charge. The Indian warriors were told to hand over their weapons. In the discussions and arguments that followed a shot rang out. A brief bloody one-sided battle followed. When the firing stopped 25 US soldiers and 200 Sioux, including women and children, lay dead or dying. Amongst the Sioux dead was Chief Big Foot, the last Indian chief to die in battle. The Battle of Wounded Knee was a sorry scrappy affair, hardly worthy of the name battle, but it symbolized the end of the Indian Wars.

The last of the redcoats

The British military campaign in West Africa against the Ashantis was typical of the small colonial wars of the latter part of the 19th century. It was also the last campaign in which the British Army wore its famous red tunic uniforms. The story of the Army's transition from brightly coloured uniforms to today's camouflaged smocks is a long one. As far back as the 1800s in the Peninsular Campaign of the Napoleonic Wars, it was realized by many commanders that clothing that allowed the wearer an opportunity to blend in with his background gave him a considerable advantage over the enemy.

In the middle of the 19th century, regular British units on the North-West Frontier in India had already started wearing 'khaki' (a Persian word for 'dusty') jackets. The move was not without its opponents. Many generals resisted with scorn and bitterness. Queen Victoria, another staunch traditionalist, was also known to be against it. By the last decades of the century, most British regiments had been kitted out with the more soberly coloured uniforms in which to fight. On being sent off on campaigns, they normally put their red tunics and fancy headgear into mothballs before marching off to battle, attired in khaki outfits.

At the end of 1895 the warriors of the Ashanti Kingdom were once again active in the British territory of the Gold Coast in West Africa. Twenty years earlier Wolseley had been sent out to crush these African tribesmen, but they were again posing a threat to British interests. An ultimatum was sent to their King Prempeh but no answer was received. A force of some 2,000 men in scarlet tunics was dispatched from Cape Coast Castle in December under the command of General Scott. The main regular British unit involved was the 2nd Battalion of the West Yorkshire Regiment. The remainder of the force was made up of supporting arms and native units.

They marched inland, hacking their way through the thick jungle, eventually arriving at the Ashanti capital of Kumasi in January 1896. Here they found the King who, despite the fearsome reputation of his warriors, spent most of his time in an alcoholic stupor. Resistance was slight and fighting was brief. The King was deposed and deported to the coast, replaced by that ubiquitous and all important member of the Empire, the British Resident, to govern in his place. There were no dramatic battles in this campaign. The 'thin red line' did not disappear for ever behind lines of smoking rifles and bellowed commands above the din of battle. These last campaigning redcoats, the West Yorkshires, were well organized in a methodical, professional and successful campaign – perhaps a more fitting tribute. Today, apart from military bandsmen, the Household Division of the British Army the 'Guards' are the only soldiers regularly to wear red jackets and dark blue trousers on parade.

The last cavalry charge

1917

Army folklore usually has it that the last British cavalry charge took place in 1898 at Omdurman where the 21st Lancers rode to death and glory against the Dervishes. Perhaps the presence in the battle of the young Winston Churchill, future prime minister and great war leader, perpetuated the myth that this action was the last of its kind. However, many years later during the First World War, old traditions and techniques lingered on in Palestine. On 8 November 1917 at Huj a force consisting of Turkish and Austrian soldiers was attacked by a mixed unit of British yeomanry cavalry in a brutally tiring charge over nearly a mile of difficult terrain.

Two squadrons of the Worcestershire Yeomanry Cavalry and one squadron of the Warwickshire Yeomanry charged the Turkish gun positions. Braving a fierce screen of machine-gun fire, the British troops galloped towards the enemy. On reaching the guns, the British cavalry used their sabres on the enemy gunners and 12 guns were captured. The successful engagement was marred by the huge casualties on the British side: of the 190 yeomen that started the charge, 36 died and 57 were wounded; 110 horses were killed.

Never again did the British cavalry in full regimental strength indulge in the glory of a galloping charge against the enemy. In the years that followed, machine guns and other more fearful weaponry gained more and more prominence and cavalry was recognized as obsolete. The two regiments involved in that last charge still live on today in the Territorial Army, still appropriately joined together, as The Queen's Own Mercian Yeomanry.

The last British soldiers to be shot for desertion

During the First World War the British military authorities court martialled over 3,000 soldiers. Most of the trials were for desertion or cowardice in the face of the enemy or some closely related offence. Possible punishment for a convicted soldier included execution. Of the 3,000 convicted soldiers only 312, none of them officers, were executed, usually by firing squad close behind the front lines. The last soldier to die by firing squad after court martial was Private L. Harris of the 10th battalion, the West Yorkshire Regiment.

Harris had originally volunteered for the Army in early 1915. He had served continuously in the trenches since March 1916 and, like many soldiers before him, he came to his fatal decision to desert in an almost casual way. On the night of 2 September his battalion was part of the formation moving towards Rocquigny. He was a member of a machine-gun team and as they advanced he held back, dumped his personal equipment and disappeared. He was arrested the next morning on a supply route well behind the lines.

After his conviction for desertion at his court martial, the General officers could find no extenuating circumstances. The last signature on his death sentence was that of the Commander-in-Chief, Field Marshal Douglas Haig. Private Harris was shot to death by firing squad at dawn, 6.30 am, on 7 November 1918, four days before the 'War to end all wars' ended.

The last military fortifications in the UK

The last military fortifications of any type to be built in Britain were the pillboxes which were part of the anti-invasion plans during the Second World War. Much of the countryside of southern Britain was covered with the concrete of brick-built pillboxes. They formed part of vast lines of defence set out at the beginning of the war to defend against the expected German invasion, Operation Lion, after the retreat from Dunkirk. The invasion never came and the pillboxes were never used. When the invasion scare was over the pillbox building programme was stopped; the last batch was built in 1942. Many of them exist today, dotted around fields and hedgerows, overgrown with brambles and, for the most part, forgotten.

The last US soldier to be shot for desertion

 1945

The USA has had a generally lenient approach to the punishment of its deserters in time of war – somewhat surprisingly considering its vigorous approach to capital punishment. The last soldier to be shot for desertion was Private Slovik during the 'Battle of the Bulge', the Ardennes offensive in the closing months of the Second World War. Slovik, never happy with the idea of fighting or laying down his life for his country, deserted from the front lines twice and had given himself up in the hope of a short – but safe – prison sentence, a result satisfactorily achieved by many hundreds of other GIs. The authorities found themselves unable to comply and Slovik was executed by firing squad at Ste Marie-aux-Mines, France on 31 January 1945.

His body, originally buried in a corner of a US cemetery in France, was disinterred in 1987 and reburied in California. He was also, for some mysterious reason, given a posthumous pardon. His execution, which had been the first in the US forces since the American Civil War some 80 years earlier, was the only one in the Second World War.

The last serving British soldier from the Second World War

 1986

The last serving member of the armed forces in Britain who also served in the Second World War was General Sir Michael Gow. James Michael Gow enlisted in the Scots Guards aged 18 in 1942, at the height of the war. After the war he saw service in most of the theatres of operation where the British Army was involved. In 1984 he took up his last posting, as the Commandant of the Royal College of Defence Studies in London. He retired in 1986, the senior general in the British Army.

AERIAL MANOEUVRES

The last Spitfires in service

 1955

The Spitfire was probably the most famous fighter aircraft ever to take to the sky. It is associated with the defiant spirit that emerged in Britain in the darkest days of the Second World War when, along with its sister type, the Hurricane, it fought the mighty German Luftwaffe. It was extensively developed and improved during its service life. The last Spitfire, a Mark 24, was made in February 1948. Service in the RAF continued until March 1954, when a photo reconnaissance squadron serving in Malaya eventually switched to Meteor jets. The Hong Kong Auxiliary Air Force continued to fly Spitfires until April 1955. Many Spitfires are still being flown today, The RAF's Battle of Britain flight displays include carefully preserved flying Spitfires which are seen by thousands of spectators every year.

The last Lancasters in service

The RAF's most famous bomber was the Avro Lancaster, which saw all of its active service in the Second World War. The last Lancasters in RAF Bomber Command left on 8 March 1950 to move to other duties. Service in other roles continued until 1956 when the last serving Lancaster in the RAF, 'D-Delta', used in maritime training, was decommissioned at RAF St Mawgan on 15 October. Lancasters saw service in overseas air forces, notably the Royal Canadian Air Force, the French Navy and the Argentine Air Force, until 1964. The last flying Lancaster in the RAF is currently with the Battle of Britain Flight.

The RAF's last flying Vulcan

One of the RAF's most famous postwar bombers, the Avro Vulcan with its uniquely styled delta wing shape, was last flown by the RAF in March 1993. The first Vulcan had flown 41 years earlier in August 1952 and entered service in the RAF, in the nuclear bomber V force, in 1959. In the early months of 1993 the Vulcan XH 558, the last surviving flyable example, was waiting for a buyer. Estimates by the RAF of the cost to keep it flying were an immediate £2.5 million refit and an extra £250,000 more a year.

The sealed bids from a number of air museums and scrap-metal merchants were at last opened and the government announced the winning bid in Parliament. The new owner was David Walton, proprietor of an aircraft collection in Leicestershire. Vulcan XH 558 had its last flight from its base at RAF Waddington in Lincolnshire on 23 March 1993. The pilot, Squadron Leader Paul Millikin, took the Vulcan on an aerial tour of many of the RAF stations associated with Vulcans in service. It landed at its final home at Bruntingthorpe in front of a crowd of thousands of enthusiasts, gathered to see a Vulcan in the air for the last time.

The famous delta-wing bomber, the Royal Air Force's Vulcan. It was originally armed with free-falling atomic bombs, but saw action only once, in the Falklands campaign in 1982, when it dropped conventional bombs on Port Stanley airfield. This particular aircraft, XH 558, the last flying example, made its last flight in March 1993. (Rex)

SCIENCE AND NATURE
5

SCIENCE

The last planet to be discovered

1930

Pluto is the last planet in our solar system, the most distant from the sun and the last to have been discovered. It has, however, a much more elliptical orbit than any of the other planets; in fact at its nearest to the sun its orbit comes inside that of the neighbouring planet Neptune.

In the 19th century, before the discovery of Pluto, the orbits and minor movements of other planets at the outer edge of the solar system were being studied by astronomers, particularly the American Perceval Lowell. He postulated that another planet might exist; it was, he believed, the only explanation for fluctuations in the orbit of Neptune. It took until 1930 to track down the mystery planet. With a programme of systematic photography, Clyde Tombaugh finally discovered the missing member of the solar system while working at the Lowell Observatory in Arizona, USA.

Pluto is relatively small, smaller than the size of the earth, and is accompanied in its dark distant orbit by the moon Charon; the existence of other moons is a possibility. Pluto's average distance from the sun is nearly 4 billion miles and it takes 248 Earth years to complete an orbit of the solar system. Pluto is the least well known of all the solar system's planets. It was the only planet to avoid the detailed scrutiny of the USA's *Voyager* spacecraft in the 1980s, the decade of planetary discovery.

Planets beyond Pluto's orbit are, of course, still a possibility. The discovery in 1992 of a 120-mile wide object, an asteroid or comet, at an even greater distance than Pluto raised the probability of confirming such a planet.

The last element to be discovered

1945

The last chemical element to be discovered was the metal Promethium. In the world of science and chemistry, it was recognized that there is a definable number of separate individual elements, pure substances unable to be broken down further without the disintegration of the atom. The first in the Table of the Elements is Hydrogen, atomic number 1, with the lightest atomic weight. Of the stable elements, at the other end of the scale, the heaviest is Uranium, atomic number 92.

By the beginning of the 20th century scientists were able to predict the existence of all the elements, categorized by their atomic numbers and the make-up of their nuclei. In 1945 there was just one gap in the table: at atomic number 61. In Oak Ridge, Tennessee a team of scientists, J. A. Marinsky, L. E. Glendenin and C. D. Coryell, used advance spectroscopy on Uranium fission products to isolate and identify the last of the elements. A rare earth metal, they named it Promethium after the Greek God, Prometheus, the 'fire stealer'. Its atomic symbol is Pm and, although rare and of limited practical use, it can be used as a power source in miniature batteries where its beta radiation is converted into electricity.

1972 *The last man on the Moon*

In 14 December 1972, the USA's short programme of manned exploration of the Moon came to an end. Gene Cernan, the commander of the Apollo 17 mission, stepped off the Moon's surface and boarded the lunar excursion module, *Challenger*. A few hours later he and his fellow crew member, Harrison Schmitt, completed a successful rendezvous with Ronald Evans in the orbiting Apollo command capsule *America* to make an uneventful return to Earth a few days later. The Moon has not experienced a (human) footfall since that day.

In 1961 President Kennedy had been stung by the Soviet Union's initial successes in manned spaceflight. He vowed that NASA, the American Space Agency, would land an American on the Moon before the end of the decade. In 1969 Neil Armstrong did set foot on the Moon, winning the space race for the USA, but it had taken a supreme effort and over 25 billion dollars. The USA's Apollo programme had tackled an enormous number of technical problems and solved them all. It was one of mankind's greatest technological achievements. Sustaining the interest of the American people and – more importantly – the flow of funds from the United States Congress proved more difficult. Each Apollo mission was a $400 million exercise that became of less and less concern to the American nation. By the time of Apollo 17 in late 1972, the United States had no further use for Moon exploration.

The USA's peaceful intentions in Moon exploration were summed up by Cernan's own carefully rehearsed words in a final TV broadcast just before he and Schmitt left the Moon, 'We leave as we came and, God willing, as we shall return – with peace and hope for all mankind.' As they blasted off the Moon's surface for their last rendezvous he added, 'Let's get this mother out of here!' A rejuvenated NASA may well develop a manned mission to Mars in the 21st century. Until then, Cernan will retain the honour of being the last human to set foot on another world.

Eugene Cernan, mission commander of Apollo 17 and the last man on the Moon, saluting the US flag. (SPL)

Lasts in Manned Spaceflight Programmes

Mercury

Date: 15–16 May 1963
Spaceflight: Mercury-Atlas 9 ('Faith 7')
Crew: Gordon Cooper

The last American to venture into space on his own.

Vostok

Date: 14–19 June 1963
Spaceflight: Vostok 5
Crew: Valeri Bykovsky

The USSR's second joint mission, Vostok 5 and 6, achieved visual rendezvous in orbit. Bykovsky's 81 orbits and nearly 5 days in space is the longest solo flight. (Vostok 6, crewed by Valentina Tereshkova, the first woman in space, was launched after Vostok 5, but returned to Earth before Bykovsky.)

Voskhod

Date: 18–19 March 1965
Spaceflight: Voskhod 2
Crew: Pavel Belyayev and Alexei Leonov

Leonov was the first man to walk in space.

Gemini

Date: 11–15 November 1966
Spaceflight: Gemini 12
Crew: Jim Lovell and Edwin 'Buzz' Aldrin

The last US two-man capsule mission.

Skylab

Date: 16 November 1973–8 February 1974
Spaceflight: Skylab 4
Crew: Gerald Carr, Edward Gibson and William Pogue

Apollo spacecraft were used to ferry the crew to and from the orbiting laboratory. The unmanned Skylab remained in orbit until it disintegrated and crashed to Earth in July 1979.

Apollo

Date: 15–24 July 1975
Spaceflight: Apollo 18. The Apollo-Soyuz Friendship Mission
Crew: Thomas Stafford, Vance Brand, Donald 'Deke' Slayton (Rendezvous with Soyuz 19. Crew: Alexei Leonov and Valeri Kubasov.)

The last Saturn Rocket Launch.

The last smallpox

1978

Smallpox was once one of the classic epidemic diseases to regularly infect the human race. It is also one of the few to be entirely eradicated by the efforts of the human race. The disease originated in prehistoric times in Africa or Europe and by the 18th century had spread to the rest of the world. Waves of smallpox epidemics regularly swept through the populations of all continents causing death on a huge scale. An acute and highly contagious viral disease, it was characterized by high fever, severe prostration and a pinkish rash that developed into pustules. Infection would result in one of two outcomes, death or eventual immunity. A mortality rate of one in four was common. It is estimated that in Europe, even in a normal year, between 10 and 15 per cent of all deaths were caused directly by smallpox. Disfiguring scars on the survivors were commonplace.

By the 18th century a form of rudimentary protection against the fatal disease was possible. Patients infected with material from the pustules of a smallpox sufferer contracted the disease and, if administered carefully, this form of the disease resulted in very low death rates and the patient, on recovery, had lifelong protection. This method, known as variolation, was practised throughout the British Empire, in some parts of Europe and America, and it was also known in Africa.

In 1798 the English physician Edward Jenner published his experiments on infection with the related disease, cowpox. He noticed that patients infected with the non-fatal cowpox, either accidentally or deliberately, were immune from smallpox infection. His inoculation method (which he named vaccination after the Latin word *vacca* for cow) quickly found favour throughout Britain, Europe and America. Vaccination programmes spread rapidly and by the early part of the 20th century smallpox had become a rare disease in the western world.

In 1966 the World Health Organization took on the job of total world eradication. There were actually two strains of smallpox in existence: *variola major*, with a fatality rate of up to 30 per cent, and *variola minor*, a much less dangerous kind. By October 1975 the last case of *variola major* was recorded in Bangladesh. In 1977 in Somalia, a patient called Ali Maow Maalin was the last ever to suffer natural infection of smallpox, this time of *variola minor*, and he survived.

In 1978 a tragic postscript served to remind the world of the scourge that had been so successfully defeated. In a laboratory in Birmingham Janet Parker was infected by an escaped virus and subsequently died. She was the world's last known smallpox victim. Smallpox now only exists in storage as laboratory specimens in two locations, in the USA and in Russia.

The last appearance of Halley's Comet

Comets are objects which orbit the sun, usually in a highly elliptical orbit. They are thought to consist of a relatively small nucleus of frozen matter. As the comet nears the sun particles of it are heated and break away from the nucleus, streaming away from the sun to form a tail. At the extremity of its orbit, in deep space, the comet is invisible; the nearer it gets to the sun the more its tail develops and is illuminated by the sun, becoming visible to observers on Earth.

Halley's Comet is the brightest and one of the most spectacular of all the regularly appearing comets. The time a comet takes to orbit the sun is called its period; Halley's Comet has a period of about 76 years. It was the discovery of this and the accurate prediction of its reappearance by the astronomer Edmund Halley that has given it its name. Halley conjectured in 1705 that the comet observed in 1682 was the same one recorded in 1607 and 1531. When the comet reappeared in 1758, 16 years after his death, his case was proved.

Regular records of sightings of 'Halley's' comet go back at least to 240 BC and possibly to 1059 BC. Down the centuries it has been regarded by the superstitious as a sign of great portent. It appeared in 1066 and is shown on the Bayeux Tapestry commemorating William the Conqueror's invasion of England. The last appearance, or more strictly the most recent appearance, of this most famous of all comets was in 1986. It reached its perihelion, the point of its orbit where it is closest to the sun, on 9 February 1986. As predicted by astronomers, the Comet's 1986 visit to the centre of the solar system was one the least favourable for viewing. Few people in the northern hemisphere saw it at all and even observers in Australia, in the southern hemisphere found it disappointing.

What made this visit of Halley's Comet special was that it was the first time it was met by a flotilla of spacecraft from Earth. Five space probes were sent to meet it. All were spectacularly successful in studying a large comet at close range and sending back a bonanza of scientific data for the first time in history. Halley's Comet is due again in the year 2061 – the date of its next 'last' appearance.

NATURE

The last mammoths

c. 1700 BC

The woolly mammoth, a large mastodon related to the African and Asian elephants of today, died out after the end of the last ice age some 10,000 years ago. The mammoth was a grass eater, superbly adapted to the climatic and geographic environment at the frontier of the ice sheet. When the ice age ended, the mammoth herds, which had spread throughout the northern hemisphere, moved further and further north to stay with vegetation and climate which they required. Just as their habitat was decreasing they encountered human hunters. It was widely thought that the combination of climatic change and hunting by humans brought about the end of the mammoth some 10,000 years ago.

However, recent evidence from within the Arctic Circle has shown that a mammoth population survived for longer. Isolated from humans on Wrangel Island off the north coast of Siberia, inside the Arctic Circle, the mammoths lived on. Smaller than the extinct older mammoths, these recent survivors had found the grasses that they required. Some minor change to their environment, possibly the arrival of human hunters, caused their final extinction about 3,700 years ago. Against all the odds, this fascinating species so nearly survived to modern times.

The last aurochs

1627

The aurochs, *Bos primigenius*, was the legendary wild ox of Europe well known by humans from prehistoric times until the 17th century. Ancient man hunted it for its meat and skin. He painted it on the walls of caves and used its bones to make tools. The aurochs is probably the wild black bull of ancient mythology. Disguised in such a body, Zeus is supposed to have abducted the maiden Europa.

The aurochs's main enemy was undoubtedly humans. By the middle ages it was a favourite quarry for sport hunting in much the same way as deer are today. Attempts were made to domesticate the small herds of aurochs, but their diminishing numbers, even in the 16th century, were probably preserved by the nobility specifically for hunting.

A representation of a large mammoth in a Russian museum in the 19th century. The huge creatures died out at the end of the last ice age, although smaller mammoths survived almost until modern times. The last 'pygmy' mammoths died on Wrangel, a Siberian island, around 1700 BC. (ME)

The last herd was maintained in the Jaktorow Forest in west Poland, but their numbers fell rapidly; by 1599 only 25 were left. The last aurochs, a cow, died in 1627. The glamour of the aurochs lives on. Today's Spanish fighting bulls are supposed to be descended from them. Recently there have been some attempts to re-create the species by the cross-breeding of European cows.

 ## The last Black Death

The Plague or the Black Death were names given to the epidemics of Bubonic Plague which first swept through Europe in the years 1346 to 1353. A ghastly virulent affliction, fatal in up to half those infected, Bubonic Plague re-occurred year after year in Europe in a frightening series of epidemics from the 14th to the 18th centuries. The Black Death spread rapidly during the warm summer months. It left the countries it passed through devastated in population numbers and usually in widespread social chaos. The disease is spread to humans from infected carriers, usually rats or other small animals, by fleas. Once infected, the victim quickly develops swellings in the lymphatic glands in the armpits and the groin and purple and black blotches appear on the skin. In the middle ages there was no known cure and death often followed within a few days.

The last outbreak of the Plague in Britain was in the 1660s, in the reign of Charles II. London was in the throes of a particularly virulent outbreak of the Plague when the Great Fire of London broke out at the end of a long hot summer in September 1666. The fire wiped out large areas of the city and with it much of the Plague infestation. It never appeared in Britain again. The Plague struck for the last time in Europe in 1720 in Marseilles and the Provence region of France. Increasing awareness of the necessity for proper public health and sanitation measures, and a good dose of luck, eliminated the Plague in Europe. However, in the 20th century America and other parts of the world have suffered epidemics. Bubonic Plague as a disease in individual humans still exists today; in Europe there are several cases a year, usually treated successfully with modern medicines.

The last dodo   ◁ 1790 ▷

The dodo is probably the most famous of any extinct species of animal known to man. It was a large flightless bird of the dove family that was found only on the island of Mauritius in the Indian Ocean. The bird was first seen and reported by Portuguese sailors around 1507. It was regarded as a comical creature, quite harmless and almost completely defenceless. The dodo, *Raphus cucullatus*, was a little larger than a turkey, weighing up to 55 pounds. It had blue-grey plumage with a tuft of curly feathers at its rear end. It was equipped with a pair of yellow stout legs and a black bill with a hooked tip.

The birds soon became a regular source of food for passing sailors as Mauritius was a regular port of call for much of the shipping en route to India and the East. Many people were fascinated by the clown-like appearance of the dodo, and their numbers were further depleted when many were captured and taken on board ship to be transported back to Europe. They seldom survived for more than a few months. By 1681 the last dodo on Mauritius was dead. The Mauritius dodo had two close relations, the white dodo, *Raphus solitarius*, found on the nearby island of Réunion, and the brown *Pezophops solitaria* of another island, Rodrigues. The last white dodo died in 1746 on board a French ship returning home. The very last dodo, a Rodrigues solitaire, died in 1790. The dodo was extinct.

The demise of the dodo has an interesting postscript in the story of the so called dodo tree or *Calvaria major*. The dodo tree is also indigenous to Mauritius and acquired its name from the fact that the fruit of the tree was a major source of food for the bird. It was observed that since the demise of the dodo not one new sapling had grown for over two hundred years. The powerful gizzard of the dodo was necessary to crush the seed casing, which passed out of the dodo, to allow the seed to germinate. By 1970 a bare dozen trees remained. In 1973 a botanist had the idea of feeding the fruit to some turkeys and three of the excreted seeds germinated. The seedlings survived and a new method of reproducing the tree has been assured.

 ## The last great auk

Despite the ravages of man upon his environment, the British Isles have witnessed surprisingly few extinctions of animal species in recorded history. An exception to this was the demise of the great auk, a sea bird which finally disappeared in 1840. The great auk, *Alca impennis*, was a large flightless sea bird of the North Atlantic area. Extremely vulnerable to human attentions through its inability to fly, it resembled a huge razorbill. It existed in North America, Greenland, Iceland and northern Britain, living on exposed cliff and coastal sites. When nesting it laid a single egg. The last recorded breeding in the wild in Britain was in 1812 when a bird was seen on its nest in the Orkneys. The species was eventually 'collected' and hunted to extinction in the British Isles in 1840 when the last specimen was killed on the island of St Kilda. In Iceland the great auk struggled on. According to records, the last living specimen was killed in June 1844. The great auk now lives on only in memories and watercolours.

 ## The last Tasmanian Aborigines

Before the arrival of European explorers and settlers in Tasmania, the island off the southern coast of Australia supported a human population of aboriginal people. However, with an area of over 26,000 square miles of forests and grasslands it seemed an ideal country for settlers from Europe to make a new start. The aboriginal natives had to learn to live with their new neighbours. But new diseases from Europe and blatant aggression from the new farmers soon made co-existence impossible, and the Tasmanian peoples died out rapidly over the 19th century. The last living Tasmanian Aborigine, Queen Lijwiji Trucannini, known as Lalla Rooth, died on 23 May 1876, at the age of 76. Her husband, the last male aboriginal survivor, had died seven years earlier.

 ## The last Quagga

The quagga, *Equus quagga*, was a form of zebra found in southern Africa. Its stripes were brown rather than black and there were fewer of them on the animal's hindquarters. Despite some successful attempts to domesticate the quagga – some were even employed as draft animals in Europe and South Africa – it could be an aggressive and vicious animal. Some cattle farmers would keep one or two in their herds of cattle to warn against predators. The quagga was also hunted for food and for its attractively patterned skin. Some live specimens were captured and sent to Europe. However, the last known specimen killed in the wild in South Africa was in 1878. The last known living specimen, in Amsterdam Zoo, died in 1883.

The last passenger pigeon ◆1914◆

The attractive pink-chested passenger pigeon of North America existed in such vast numbers until the 19th century that it was almost impossible to have envisaged them ever becoming extinct – yet it happened. In 1800 it was estimated that 40 per cent of the entire North American bird population was of one single species: *Ectopistes migatorius*, the passenger pigeon.

They had been hunted as food for centuries by the indigenous Indian population but the coming of the white man with his firearms changed the rules. Even so, with single flocks of birds numbering several million, it must have seemed an ideal source of food. By 1860 professional pigeon hunters would shoot thousands of birds in a single day; hunting parties could easily kill a million at one session. After a shoot the dead birds were sent to the cities and sold for their meat. Those corpses that were too mangled for human consumption were used as pig food; the vultures and other carrion would clear up the rest.

The last flock was seen in 1896. It numbered a quarter of a million but nevertheless a hunting party managed to massacre most of them; perhaps only 5,000 escaped. About 200,000 of the dead birds were sent off by rail to be sold. A derailment further up the line caused a 24-hour delay and every single carcass rotted; the entire load was dumped, an ignominious end for any wild bird species. The last passenger pigeon seen in the wild was a single bird on 24 March 1900 in Pike County, Ohio. The last living bird, named 'Martha', died in Cincinnati Zoo on 1 September 1914. It was 29 years old and the very last of billions of passenger pigeons killed by man in less than a century.

The last Tasmanian wolf ◆1933◆

The thylacine, also commonly known as the Tasmanian wolf, was a voracious predatory marsupial wild dog. At one time the animal lived on the Australian mainland, but competition from the dingoes probably led to its demise there. In the exotic new world of Tasmania the Europeans found many new animal species that had to be dealt with. The Tasmanian wolf was one of the most vicious. The thylacine fed on kangaroos, wallabies and, soon after the arrival of the Europeans, the farmer's flocks of sheep and even his dogs.

The animal's many other nicknames – 'Tasmanian tiger', 'kangaroo wolf' and 'zebra wolf' – are a good description of its appearance. It was said to have the head and teeth of a wolf, the stripes of a tiger on its rear and the tail of a small kangaroo. It carried its young in a backward opening pouch similar to the opossum. The menace of this predatory animal to farming was recognized by the Tasmanian government and towards

The Tasmanian wolf, or thylacine, was a curious looking dog-like creature with yellow and brown stripes on its hindquarters. Although a 1961 expedition to the forests on the west coast of Tasmania reported seeing footprints, the thylacine is generally reckoned to have been exterminated in the 1930s. (ME)

the end of the 19th century the authorities offered bounties for each one destroyed. The species became doomed and in 1930 the last known killing of a thylacine in the wild, a young male, took place. The last specimen to be captured alive was in 1933 but it died the same year in Hobart Zoo. The Tasmanian wolf was gone. The government withdrew the bounty scheme three years later.

◁1941▷ *The last Arabian ostrich*

The African ostrich is a bird as well known for its size as for its plumage. Its fine long feathers were in great demand in the fashion world for much of the 19th and 20th centuries. Today it is farmed in some parts of southern Africa for its meat as well as its feathers. There were at least two other species of ostrich, one in China, last sighted around 1900, and the other in Arabia.

The Arabian ostrich, known as the na-ama, was smaller than the African species but had the same fine feathers which were to be its downfall. It was widely hunted for its plumage and, although quite plentiful in Syria and the Arabian peninsula before the First World War, by the 1930s it had become rare. The last known specimen was shot in Bahrain in 1941. Rumours lived on: a German tank crew is reputed to have shot and eaten one in 1944 and parts of a body were found in 1966.

The last London 'pea-souper' 〈1952〉

Ever since the industrial revolution, Britain's large towns and cities have suffered from the smoke generated by thousands of coal-burning fires. Before the widespread introduction of domestic central heating many homes used coal as the main form of heating. Combined with the effect of industrial coal-burning processes, the accumulation of smoke caused the bigger cities to be covered in palls of smoke that hung in the air undisturbed for many days. Under certain weather conditions the smoke would combine with natural fog causing a dense blanket of acrid, dangerous, blinding smog.

Apart from the obvious hazard of lack of visibility, the health problems suffered by city residents became more and more critical. The last heavy smog to hit London was in December 1952. London's last 'pea-souper' caused many road accidents and brought on severe bronchial problems for thousands of residents. In the 1950s a series of measures were introduced to curb smoke emissions. The Clean Air Act of July 1955 finally got to grips with the problem. Restrictions on the use of coal on domestic fires were brought in and smokeless fuels introduced. Smoke-free zones were established and rules on the minimum heights for industrial chimneys brought in. True smog is now unknown in Britain, although no Victorian melodrama on television could be without it.

The last English elms 〈1975〉

Dutch elm disease struck the elm trees of Europe and America in the late 1960s. A decade later few of these great trees survived to grace the British countryside. The fungal disease, which had caused this devastation, is usually spread from tree to tree by the bark beetle. The fungus causes growths inside the tree, blocking the passage of vital sap. The tree – all kinds of elm are susceptible – can take several years to die. Some elms have been kept alive by regular injections of fungicide, some others seem to have developed a natural immunity.

This most recent outbreak of the disease, which ended in the mid-1970s and destroyed most of the large elm forests in Britain, is only the last of many such visitations. Archaeological and other records show that the elm populations have been attacked before – and recovered later. The disease was certainly known in Europe in 1838. An outbreak spread in Europe, including Britain, in the 1920s and many trees, only partly infected it seems, went on to recover. One day elms might re-populate the hedgerows and fields and bring their particular style of majesty to the landscape again.

6 TRANSPORT

 ## *The last inland waterways*

The 18th century saw a rapid expansion of the inland waterway system throughout Britain. As the roads had proved quite unsuitable for heavy loads and constant traffic, it was the canals that were developed as the very sinews of industry. Without them neither the raw materials nor the finished products of the industrial revolution would have reached their destinations. By the 1830s, however, the railways had done to the canals what the canals had done to the roads – 'railroading' them off the map. The last major inland waterway to be constructed in Britain was the Birmingham and Liverpool Junction Canal in 1835.

The Chester canal system was isolated from the main canals around the 'engine room of industry', Birmingham. In an Act of Parliament of 1826 permission was given to build a canal to join the two systems. The most famous engineer of his day, Thomas Telford, was hired to build it. It ran for 40 miles, much of it in a straight line, from Autherley Junction near Birmingham north to Nantwich. It had 26 narrow locks and one short tunnel. It was opened in 1835 a few months after Telford's death at the cost of £16,000 per mile.

It was not long before the financial power of the railways was felt by the canal companies. The canals had enjoyed their own way for many years, holding a virtual monopoly in transport. The railways broke that monopoly and received much support for doing so. Ironically the canals were used to transport much of the material required to build the railways. The railway companies then bought them out and often used the actual canal routes on which to lay more tracks. The Birmingham and Liverpool Junction Canal was taken over by the Ellesmere and Chester Canal Company in 1846. Almost immediately it was bought out by a new company, the Shropshire Union Railways and Canal Company, formed to exploit both canals and railways.

The Manchester Ship Canal was opened in 1893, but as it was designed for sea-going ships, it was not, strictly speaking, an inland waterway. Although many of the canals continued to operate effectively – the system was maintained, modernized and in some cases further extended – no new major inland canals were built in Britain after 1835. Telford's last canal was the beginning of the end for the inland waterways. Today, very few are used for commercial transportation but many miles have been successfully restored for pleasure cruising, including Telford's Birmingham and Liverpool Junction.

Walter Hancock's steam omnibus *Automaton* (opposite), operated by the London and Paddington Steam Carriage Company was the last of the road steamers. It was killed off in 1840 by the powerful railway lobby and the lack of serious investment in roads. (AR)

The last steam omnibuses

◇ 1840 ◇

One of the most magnificent means of transport devised in the 19th century was the steam-powered omnibus. It was based on the horse-drawn coaches of the day, but with the addition of some brilliant engineering innovations that were far ahead of their time. They competed successfully with horse-powered omnibuses and coaches, and for a time they also threatened the 'invention of the century', the railways. Eventually, however, a combination of the railway companies' vested interests and the short-sightedness and conservatism of the Turnpike Trusts managed literally to drive the road steamers off the roads in 1840.

In 1801 a Cornishman named Richard Trevithick built the first successful steam carriage, but it had to wait twenty years to be developed into a reasonable commercial proposition. Sir Goldworth Gurney constructed a succession of steam-powered coaches for Sir Charles Dance in the early 1820s. These road steamers incorporated a number of features such as speed changing gears, compensating steering geometry and the differential drive hub and back axle found in all road vehicles today. They were capable of over 10 miles per hour and they travelled the nine miles between Cheltenham and Gloucester with fare-paying passengers three times a day. Despite highly competitive prices, Sir Charles's steamers were not the commercial success they should have been.

There was a deeply ingrained opposition to the steam carriages, mainly due to prejudice fuelled at every opportunity by the fast developing railway companies. Also, the roads at that time were not really capable of taking heavy traffic. Rather than improve

the roads, the Turnpike Trusts put every obstacle in the way of steam road transport. The toll structures were deliberately set up to penalize the steamer, its toll being over ten times that for an ordinary horse-drawn coach. This was despite the existence of more than adequate proof that a coach pulled by horses would actually cause more damage to a road surface than a steam carriage. Fear of the steamers' boilers exploding added to the reservations about the invention. This was very much exaggerated and in any case was no more likely to occur than on the railways.

Walter Hancock in London had more success. He set up the London and Paddington Steam Carriage Company in 1833 and ran a series of trial routes in London in his grandly, if obscurely, named vehicles *Enterprise* and *Autopsy*. He then travelled the country demonstrating the ability of his new vehicles. Many other companies followed. In 1834 the Steam Carriage Company of Scotland began services between Glasgow and Paisley. It had six vehicles and for a number of years undertook the 40-minute journey every hour throughout the day until sabotage put it out of business. In the same year Telford and Stephenson had given their backing to the London, Holyhead and Liverpool Steam Coach and Road Company. With remarkable foresight this company intended to address the real problem, the roads, by building and maintaining its own.

In London, Hancock held out longest against the opposition. His latest vehicle, the splendid *Automaton*, capable of 20 miles per hour, ran regularly for a number of years. Finally in 1840 it was withdrawn from service forever. It was the last road steamer in service. The demise of the steam-powered omnibus and the rise of the railway train was not inevitable. Had the proponents of road steamers managed to convince some really powerful and influential backers early enough, and had the Turnpike Trusts been more adventurous, history might have had a different story to tell about that curious invention, the railway.

Steam power on the roads was left to the plodding traction engines which in 1865 were further restricted, on poor roads, by the Red Flag Act which decreed a ponderous maximum speed of four miles per hour. In the 20th century a revival of interest in the idea showed that it was practicable when steam-powered lorries ran successfully for many years before the Second World War.

The last stage coaches

Stage coaches have an important place in the reality and the romance of British history. Every bouncing, gaudily painted, fragile, enclosed carriage – its swaying driver nobly controlling the straining horses – is a gem from the past. But stage coaches were overtaken, in more ways than one, by the technology of the Victorian age.

The stage coach had its golden period in Britain in the first few decades of the 19th century – it was developed further and lingered for much longer in the north. Regular services had been introduced in the 17th century and were improved and augmented by the expansion of the turnpike roads and the increasing network of coaching inns. At the peak there were dozens of routes out of all major cities. The roads through most towns and villages throughout Britain were bustling with coach traffic running in all directions. In the late 18th century some coach routes started to carry the Royal Mail, replacing the slower post-boys on horseback. The route from London to

Bristol in the West Country in 1784 was the first. Protected by armed guards, the mail coaches carried the post to all parts of Britain for over 50 years.

The railways arrived in the 1830s and within a few years were providing a superior, faster and more reliable service for both the passengers and the mail in much of southern Britain. The decay of the turnpike road system, deliberately encouraged by the rail lobby, did not help. The last mail coach service out of London closed down in 1846. Further north the railways were not so dominant. The last great long-distance coach services, carrying the mail, were to be found in the Scottish Highlands. As the years of the century passed the railways spread throughout the country and, one by one, the coach services were replaced. The last long distance coach service, the *Royal Mail,* was from Inverness to Thurso. It ceased in October 1874, much regretted and mourned even in its day.

Today the romance of the days of coaching still lives. The love of horses, the coaching prints and the magic of 'Dickensian' style Christmas cards has burnished the folk memory of the forerunner of today's public transport system. The combination of fact, fiction and myth that surrounds the image of the stage coach remains a powerful one.

The last of the broad gauge ◁ 1892 ▷

During the 19th century Britain led the industrial world in many fields, no more so than in the area of railway engineering. In the 1830s and 1840s Isambard Kingdom Brunel had left the railway world gasping – in some cases spluttering – with his brilliance and vision as chief designer for the Great Western Railway. Always controversial, one of his main features for the Great Western, perhaps his most daring, was the 7-foot 'broad' gauge of the railway tracks. Most other railway companies, and there were several spread throughout mainland Britain, were content to go along with the more common, narrow width of 4 feet and 8½ inches.

Brunel had always thought a wider gauge would be superior; not merely because the ride would be smoother and more comfortable. It was really a matter of engineering efficiency. Friction was the greatest obstacle to higher speeds (40 miles per hour was considered fantastically fast) and reduction of running costs. Friction could be reduced by having larger wheels. Larger wheels meant higher, less stable carriages unless they could be mounted between the wheels instead of above them; at a gauge of 7 feet this became possible without reducing carriage width. In fact, Great Western carriages were still wider than others and consequently very popular with passengers.

By the 1880s the Great Western Railway was running a large network, much of it broad gauge, throughout the south, the west and the south midlands of England and in south Wales. Their Bristol and Exeter track was served by their fastest locomotives and had, in the 1840s, provided the first 'express trains' in the world. But technical superiority was not enough. From the start, the great inconvenience of the broad gauge system – its incompatibility with the rest of the railways – was a major problem. Passions ran high whenever there were discussions on the merits of different gauges – and broad gauge devotees were always the loudest in the arguments.

But the broad gauge was doomed just a few years after its inauguration when the folly of having different systems was realized. Some of Great Western's own track and rolling stock was already narrow gauge by the 1880s and most of their track had been given a third rail, 'mixed gauge', so that both narrow and broad gauge could use the same line. In 1861 they were already running their own narrow gauge trains from Paddington to Reading. Much of their rolling stock was designed so that it could later be easily converted to narrow gauge.

The last stretches of track that were still purely broad gauge were found on the Exeter to Truro main line and its branch lines. Much of the line was single track, so working on one line while another was still in use would have been impossible. It was decided that this last broad-gauge stretch would be converted to narrow gauge over one single weekend, 21 and 22 May 1892. A track conversion team of 5,000 specially trained men was readied for the occasion.

On Friday 21 May, the last broad-gauge passenger train, the *Cornishman*, left Paddington at 10.15 am amid much ceremony. Crowds had gathered to see it leave and thousands lined the track all the way to Penzance. Many a coin was placed on the track to be flattened as a memento. West of Exeter the station masters received certificates authorizing work to start immediately on the down track. The train reached Penzance at 8.20 pm and began its return, now empty of passengers, at 9.10 pm. It stopped at every station to Exeter and then steamed off to await its turn to be broken up at the Great Western's works at Swindon. At daylight the next day the track team swung into action. The conversion was done without a hitch – 30 hours later the West Country broad-gauge track had gone. On Sunday night the mail train from Paddington ran on schedule – on narrow gauge.

One of the many gangs employed to convert the broad-gauge tracks of the Great Western Railway to the standard gauge over a single weekend in May 1892. Isambard Kingdom Brunel's 7-ft broad gauge was vastly superior, but had to make way for the almost universally accepted narrower railway tracks throughout Britain and abroad. (ME)

The narrow gauge won in the end. It had originally been chosen in the early part of the century, having gradually developed out of the early horse drawn colliery railways in the north of England. At the time it seemed that 4 feet and 8½ inches was a naturally suitable width for these horse carts on tracks. Today the same gauge is used throughout many parts of the world and has even undergone metrification – it is now regarded as the international standard of 1432 mm.

The last steam-powered flight 1894

Today steam-powered heavier-than-air flight seems such an anachronistic dead-end in the development of the aeroplane that it is difficult to believe that it ever happened. The last recorded successful attempt at flight using steam power was in England in 1894. The experimenter was none other than Sir Hiram Maxim, an American-born naturalized Briton, already famous as the inventor of the Maxim machine gun.

During the latter half of the 19th century numerous attempts at flying in the USA, France and Britain involved the use of steam power. Many of these experiments used models but a small number actually achieved a limited success in manned flight. Perhaps powered 'hops' would be a more accurate description but they certainly attained some sort of aeronautical mobility.

One of the most notable successes was in France in 1890. Clément Ader constructed his 'bat-wing' style monoplane *Eole* relying on an ingeniously designed steam engine which produced 20 horse power. It flew a series of short flights, not long enough to be categorized as completely successful, but it was the very first aeroplane to take off under its own power. Steam power, however, was by this time already obsolescent. The first internal combustion engines had been built in the 1870s and were far more promising as a potential source of power for a heavier-than-air aircraft.

Sir Hiram Maxim was an archetypal 'inventor' of the period and had turned his attention to flying machines in the 1880s. Careful experiments with wind tunnels had produced designs for aerofoils and propellers. An extremely efficient power plant, driven by steam, was designed to power an enormous biplane. With two gigantic propellers, the aircraft was designed to run along 1800 feet of railway track constructed at Baldwyns Park. An extra set of guide rails was fitted to prevent it leaving the track entirely.

After several experimental runs success came on 31 July 1894. Sir Hiram, with an additional two crew members on board, finally got his aeroplane, puffing and steaming, to lift off after a 600-ft run. But this huge machine was only ever intended as a test rig. It would have been impossible to control it in free flight. Many demonstration runs followed, but with parts of the outer wing panels removed to prevent proper flight.

Unfortunately Sir Hiram abandoned aviation for many years, to return only after the Wright Brothers had made history with their own biplane, powered by their own power plant. This time it was a modern internal combustion engine which eventually gave the vital contribution to successful powered flight.

The last turnpike

Turnpike roads were toll roads run by private companies, the Turnpike Trusts. They enabled the improvement of some roads which would otherwise have been left undeveloped and thereby allowed a fast coaching service to be established in the 18th century. They encountered severe competition in the 1830s when the railways started to expand rapidly throughout Britain. The turnpikes gradually declined in importance during the rest of the century, many falling into disuse, and the last Turnpike Trust, in Anglesey, abolished its tolls in 1895.

The name turnpike comes from the 'pike', or bar, which was 'turned', much like a gate, to let the traveller pass after the toll had been paid. They were originally set up by an Act of 1663 which empowered magistrates to erect gates and charge a fee to anyone travelling over a given stretch of road by horse or carriage. Later, trust companies were created to manage the roads and to ensure that they were adequately repaired and maintained. Never popular, always accused of overcharging for the use of poorly kept roads, the Turnpike Trusts in their heyday controlled about 6 per cent of Britain's roads. There were 21,000 miles and 8,000 toll gates, but 1871 saw the last toll roads in London, and 1895 the last toll roads anywhere in Britain.

Ironically, just as motor vehicles started to appear the last turnpike roads disappeared. The development of an adequate road system for a modern age was left to the central and local government authorities. Most UK roads are still free of tolls with the exception of some motorway bridges and tunnels. Throughout the country the turnpikes have left a legacy of the toll houses often still standing – usually beside a once important road junction – where the toll-gate keepers used to live.

The last of the 'Red Flag' Act

The year 1896 was crucial to the development of the motor car in Britain. The abolition of the so-called 'Red Flag' Act of 1865 brought an end to the restrictions placed on mechanical transport, including the new 'horseless carriages'.

For most of the latter half of the 19th century the railways provided the supreme method of efficient long-distance travel. People of all classes could ride in relative comfort, for little cost, to all parts of the country. What roads existed outside the towns had been neglected and were suitable only for country folk for local travelling about their business. Rather than repair and maintain the roads, the government tried to restrict their use. Motorized transport, steam-traction engines and some other steam vehicles were severely limited by the passing of the 'Red Flag' Act of 1865. It restricted speeds to 4 miles per hour and required the vehicle to be preceded by a walking man carrying a red flag. There probably was some danger – to passengers and others – in travelling too fast, but pressure from the railway owners had a not inconsiderable influence in getting this Act onto the statute books.

In 1885 Germany's Karl Benz invented his motor car and in 1894 the first of the new-fangled machines from Germany and France began to be imported into Britain by intrepid 'motorists'. By this time the red flag of the 'Red Flag' part of the Act had been abolished but the speed limit of 4 miles per hour and the man on foot still remained in law. What was suitable for slow moving, steam-driven contraptions was clearly inappropriate for the modern motor car of the 1890s. Despite a general resistance to these dangerous 'horseless carriages', something had to be done to help the fledgeling motor industry.

Pressure on the government to change the law came from several quarters. One of them was Harry Lawson, a colourful entrepreneur who recognized the potential for motor cars if only they could be given unrestricted access to the country's highways. He really did seem to appreciate how the motor car could develop and radically affect the transport system forever. In 1896 the government eventually relented. It was agreed that the speed limit would be raised to 14 miles per hour (to be lowered by local government boards to 12 miles per hour) and the necessity for a foot man would be abolished.

The new Locomotives on Highways Act came into force in November. The last day on which motorists were restricted to 4 miles per hour was 13 November. On 14 November, in celebration, Harry Lawson organized the first of the 'London to Brighton' runs that are still an annual event today. Some 30 cars took part and with some foresight Lawson told those who reached Brighton that history would remember their 'immortal ride'. The British motor industry began to develop almost immediately. By the end of the century, just a few years later, Britain could boast dozens of firms in the car-making business, competing with the best that the continental and American firms could offer.

The last main line railway ◁ 1899 ▷

Throughout 19th-century Britain there was an explosion in the development of transport. Among the early methods of transport available to the Victorian traveller was the railway. From its beginnings in the 1820s, it developed into a popular nationwide network by the end of the century. The last trunk line in the country to be completed was the Great Central Railway Company's link from the Nottinghamshire coalfields that joined the Metropolitan's link from London at Aylesbury. Marylebone Station, the Great Central Railway's new terminus in London, was the last main line station to be constructed in the capital.

The Manchester, Sheffield and Lincolnshire Railway, the MS&L, covered the greater proportion of central England from Southport and Liverpool in the west to Grimsby in the east and Rugby in the south. It had been formed from an amalgamation of several smaller companies in 1846. The success and expansion of railways at that time were all about alliances. It was an alliance that the chairman of the MS&L, Sir Edward Watkin, planned to fulfil his grand desire of a 'Manchester to Paris' railway. The vital missing link was, of course, London. He became a member of the board of the Metropolitan Railway in 1872 and, using his influence, gained access to the capital over the Metropolitan's line between Quainton Road just north of Aylesbury and Harrow-on-the-Hill north of London.

The MS&L built new track from the north to Quainton Road and from Harrow-on-the-Hill to the brand new terminus at Marylebone in north London. On completion of the new link the company was renamed the Great Central Railway. Marylebone

Station, modest by the standards of the other main line stations in London, was opened with great ceremony on 9 March 1899. It had four platforms. The inaugural passenger service from Manchester to Marylebone took place on 15 March.

The Great Central Railway was never a great success in comparison with the other, larger railway companies but it set certain standards that were followed. Its rolling stock was considered amongst the best; its slogan 'Rapid Travel in Luxury' began to mean something in the early part of the 20th century. Perhaps the Great Central's greatest achievement was the creation and development of the port of Immingham near Grimsby between 1906 and 1912.

The Great Central Railway was absorbed by the London and North Eastern Railway, the LNER, in 1923 and nationalized along with all the others in 1948. Marylebone Station then came under the control, in succession, of Eastern Region, Western Region and London Midland Region. It now serves only two suburban lines, to Aylesbury and High Wycombe, but with great gentility. Its listed building frontage and its largely unaltered interior are in great demand by film companies for those tearful departures required in so many of today's 'period' films.

 ## The last square riggers

A square-rigged sailing ship is generally recognized to be one of the most beautiful of man's technical creations. Before they were replaced by steam ships in the latter half of the 19th and early part of the 20th centuries, the square riggers of the merchant marine and the navies of the world represented the pinnacle of the development of ocean transport.

The last working square rigger in British waters was the *Waterwitch*, built in Poole, Dorset in 1871. Originally a collier brig it was converted to the more convenient barquentine rig in 1884. At the end of its working life it was owned by Edward Stephens and its home port was Fowey in Cornwall. *Waterwitch* made its last commercial voyage in 1936.

In other parts of the world commercial tall ships continued for many more years. In 1952 several square rigged brigantines survived the Second World War to operate out of Colombo in Ceylon, carrying cargoes to Madras. They were the last genuine commercially operated square riggers in the world.

 ## The last passenger-carrying airships

In the early days of scheduled aircraft services, there existed a glorious parallel – airships carrying a privileged band of passengers in extraordinary comfort and glamour. While cumbersome biplane bombers from the Great War were being converted for use by hardy aviation passengers on short hops about Europe and America, the Zeppelin Company of Germany was settling down into what was then thought to be the most practical form of air transport, the hydrogen-filled rigid airship.

In the 19th century many airships had been built and flown but not until 1900, when Count von Zeppelin's rigid airship design showed the way, did safe passenger aviation seem possible. Zeppelin spent many years developing his huge aerial monsters for use in peace and in war. He gave his name to these strange aircraft and his own company was the first – and last – to take passengers on regular flights.

By the time Hitler came to power in Germany in the early 1930s the huge *Graf Zeppelin*, and later the even larger *Hindenburg*, held exclusive sway over the select transatlantic routes between Germany and South America and the USA. Their future, however, was doomed. Hydrogen was highly inflammable and despite the Zeppelins' good safety record it was recognized that helium gas, a completely safe alternative, would have to be used in future. The latest Zeppelin, *LZ 130*, was under construction but waiting for a decision on supply of the necessary helium from the USA, the world's only supplier of the gas. The future for airship travel was in the balance. That balance was tipped irrevocably in 1937.

On 3 May 1937 the *Hindenburg* and the *Graf Zeppelin* both set out on what were to be their last commercial flights. The *Hindenburg*, coming in to moor at Lakehurst, New Jersey on the evening of 6 May, mysteriously caught fire. Its hydrogen exploded and thousands watched as the airship sank slowly to the ground torn apart by the flames killing 36 people. At that very moment the *Graf Zeppelin* was on a return flight from Brazil

The grand passenger lounge on the British airship, R 101. Windows and promenade decks allowed the passengers to watch the world drift by below. On 5 October 1930 the R 101 crashed in France on its maiden commercial flight, killing 48 passengers and crew. (Topham)

to Friedrichshafen in Germany. The passengers only heard the news after their safe return – they were the last fare-paying passengers to travel a regular airship route. In 1940, during the Second World War, both the remaining Zeppelins, now hopelessly obsolete, were deliberately destroyed on Hermann Goering's orders.

1940 The last Thames steamboat service

Introduced during the Second World War, in September 1940, the Thames steamboat service was run by London Transport using steam-powered boats provided by the Port of London Authority. The boats plied their trade from Westminster to Woolwich. The journey unfortunately took over two hours and the resulting service was a failure. It was withdrawn on 2 November after less than a month.

1961 The last London Transport steam Underground

Today the Underground railway system in London is all electric but it was not always so. The original 19th-century system had been set up with steam locomotives. It was only in 1899 that the first electric-powered trains entered service. Over the next 20 years all the regular services went electric.

There was one small steam pocket on the Underground that lasted for many more years. On the Metropolitan line, electric locomotives were replaced at Rickmansworth with steam engines, a process costly in both money and time. This section was eventually modernized, and on 11 September 1961 passenger services under steam power came to an end. Steam locomotives, originally from the Great Western Railway, continued hauling engineer trains and other background duties until they too were retired after a special commemorative run on 6 June 1971 between Barbican and Neasden, ending the 108 years of London Transport's steam era.

The last trams

The London trams ended their service in the nation's capital on 5 July 1952. It was an occasion much heralded and celebrated. During the week passengers on the trams were issued with special tickets with the inscription 'Last Tram Week'. On the last day, thousands packed the trams to savour their last moments. The last official tram in service in London, number 1951, ended its trip well past midnight and into the next day, barely mobile and denuded of all its fittings by souvenir hunters. Trams in Manchester had already ground to a halt. The last service run had been watched with similar nostalgia in 1949.

British city-centre tram services continued in Glasgow for many more years, but by the early 1960s the end of the line loomed large. In its heyday the Glasgow system was second only to London in size, in the 1950s it was the largest. Just before its demise it had shrunk to just three operational routes. The last of these routes to survive was No 9, from Dalmuir West to Auchenshuggle. It was last operated on 4 September 1962.

Blackpool's famous trams survived, of course, running out to Fleetwood, for the delight of the many visiting holidaymakers, but it cannot be regarded as a complete city system. Today's renewed interest in tram systems gathers pace in Britain. Manchester is already operating a modern metrolink system, part of which is on a street section and could herald a return of the much-loved tram.

The last steam trains in Britain   ◇ 1968 ◇

It is unlikely that the complete and utter demise of steam locomotives in Britain will ever be documented, such is the romance and glamour associated with them. Museums, preservation societies and the formal British railway network itself will probably always retain at least a toe-hold in what has become a lucrative leisure industry. However, genuine regular scheduled steam railways came to a well publicized end in the late 1960s.

British Railways had built their last steam locomotive, the *Evening Star*, in March 1960 and steam power gradually gave way to diesel-electric during the 1960s. The Brockenhurst to Lymington branch line in Hampshire ran under steam power until 30 May 1967, a line that was itself over 100 years old. This was the last regular British passenger service using steam locomotives.

Steam operation continued fitfully for a few more months, outside the public gaze of any passengers until 8 August 1968. British Railways laid on a commemorative 'Farewell to Steam' return trip from Liverpool to Carlisle on 11 August 1968. Perhaps this can be regarded as the end of steam travel . . . or can it?

POLITICS AND GOVERNMENT

7

 ## The last Scottish Parliament

After the Act of Union on 1 May 1707, the 45 Scottish MPs and the 16 Representative peers were absorbed into the British Parliament. A large amount of autonomy for the Scots, such as the separate legal system, was guaranteed by Queen Anne's ministers to persuade the Scots MPs to agree to this Act. The Scots gained free trade with England and representation at Westminster but had to give up their own Parliament.

 ## The last royal veto

Bills of Parliament, before they become Acts of Parliament, have to receive the Royal Assent. This used to be given, by the monarch in person, in a ceremony in the House of Lords. In more recent years the assent was given by a Royal Commission, a number of lords sitting on a bench immediately below the royal throne. This ceremony has also passed away and was last performed in July 1967. Now the Royal Assent is given without public ceremony at all.

Of course many years ago the monarch would actually be involved in the decision-making process, assenting or not as they thought fit. The last time a sovereign gave a public *dis*approval to a Bill of Parliament was in 1708 when Queen Anne, unhappy with the Scottish Militia Bill, was heard to announce 'La Reyne s'avisera', Norman-French, perhaps, for, 'the Queen is not amused'.

 ## The last of the Two Secretaries

From the reign of George I (1714–27), there were two major Secretaries of State, both essentially doing the same job. The post of Secretary of State had developed as one through which the royal will could be expressed. The secretariat available to this major office holder was small by today's standards and by 1714 it was realized that it was too much for one man, so the job was shared between two.

Both secretaries were responsible for foreign policy matters and for internal order within the country, or at least those matters that could not be handled by the magistrates.

A certain amount of job demarcation between the two holders was provided by dividing the jobs geographically. The two posts were thus called the Secretary of State for the Northern Department and the Secretary of State for the Southern Department. Generally speaking the foreign affairs were also divided on a geographic basis, with the Southern Secretary taking responsibility for Ireland and the colonies.

This rather convoluted system came to an end on 27 March 1782, when the Secretaryships of State were divided along the lines found today, home and foreign affairs. That year the government of Lord North resigned and the Marquess of Rockingham took over. The two outgoing Secretaries, Viscount Stormont who held the Northern Secretaryship and the Earl of Hillsborough who held the Southern Secretaryship, were the last to hold these posts. Lord Stormont, or David Murray, was an experienced diplomat and an elected Scottish Peer who later became the Earl of Mansfield. Wills Hill, the (Irish) Earl of Hillsborough, sat in the House of Lords by right as the (English) Baron, Lord Harwich. He was more a courtier than a diplomat and eventually succeeded to the title of the Marquess of Downshire. Charles James Fox took over the Northern Department which was converted into the Foreign Office and his rival, Lord Shelburne, took over the Southern Department which was converted into the Home Office.

The last of the Irish Parliament

◇ **1800** ◇

Westminster, the 'Mother of Parliaments', reigned supreme in Great Britain and without real challenge throughout the 19th century. This was not always the case. Both Scotland and Ireland had independent sovereign parliaments, under the same crown as England, at certain times in the past. Scotland's independent Parliament disappeared in 1707, to be subsumed in the English Parliament at Westminster. Ireland's Parliament lasted until the first day of the 19th century, 1 January 1801.

In the last years of the 18th century, while Britain was at war with France, Ireland was experiencing considerable unrest. Catholics were strongly discriminated against, unable to vote, be elected to office or occupy the most important positions in public life. The Irish Parliament in Dublin was modelled on that at Westminster. It had an upper House of Lords and a lower House of Elected Members. Whilst nominally independent, it could not pass legislation that was against the interests of mainland Britain. It was in any case strongly manipulated and controlled by the British government through the powers of its mouthpiece in Ireland, the Lord Lieutenant installed in Dublin Castle.

Moves for radical political and religious reform were strong and growing stronger. One reforming movement, led by a group called the 'United Irishmen', was inevitably exploited and supported by the French. An insurrection in 1798 was put down by the British military with the usual ruthlessness. The British government decided that it had had enough. After much debate it was decided to unite the Irish and British Parliaments. In 1800 the Act of Union was passed, in both houses of both Parliaments. This act abolished the separate Irish Parliament in Dublin and, in effect, created the United Kingdom of Great Britain and Ireland.

The Irish were given a hundred seats in the Westminster Parliament. In addition, they were granted 28 places in Westminster's House of Lords for Irish peers, elected for life from among their own number by fellow Irish lords, and four Irish bishops from the now unified Anglican Church of England and Ireland.

In the process of persuading the Irish to relinquish their own Parliament open bribes had been paid to the patrons of the Irish 'pocket boroughs'. They made up the bulk of the old Irish House of Commons, and their constituencies, without a broad franchise or a secret ballot, were totally in the control of the owners of the land. To compensate the landowners for their loss of influence and power they were paid £15,000 per seat. A total sum of £1.25 million was paid out by the British government. The Marquess of Downshire, ironically a vigorous opponent of the Act, was reputedly the most generously compensated for his many pocket seats.

The last sitting of the old Irish Parliament was on 2 August 1800, the day after the Act of Union received the royal assent. A 500-year-old institution was dead. Dublin remained the centre of governmental administration for Ireland but its political heart had been torn out. The splendid Parliament buildings were sold to the Bank of Ireland but on condition that the interior be altered so that all trace of its previous use be obliterated. Despite this, the House of Lords, 'the Old House in College Green', remains today much as it was in its 18th-century glory.

As a result of the Act Ireland became part of the UK on 1 January 1801. Westminster would provide direct rule for over a hundred years until 1922 when the Irish Free State formed its own Parliament, the Dáil, but alas, not in the old buildings. The Act did not solve the religious problems of Ireland. Although it gave Catholics the vote, it did not give them the right to become MPs. The ascendancy of the Protestant minority over the Catholic majority was maintained for many more years. As for the political problems, agitation for Irish Home Rule started almost immediately.

The last official discrimination against Catholics

1829

Religious liberty has only been grudgingly granted to British citizens. The freedom to practise virtually any religion was established by the 18th century but bigotry was still rife. Open discrimination, particularly against Catholics, was still quite legal at the beginning of the 19th century. The ultimate test of full citizenship is widely regarded as whether any person can become a Member of Parliament. In 1829 Daniel O'Connell was the last Christian to be barred from Parliament for refusing, as a Roman Catholic, to take the oath of supremacy.

In 1673 and 1678 the British government introduced the Test and Corporation Acts which made the holding of public office conditional upon a denial of the transubstantiation in the Mass, as believed by Roman Catholics, and a certificate of attendance at Anglican communion. Many exceptions had been allowed to these laws, framed in the time of King Charles II, to allow almost all Protestants – dissenters included – to take part in public life. By the beginning of the 19th century Catholic emancipation was the real issue of the day and it was being fought out in the towns and villages of Catholic Ireland. The Duke of Wellington, as prime minister, was eventually forced to deal with this near intractable problem.

The Catholic Association, led by the Roman Catholic priesthood and with Daniel

O'Connell as its main spokesman, was in a very strong position and agitating for the right of Catholics to sit in Parliament. In County Clare, in a parliamentary by-election, O'Connell, a Catholic and thus disqualified from taking his seat, stood against Vesey Fitzgerald who was offering himself for re-election. O'Connell won and set in action a series of events that swiftly led to Catholic emancipation.

O'Connell's election fuelled agitation in Ireland. To the alarm of the government, it spread to England where open conflict and cries from anti-Catholic mobs of 'no popery' were increasingly heard. The government soon admitted the justice of the Catholics' cause and that nothing short of full emancipation would satisfy them. Action was needed quickly to avoid prolonged demonstrations and dangerous conflict.

Although personally against the measure, the Duke of Wellington was a realist. He and his ministers, particularly Robert Peel as Home Secretary, accomplished a *volte-face* and brought in legislation for 'Catholic relief'. This altered the oath of allegiance to the Church of England required of all Members of Parliament. An amazing amount of hard work was required to persuade his Tory party to support the measure, the House of Lords to approve it and the King not to obstruct it. The job was eventually done on 13 April 1829.

On 15 May O'Connell arrived at the House of Commons to take his seat. As he had been elected under the old rules the clerk presented him with the old oath which included a denial of fundamental Roman Catholic beliefs and a declaration of the supremacy of the sovereign in all religious matters. He refused and from the bar of the House argued his case. The debate continued on 18 May, but after a long and very eloquent statement the use of the new oath was again refused to O'Connell. He returned to Dublin to a very enthusiastic reception from his supporters who knew that the case was all but won. A triumphal progress to County Clare was followed by his decisive re-election for the seat on 30 July. He was duly sworn in under the new oaths and at last took his seat in Parliament.

A significant side issue to this legislation was that it now allowed Roman Catholic peers to enter Parliament. There were eight English, twelve Irish and two Scottish lords who were immediately enabled to take their seats in Parliament in the Upper House. *Official* concern at 'popery', in the form of open discrimination against Roman Catholics, drew to an end when Catholics entered Parliament. The Jews had to wait another 30 years before they were granted the same right.

The last of the rotten boroughs 1832

The representation of the towns and shires of Britain in Parliament was developed over several centuries. Never democratic in the modern sense, the system had, by the 1800s, become obviously unequal and notoriously unfair. Pressure for change grew; the parliamentary battles over the Great Reform Bill, attempting to abolish the 'pocket' and 'rotten' boroughs, were a nationwide sensation that lasted for more than two years.

Large areas of the country, such as Birmingham, Britain's second city, were completely unrepresented in Parliament. Other areas, whose populations had dwindled to mere handfuls, were over-represented, the infamous rotten boroughs. Bute in Scotland had only twelve voters; Old Sarum in Wiltshire had just seven; Dunwich in

East Anglia, which had been swallowed up by the advances of the North Sea, still loyally returned two members to the House of Commons every election.

Voting was based on the ownership of the land; a pocket borough was 'in the pocket' of a rich landowner who could, if he owned enough of the land, literally and legally own a majority of the votes required to elect the Member of Parliament. Seats in Parliament were openly bought and sold. Many important landowner peers each controlled several seats in the House of Commons.

The franchise, those entitled to vote, was also very small. Only 22 seats out of over 600 had an electorate of more than 1,000; most had less than 500, usually enough to elect two or more Members of Parliament. Among the voters there were no women, no working class, not even what today would be called the middle classes. In addition, with no secret ballot the practice of open bribery was common.

By the beginning of the 19th century there had developed considerable pressure to bring this corrupt system to an end. The prosperous, respectable middle classes wanted their share of power. The working classes were bitter and angry; they too wanted change and they talked of violence and seemed prepared to use it. Reform, however, was not a foregone conclusion; it was fiercely resisted, especially by the old Tories with their belief in property, and even by the Church which saw a threat to its view of the established order of society.

The Duke of Wellington, prime minister in 1830, dug in his heels. He could envisage no useful improvements to the current political system. He said that 'beginning reform is beginning revolution' and believed that in a reformed Parliament no 'real

Lord John Russell introducing his Reform Bill at the dispatch box in the House of Commons. He spent two years fighting for and steering the legislation through Parliament. In the end the Great Reform Act of 1832 brought an end to the rotten boroughs and severely restricted the pocket boroughs but failed to extend the franchise to the working classes. (ME)

gentleman' would be able to take any further part in public affairs. As Wellington and the Tories refused to tackle the reform issue, the King, William IV, reluctantly called on the Whig leader, Earl Grey, to form an administration and carry through the necessary legislation. Earl Grey appointed his Paymaster-General, Lord John Russell ('Lord' was a courtesy title as he was the younger son of the Duke of Bedford), to lead the Whigs in the House of Commons. So began the battles over the Great Reform Bill.

The Bill planned to sweep aside 143 rotten boroughs and to give the large towns and cities of the Midlands their own Members of Parliament for the first time. It also proposed to increase the number of voters by using various different property qualification schemes. At the first attempt, in the House of Commons, the Bill unsurprisingly foundered – it had, after all, at least 143 self-interested opponents. Grey asked the King for a dissolution, and an election on the single issue of Parliamentary reform followed. The Tories were trounced. On the second attempt the Bill was passed in the House of Commons but was rejected by the House of Lords. The battle shifted back to the Commons. The Bill was presented to the House for the third time by the indomitable Russell and was passed by two to one. Back in the House of Lords in May 1832 it was rejected again. The country was in uproar. This single issue dominated political thought and talk throughout the land.

Grey approached the King again. He brought a more severe message. He needed the King to create enough friendly Whig peers to ensure the smooth passage of the Bill. The King refused and asked Wellington to take on the job. The Duke became convinced that orderly government would be impossible so the premiership was passed back to Grey. Unable to manoeuvre in any other way, the King threatened the peers. When the Bill was brought to the Lords again most of its opponents stayed away. The Bill became law in June 1832 amidst sensational scenes throughout the country. Detailed Scottish and Irish Bills followed in July and August.

So ended the rotten boroughs. Although the Great Reform Act was a genuine attempt to widen the franchise and bring an end to corruption, it seems relatively tame today. Without secret voting, the very real influence of the large landowners still persisted in pocket boroughs. Britain had to wait another 40 years for that to be remedied with the secret ballot.

As for extending the franchise, the Act was a disappointment. Although another 300,000 of the middle classes were brought onto the rolls, the working class were excluded. They turned to the radical Chartist movement for help. Even today, boroughs can still go 'rotten' when populations shift. Regular Boundary Commission reports ensure that constituency boundaries are moved to maintain reasonably equitable Parliamentary representation.

The last government dismissed by a monarch ◇ *1834* ◇

The development of the unwritten British Constitution over several centuries gradually took power away from the sovereign and, in theory at least, gave it to the people. One of the theoretical powers the sovereign still holds today, although not used, is the ability to dismiss the prime minister and the government of the day and ask another person to form an administration. The last monarch to dismiss a government, without consulting any other official source, was William IV in 1834.

After the passing of the first Reform Act by the Whigs in 1832, the Whig leader Earl Grey retired from public life. In the summer of 1834 the King, after his attempts to encourage a coalition ministry failed, reluctantly confirmed the Whigs in office and the premiership fell to Viscount Melbourne. Melbourne was a skilled politician who gave the outward impression that he had no real political ambition. On receiving the invitation to become prime minister he is reported to have described it as 'a damned bore', but he took the job nonetheless and was soon in conflict with his King over policy and appointments to the government.

Lord Althorp was the Whigs' leader in the House of Commons, and his appointment continued to have the King's approval. When Althorp, the son of an earl, succeeded to his father's earldom and moved to the House of Lords, Melbourne wished to replace him in the Commons with Russell. Lord John Russell was a rising star in the Whig hierarchy. Unfortunately the King loathed him and found his insistence on the reform of the established Anglican Church in Ireland completely unacceptable. The King on this matter, as on most, wished it to be left well alone.

On Althorp's retirement from office the King genuinely expected Melbourne to resign too; he did not. On 14 November, after calling on the King at Windsor, Melbourne was handed a formal letter. The letter was polite and firm: he was dismissed. Melbourne was also polite and uncomplaining. He commented later, 'I have always thought complaints of ill-usage contemptible, whether from a seduced disappointed girl or a turned out prime minister.' He even offered to carry any letter to the Duke of Wellington who was to be invited, with Sir Robert Peel, to form a Tory administration.

The press and the rest of Melbourne's cabinet were not so sanguine. There was astonishment and disbelief that the King could have dismissed a government which had such a large working majority in the House of Commons. The new administration which Peel put together was, by March the following year, reeling from a succession of defeats in Parliament. Peel almost begged the King to be released. To much relief all round, even to the King, Melbourne was called back and in April agreed to form his new ministry. It is ironic, but somehow eminently suitable, that it was Melbourne who did so much to help the young Queen Victoria on the path of genuine constitutional monarchy a few years later.

The last official discrimination against Jews

At the beginning of the 19th century Jews in Britain had very few rights. But as the prejudices against Catholics, Irish immigrants and foreigners gave way to reason, so practising Jews were gradually admitted to most parts of society as respectable, useful Britons. The last bastion of prejudice against Jewry – as against Catholics – was in the Houses of Parliament, where Jews were eventually allowed to become members in 1858. The last Jew actually to be forcibly prevented from taking his rightfully elected seat in the House of Commons was Alderman Salomons, elected member for Greenwich, London, in 1851.

The Jewish race was treated with contempt by many British Christians during the

19th century. In addition to the religious overtones of this mistrust, Jews were resented for their often spectacular successes in banking and money-lending. Official, legal prejudice remained pervasive. Several Jews had been elected to high office and special Acts of Parliament had to be passed to enable them to hold these positions. Legislation was passed to allow Salomons to take up his elected post of Sheriff of London in 1835. However, it took another eleven years, until 1846, before Jews could hold elected municipal office.

Salomons had not been the first British Jew to be elected to Parliament. Baron Rothschild had made the first attempt in 1850. He had been returned for the City of London but his request to swear his oath of allegiance, before entering Parliament, on the Old Testament instead of the New Testament was refused. The next year legislation was introduced to enable Jews to take their oath without the Christian references. It was while this legislation was being debated that Alderman Salomons was elected as Member of Parliament for Greenwich.

Before Salomons took his seat he too objected to having to swear on the New Testament and use the words 'on the true faith of a Christian'. He boldly refused to leave the chamber and actually took part in the debates and the voting on whether he should be allowed to take his seat. The voting went against him and he was eventually led away by the Sergeant-at-Arms. Petitions from his constituents followed but nothing was done as the legislation to permit Jews had been thrown out by the House of Lords. In the meantime action in the Court of Exchequer had been brought against Salomons, for sitting and voting in Parliament without taking the oath, which was a criminal offence. He was fined £500.

Many more attempts were made in the House of Commons, led by Lord John Russell, to amend and reform the law. Each was blocked by the House of Lords. Eventually in 1858 the House of Commons, by a resolution of its own, allowed Jews to be admitted. Finally in 1860 an Act was passed to allow Jews to omit the Christian oath on taking office.

Disraeli, a well-known and famous parliamentarian by this time, was from Jewish stock, but a practising Christian, and had therefore been able to enter the Commons much earlier. In today's political world Jews in the British Parliament now pass unnoticed on their way to hold high office.

The last Whigs 1866

The Whigs first came together as a political party in the last decades of the 17th century. They were in power for much of the 18th century and favoured restricting the monarch's powers and increasing those of Parliament. Their demise as a single party in the 19th century followed their union with some of the old Tory party to form the Liberals. Lord John Russell was the last Whig prime minister.

At the beginning of the 19th century party politics were sometimes difficult to disentangle, as opponents one year became allies the next. The Whig Lord Melbourne, Queen Victoria's favourite prime minister in the late 1830s, had served quite happily a few years earlier under the arch-Tory, the Duke of Wellington. Without strong 'party machines' there was room for much flexibility amongst politicians. This applied as much to appointments as to party allegiance. For instance, acknowledged leaders of the parties were one thing but prime ministers were chosen by the sovereign. Thus in 1846, Lord John Russell was the Whig prime minister and the once Tory Palmerston was Foreign Secretary; 15 years later the roles were reversed – Palmerston was prime minister with Russell as his Foreign Secretary.

Also, in the 1840s, a genuine new political party was in the making. The followers of Sir Robert Peel, known as 'Peelites', were loosening their ties with the remainder of the old Tory party, mainly over the issue of free trade and the repeal of the Corn Laws. Gladstone was one of the Peelites. Palmerston had resisted parliamentary reform for 30 years. He was one of the last true Whigs. He was prime minister on his death in 1865. Palmerston left office and this world with the reassuring words, 'Die, my dear doctor? That's the last thing I shall do!' Russell succeeded to the premiership and to the leadership of the declining Whigs.

Russell was the third son of the Duke of Bedford and had been known by his courtesy title of Lord John Russell in the House of Commons. He had done sterling service 30 years earlier, steering the Great Reform Act through the Commons. In 1861 he had been created an earl in his own right and elevated to the House of Lords. When Russell took over the leadership of the Whigs there was a great public clamour for Parliamentary reform, mainly for the extension of the franchise to include the populous artisan classes in the big cities. On Palmerston's death the way was clear: Russell set to with relish.

The Peelites had found much in common with the Whigs and were part of Russell's administration. Gladstone, an ex-Peelite and now a confirmed 'Liberal', was leader in the House of Commons. Despite Disraeli's contention that 'England does not love coalitions' this was the final phase of the coalescing of the constituent parts of the Liberal Party. But Russell soon came unstuck with his Reform Bill. Moderate as it was, it could not find a majority in favour. Russell resigned in June 1866 and the last of the Whig prime ministers retired from active politics; he died in 1878.

The Tories under Lord Derby took over on 28 June. Disraeli, the Tory leader in the House of Commons, urged his own party to bring in the reforms 'to dish the Whigs'. So it was, ironically, the Tory government that finally brought in the Reform Act of 1867 to extend the vote to a large proportion of the new working class. Although Disraeli did dish the Whigs, retribution was swift. Lord Derby soon resigned and Disraeli, finding himself prime minister, called a general election. The Liberals, now including Peelites, elements of the Whig party and the Radicals, led by John Bright, finally came together. Led by Gladstone, they were swept into office on the extended franchise.

 ## The last US president to be impeached

Andrew Johnson was the last president to undergo impeachment, a trial by the Congress. He was acquitted in 1868, saved by one vote short of the required two-thirds majority in the Senate required to convict. Johnson unexpectedly came to office on the assassination of Abraham Lincoln in 1865. His lenient Reconstruction policies after the American Civil War enraged the Radical Republicans. His efforts to rehabilitate the Southern white aristocrats produced many enemies in Congress.

In 1867 Johnson dismissed Secretary of War Edwin Stanton in contradiction of the new Tenure of Office Act, which prohibited the president from removing certain Federal officers without the approval of the Senate. Despite his claim that he had the right to change his 'constitutional advisers', the Senate reinstated Stanton and the House of Representatives voted to begin the process of impeachment against the President – the first and last such instance in US history. In the vote of May 1968, the two-thirds needed to remove him did not materialize as seven Republicans voted with Johnson's supporters. However, Johnson's political credibility had collapsed and in March the following year he resigned as president.

Impeachment was being actively considered for Richard Nixon in the aftermath of the Watergate affair in 1974. He resigned on 9 August and thus avoided almost certain conviction.

US President Richard M. Nixon says goodbye to White House staff. He was very nearly impeached by Congress over his involvement in the Watergate scandal. He was forced to resign in August 1974 and was granted a full pardon by his successor, President Gerald Ford. He died in 1994. (Hulton)

The last of the public ballot

1872

In 1872 Parliament passed the Ballot Act to provide for confidential voting in the form of a secret ballot. Before this legislation, voting was quite open and the way any particular voter cast his vote was available for the public to see. The votes were usually written into a ledger and kept as a public record. This public availability of the voting records enabled bribery to flourish.

The last election in the United Kingdom to be conducted with open voting records was the by-election at Oldham held on 4 June 1872. John Platt, one of the two Liberal MPs for the seat, had died causing a by-election. In the ensuing election the Conservative candidate, J. M. Cobbett, very narrowly defeated the Hon E. L. Stanley who was standing for the Liberals.

1902

The last prime minister in the House of Lords

Robert Cecil, 3rd Marquess of Salisbury, was the last serving prime minister in the House of Lords. He formed his last ministry on 25 June 1895 and retired from the premiership in July 1902. Lord Robert Cecil was born the second son of the Marquess of Salisbury. As a young man he spent two years on a round-the-world tour after leaving Oxford University in 1850. His first-hand view of the Empire in the making stood him in good stead throughout his life. On his return he was elected unopposed to the House of Commons as MP for Stamford in 1853. He married early and, although born to privilege and power, as a younger son he had to earn his living which he did from political journalism. He succeeded to the marquesate on the death of his father in 1868, his elder brother having died earlier.

As a marquess, a rank of nobility second only to that of duke, he became a member of the House of Lords. The 'natural' authority of the aristocracy might have weakened considerably during the 19th century, but members of the House of Lords were still expected to play as full a part in government as their parliamentary colleagues in the lower House. Salisbury served in the India Office and also as Foreign Secretary before becoming prime minister for the first time in 1885. He had been out of office for three years when, in 1895, his last ministry was formed after the short-lived Liberal administration of Lord Rosebery. In fact, with a few short breaks, Salisbury dominated the political leadership of the country from 1885 until July 1902 when, with his health failing, he was persuaded to resign.

He was a true Victorian. Born fifteen years after the Battle of Waterloo – he had the Duke of Wellington as his godfather – he died in 1902 a year after the end of the Boer War. He was not greatly in favour of the parliamentary reforms passed during his career and, despite being known for his 'masterly inactivity', he was a successful and much admired politician. He was also his own Foreign Secretary for much of his time as premier. Ironically at a time of tremendous power and splendour for the British Empire he managed a foreign policy that was summed up in his own words: 'splendid isolation'.

He was a man of many talents, taking a keen interest in farming and, above all, scientific experimentation in the true Victorian style. When first called upon to form a ministry it is said that the telegraph summoning him to the Queen at Balmoral interrupted him in his laboratory at Hatfield House whilst testing a telephone. It is fitting that someone who had made it a practice, throughout his career, to resist much of the inevitable political change in Britain should have been the last non-elected prime minister.

Although most prime ministers since Salisbury have been elevated to the peerage after their time at 10 Downing Street, they were always members of the House of Commons whilst in office. There is no absolute constitutional requirement for such an arrangement but the general march of democracy since the end of the 19th century made it accepted practice. A prime minister who has neither submitted to the will of the electorate nor is able to speak in

Robert Arthur Talbot Gascoyne Cecil, 3rd Marquess of Salisbury, was the last British prime minister from the House of Lords. Conservative leader for 23 years, he retired in 1902 and died a year later. (Popperfoto)

the House of Commons – the accepted source of real democratic authority – would be completely unacceptable to the majority of the country today.

Viscount Halifax was Foreign Secretary in 1940 when a replacement for Neville Chamberlain was needed. Churchill was eventually chosen to head the National Coalition government but Halifax had been a strong contender. His peerage was one of the reasons why he never became the country's wartime leader.

On his resignation in 1963, Prime Minister Macmillan advised the Queen to choose Alec Douglas-Home, although in the House of Lords, as his successor. Because of a change in the law earlier that year the 14th Earl of Home was able to renounce his peerage. He fought and won the safe seat of Kinross and West Perthshire in a by-election to become a Member of Parliament in the Commons and to take up the reins of power at Number 10.

The last (solo) First Lord ◆1902◆

Under the British Parliamentary system today it is usual for the prime minister to be also the 'First Lord of the Treasury' and to be theoretically senior, in the Treasury, the 'Ministry of Finance', to even the Chancellor of the Exchequer. The last First Lord not to be prime minister was Arthur Balfour from 1895 to 1902. He sat in the House of Commons while his uncle, Lord Salisbury, was in the House of Lords as prime minister. Balfour succeeded Salisbury as prime minister and retained the title of First Lord of the Treasury, which has been held by every prime minister since.

The last single-sex elections ◆1918◆

In 1918 after many years of campaigning, by the suffragettes and others, legislation was passed to allow women the vote. This first legislation restricted the women's vote to those who were over 30 and were householders or married to householders. The first elections where women voted was at the general election of 1918.

The last election where women were specifically excluded from casting their votes was at a by-election held in East Finsbury in July 1918 during the Great War. The sitting MP, Joseph Barker, died, forcing a by-election which was duly called. The convention between the major parties not to contest by-elections during wartime was kept, but two independent candidates put themselves forward to force what was to be the last overtly sexist ballot in the UK. Beside the eventually victorious Liberal candidate, Mr H. E. A. Cotton, there was a Mr H. Spencer from the Vigilante Society, 'promoting purity in public life', and Mr A. S. Belsher who was the 'Patriotic get on with war' candidate.

Other later by-elections were held during that parliament, before women could vote, but they were all unopposed. Mr Hugh Morrison was elected as a Conservative for the Wilton division of Wiltshire on 6 November 1918, five days before the end of the war and less than two months before the general election. But he needed no votes from either sex as he was unopposed.

The last Liberals in Government

The last Liberal government was headed by Asquith from 1908 to 1915. On 25 May 1915 a new, wartime coalition government was formed with support from all three main parties, Liberal, Conservative and Labour. The coalition continued with various switches of allegiance, and the replacement of Asquith by Lloyd George as prime minister, until after the War. Lloyd George – the last Liberal prime minister – took up the reins of power in 1916 but continued to head the coalition government after peace came in 1918. Divisions in the Liberal Party had begun to show over the direction of the War and Lloyd George's elevation to prime minister, over Asquith, furthered the split. The election victory in 1918 of the coalition government, predominantly Conservative but with a Liberal prime minister, added to the marginalization of the Liberals. The final nail in the Liberal coffin, however, was the rise of support for the Labour Party.

Lloyd George's coalition ended four years later, in 1922. The Conservatives had become increasingly irritated with the individualistic style of government under the 'Welsh wizard' and left the coalition. The grouping of the Tory MPs that made the decision to leave the coalition formed the 1922 Backbench Committee, an organization still in existence today. Lloyd George was forced to resign as prime minister on 19 October 1922. The Conservatives took office, on their own, with Bonar Law as the prime minister, and at the general election a month later won a huge majority. The number of Liberal MPs from the two wings of the party numbered 116; this rose to 159 at the election in the following year but at the 1924 election their numbers slumped to 40. The Liberals were never to have over 100 MPs again and a Liberal has never since headed a government.

Sir Herbert Samuel was Britain's last Liberal Cabinet Minister to hold a major office of state. He was Home Secretary in Ramsay MacDonald's National Government from August 1931 to 28 September 1932. In 1938 Samuel was offered the post of Lord Privy Seal in Chamberlain's Cabinet, but he was unhappy with the Conservative government's economic policy and turned the offer down. He died in 1963. (Hulton)

The last compulsory re-election of ministers

When a Member of Parliament was appointed to certain government offices more than nine months after the date of proclamation summoning the new Parliament, he was required to seek re-election in a by-election. In some instances these re-elections were unopposed but in others, the confidence of the government was tested. Winston Churchill, for example, had to re-contest his Dundee seat in 1917 when he was appointed Minister of Munitions.

In 1919 and in 1926 legislation was passed to limit and finally abolish this requirement. The last time a minister was required to re-contest his seat was when Alexander Munro MacRobert was appointed Solicitor General for Scotland in December 1925. The by-election in his constituency of Renfrewshire, East was held on

29 January 1926. He only narrowly held off the Labour challenger, the Reverend J. M. Munroe. MacRobert had only been an MP since October 1924 and he remained in the House of Commons until his death in 1930.

On occasions the voters took advantage of the by-elections to show their disapproval of the government. The last MP to be unsuccessful in re-contesting his seat on appointment to government office was Thomas Lewis in 1922. He was appointed to the post of junior Lord of the Treasury in the Coalition government. At the by-election on 25 July in his constituency of Pontypridd he was unexpectedly defeated by the Labour candidate Thomas Isaac Mardy Jones by over 4,000 votes. He was returned in the general election later that year as the Member of Parliament for University of Wales.

The last general election not on a Thursday ⟨1931⟩

The tradition of holding public elections – particularly general elections – on a Thursday is well established today. In past years virtually every other day of the week apart from Sunday has been used. The last general election which was not held on a Thursday was that in 1931 when Tuesday 27 October was chosen by prime minister Ramsay MacDonald. All subsequent general elections and most by-elections have since then been held on a Thursday.

The last US president of more than two terms ⟨1945⟩

The last US president to be elected for more than two terms was Franklin D. Roosevelt. He was elected four times and he died during his fourth term, in 1945. He was also the only president to have been elected more than twice. The constitution was altered, by the twenty-second amendment after the Second World War, which restricted any individual to a maximum of two terms as president.

American President Franklin D. Roosevelt on the steps of his home with his family at Hyde Park, New York after his landslide second presidential victory in 1936. He went on to win again in 1940 and 1944, the last president to win more than two terms in office.
(Popperfoto)

Roosevelt was elected to the White House in 1932, at the height of the Depression. His sweeping economic programme, his 'New Deal', 'provided relief, loans and jobs' to a country in the grip of economic despair, and he was overwhelmingly re-elected in 1936. Roosevelt, at first, struggled to keep the USA out of the Second World War and his isolationist stance proved popular enough to earn him a third term in 1940. However, when America was finally drawn into the conflict after the attack on Pearl Harbor, Roosevelt played a leading role in the Allied cause and he was re-elected for a fourth term in 1944.

However, by the final year of the war Roosevelt's health had deteriorated. He had never enjoyed good health since being stricken with polio in 1921 and partially paralysed. In 1945 Roosevelt attended the Allied Leaders' conference at Yalta, a shadow of his former self. He died in office, just three weeks before the German surrender.

The last election to Westminster by proportional representation

Proportional representation for the election of Members of Parliament to Westminster was last used for the university MPs in the 1945 general election. As most of the universities elected more than one member per seat the use of a PR system was quite useful. The form of proportional voting employed was the single transferable vote; when electing more than one member the system allows the voter to choose between candidates, placing them in order of preference.

There was a by-election in 1946 for one member in one of the university seats. However, as there was only one vacancy this election was conducted under the normal 'first-past-the-post' rules. The single transferable vote system is still used in the UK, in Northern Ireland, for all local elections and for elections to the European Parliament.

The last multi-day elections

In the 18th and 19th centuries, elections were spread over several days and, for general elections, not necessarily on the same days for all parts of the country. The last general election to be conducted over more than one day was the second election of 1910, held from 2 to 19 December. There was one exception to this; the Orkney and Shetland constituency had their election conducted over two days up to and including the general election of 1929. As transport and communications were improving steadily, the arrangements were finally changed for all succeeding elections to be conducted all on a single day. The last election to be conducted over a period of more than one day was the by-election for the Scottish Universities seat conducted over several days, from 22 to 27 November 1946.

The last of the Common Wealth Party

One of the more interesting of the smaller political parties of the 20th century was the Common Wealth Party. It was founded by Sir Richard Acland, the (previously Liberal) Member of Parliament for Barnstaple in Devon. He had first formed the 'Forward March' movement which in 1942 joined up with the '1941 Committee' formed by J. B. Priestley. The Common Wealth Party claimed to be a socialist party founded on Christian morality.

It had three by-election successes during the war but during the 1945 general election, out of 23 contests, it secured only one Member of Parliament, E. R. Millington, who held the Chelmsford seat. Millington was their last MP. He left the party and joined the Labour Party in 1946.

The last Independent Labour Party MP

The first Labour Member of Parliament, Keir Hardie, was also a member of the Independent Labour Party (ILP). After taking his seat in 1892, Hardie helped establish the ILP the following year. As a group they were affiliated to the Labour Party until 1932 when they terminated their association in protest at Ramsay MacDonald's leadership of a Tory-dominated 'National' coalition government.

In 1935 the ILP had four MPs, all from Glasgow, and after the 1945 election it was down to three. It fought its last successful election in a 1946 by-election after the death of its sitting member for Glasgow Bridgeton, James Maxton. This time the seat was contested by the Labour Party but the ILP candidate, J. Carmichael, narrowly squeaked home. Within a year, however, he and his two colleagues had joined the Labour Party anyway. The ILP were to have no further parliamentary success. The last candidate to contest a seat for them was A. J. Graham, who stood for Halifax in the 1970 general election but gained only 847 votes and lost his deposit.

The last multi-member constituencies

Some parliamentary constituencies used to have more than one Member of Parliament to represent them. In the 18th and 19th centuries this was a common arrangement but as parliamentary constituency boundaries were reviewed again and again throughout the years this system gradually died out. The last general election where there were multi-member constituencies was held in 1945. The Northern Irish seats of Fermanagh and Tyrone, Down and Antrim and the Scottish seat of Dundee all had two members. Also many of the university seats elected more than one MP. All these arrangements were swept away before the 1950 general election, when all the constituencies were adjusted to provide for one MP only.

The last university Members of Parliament

Until 1948 the British House of Commons had a certain category of member, unique in the democratic world. If you were a graduate of one of the principal universities and had kept your name on their electoral list, you could vote twice, once in the constituency where you resided and once for a Member of Parliament to represent your old university. This extraordinary enclave of academic privilege was abolished by Act of Parliament in 1948 and the last university members were those who left the House of Commons just before the 1950 election.

The idea of university members was introduced by King James I in 1603. Until the early 19th century it was limited to Oxford and Cambridge. As new universities were founded in the 19th century the university representation was actually extended to keep pace. When the common man and woman were fighting for the franchise throughout the 19th and 20th centuries, the number of university Members of Parliament also increased. At the time of their abolition there were 12 in all. Some universities were grouped together, while others such as Oxford and Cambridge had two MPs each.

Some famous Members of Parliament had university seats; among them were prime ministers Pitt, Sir Robert Peel, Palmerston, Gladstone and even, reluctantly, when he lost his other seat, Ramsay MacDonald. When the Labour government finally abolished the system in 1948, Winston Churchill promised to restore it when the Conservatives were re-elected. There were, however, more pressing matters to occupy his time when he regained the premiership in 1951.

The last member to be elected to serve for a university was Walter Elliot, who was elected in a by-election for the Scottish Universities seat after one of their three MPs, Sir John Boyd-Orr, resigned to become a United Nations official. The Rt Hon W. E. Elliot, a Conservative government minister who had lost his seat at the 1945 general election, stepped into the breach. On 27 November 1946 he was elected with a huge majority, all four of the opposing candidates losing their deposits.

The idea of university MPs lived on for yet a few more years. In Northern Ireland, the Stormont Parliament continued to include four MPs representing Queens University Belfast until 1963 – the last election for the university MPs taking place in the Northern Ireland general election on 31 May 1962.

The last unopposed MP

Today most parliamentary candidates and all elected MPs have to work hard during elections. Even in 'safe' seats, party candidates put in a considerable amount of time underlining their own merits and their party's policies, even when their victory is certain. All major parties require nationwide statistical results and now always put up candidates even in seats where chances of success are non-existent.

In more sedate political times an MP's right to a seat or a party's inevitable victory were more readily acknowledged by others. It was common for some candidates to be unopposed and therefore for a registering of votes to be unnecessary. The last time for any seat in the UK to be unopposed in a general election was in 1951. In Northern

Ireland, Londonderry, Armagh and North and South Antrim were all unopposed and the Conservative and Unionist candidates declared elected.

In by-elections, the last time a poll was unopposed was in Armagh on 20 November 1954 when C. W. Armstrong was elected unopposed for the Conservative and Unionist Party. The lack of effective opposition party support in Northern Ireland was underlined in the 1959 general election when the Conservative and Unionist candidate in North Down received 98 per cent of the votes.

The last MP expulsions

1954

Members of Parliament, of the British House of Commons, are members of one of the finest 'Gentlemen's' clubs in the world. Apart from the little matter of getting re-elected from time to time there is very little they have to do to remain there apart, that is, from avoiding bankruptcy, prison sentences and lunacy. The last MP to be forced from membership of the House of Commons was the Conservative member for South Norfolk, Peter Baker. After an honourable war – he was awarded the Military Cross in 1944 – he was elected by the voters in South Norfolk in 1950. His parliamentary career came to an unexpected end in 1954 at the Old Bailey. In November of that year he was found guilty of forgery and sentenced to seven years imprisonment. On 16 December 1954 he was expelled from the House of Commons and his seat declared vacant.

In 1976, John Stonehouse, the Labour member for Walsall (and the last Postmaster General), nearly suffered a similar fate. He had faked his own disappearance from a Miami beach in 1974. He was soon discovered in Australia travelling under false identity and was arrested on Christmas day. Returning to Britain to stand trial on fraud, conspiracy and theft charges, he refused to resign from the House of Commons, although he did eventually resign from the Labour Party. He was found guilty of the charges and sentenced to seven years in jail on 6 August 1976. He saw the writing on the wall and on 27 August he did at last resign from the House of Commons – just before he was expelled.

Former Labour Cabinet Minister John Stonehouse being escorted into a Melbourne court house. He was sentenced to seven days in jail for entering Australia illegally. Extradited to Britain, he became the last MP to serve time in a British prison. He narrowly avoided being expelled from the Commons when he resigned a few days into a seven-year sentence for fraud. (Popperfoto)

The last MP to be adjudged bankrupt and thus forced to leave the House was the Conservative Cornelius Homan, member for Ashton-under-Lyne. His time in the House, he was elected in October 1924, was terminated after four years when he was declared bankrupt in October 1928. His seat was declared vacant and at the following by-election the voters chose the Labour candidate Albert Bellamy to represent them as their MP.

Lunacy is an uncommon reason for leaving the House of Commons. The last recorded instance took place during the First World War when the Liberal MP for Colne Valley, Charles Leach, was removed from the House in 1916 under the Lunacy Act. He died three years later.

The last of the automatic discharge

Membership of the Armed Services used to be automatically terminated if the serving officer or soldier was a candidate in a parliamentary election. Indeed many ex-servicemen who went on to become distinguished Members of Parliament openly confessed that they had been persuaded to stand in the 1945 general election by the prospect of early release from the forces still fighting in the Far East at the time.

This candidature rule was occasionally used, perhaps abused, by servicemen deliberately seeking to be released from national service during the 1950s and 1960s. It became clear that the large number of 'Independent Servicemen' candidates standing in by-elections were servicemen willing to forego the £150 election deposit to gain their freedom from the military, and rules were changed. The last man to use this as an escape route to 'civvy street' was M. Thompson. He was a candidate in the by-election in Middlesbrough West on 6 June 1962. Thompson's 117 votes, a mere 0.3 per cent of the poll, cost him £150 for his lost deposit but ensured his release from HM forces.

The last US president to be assassinated

Historically America has had more of a propensity for political assassination than Britain. For the United Kingdom's one assassination – of Spencer Perceval in 1812 – four US presidents have met a violent end. Abraham Lincoln, James Garfield and William McKinley were all murdered whilst in office. The fourth and last presidential assassination was that of John F. Kennedy in 1963.

The young charismatic president had encouraged a fresh and optimistic outlook across America on becoming president in 1961. He declared in his inaugural address a campaign 'against the common enemies of man: tyranny, poverty, disease and war itself'. His first foray into foreign affairs – the CIA-sponsored Cuban Bay of Pigs invasion in April 1961 – was a fiasco, but he won plaudits for his handling of the Cuban Missile Crisis a year later. His attempts to introduce sweeping civil rights measures at home, however, were largely thwarted by the conservatism of Congress. Despite these setbacks he retained an immense popularity at home and abroad.

In 1963 Kennedy expected to win the following year's presidential election with a large enough mandate to push through major reforming legislation. But on Friday 22 November 1963 these dreams were cut short. On a motorcade visit to Dallas, Texas, President Kennedy was shot in the neck and head by assassin Lee Harvey Oswald. He was dead upon arrival at hospital. Oswald – who was himself assassinated two days later – insisted he had worked alone. Later that fateful day vice-president Lyndon Johnson was sworn in as president.

Various conspiracy theories, involving the CIA, the KGB, the Mafia and many others, have come to light over the years, but the reason why America lost one of its most popular leaders will probably never be known. Although Johnson introduced most of the reforms Kennedy had planned many Americans still mourn the loss of a much-loved president.

The last ministries

Ministry: Admiralty.
Position: First Lord of the Admiralty. Position last held by Earl Jellicoe. Post abolished 1 April 1964.

Ministry: Economic Affairs.
Position: Secretary of State for Economic Affairs. Position last held by Peter Shore. Post abolished 8 October 1969.

Ministry: Foreign Office.
Position: Secretary of State for Foreign Affairs. Position last held by Michael Stewart. Post abolished 17 October 1968.
Michael Stewart continued in the new post of Secretary of State for Foreign and Commonwealth Affairs until the end of the Labour government in 1970.

Ministry: Air Ministry.
Position: Secretary of State for Air. Position last held by H. Fraser. Post abolished 1 April 1964.

Ministry: Colonial Office.
Position: Secretary of State for the Colonies. Position last held by F. Lee (from 6 April 1966). The post came under Department of Commonwealth Affairs 1 August 1966. Post abolished 6 Jan 1967.

Ministry: War Office.
Position: Secretary of State for War. Position last held by J. Ramsden. Post abolished 1 April 1964.

Ministry: MOD.
Position: Secretaries of State for Air Force, Army and Navy. Position last held by Lord Shackleton, G. Reynolds, J. Mallalieu. Posts abolished 6 Jan 1967.

Ministry: Commonwealth Affairs.
Position: Secretary of State for Commonwealth Relations. Position last held by A. Bottomley. Post renamed Secretary of State for Commonwealth Affairs 1 Aug 1966. Position last held by G. Thompson. Merged with Foreign Office and post abolished 17 Oct 1968.

Ministry: India and Burma.
Position: Secretary of State for India and Burma. Position last held by Earl of Listowel. Post abolished 14 Aug 1947 (India) and 4 Jan 1948 (Burma).

Ministry: Irish Office (abolished 1924).
Position: Lord Lieutenant of Ireland. Position last held by Viscount FitzAlan, until 19 October 1922. Post abolished 6 Dec 1922.

Ministry: Ireland.
Position: Chief Secretary for Ireland. Position last held by Sir H. Greenwood, until 19 October 1922. Post abolished 6 Dec 1922.

Position: Postmaster General. Position last held by John Stonehouse. Post Office became Public Corporation 1 Oct 1969. The position of Minister of Post and Telecommunications was created and first held by John Stonehouse and last held by Tony Benn (7 Mar 1974). Post and Office abolished 29 Mar 1974.

The last of the old Service departments

The last moments of Britain's old service departments, the Admiralty, the War Office and the Air Ministry, came in 1964 after a complete re-organization. On 1 April 1964 out went the old names as the departments were merged into the single Ministry of Defence. The upheaval affected all the government ministers and hundreds of civil servants concerned with the Royal Navy, Army and Royal Air Force.

The last of the National Liberals

During the First World War, the Liberal Party split after Lloyd George ousted Asquith from the premiership of the coalition government. The quarrel was patched up after the 1922 election. Before the 1931 election the Party split again, 23 MPs forming the Liberal National Group. Apart from the 1931 election, members of the group were never opposed by the Conservatives. The members of the group moved further and further from the Liberal Party and closer to direct support of the Conservatives. After the 1935 election they were, in effect, counted as Conservatives. In 1948, with their constituency associations almost universally merged with the Conservatives they renamed themselves the National Liberals.

By the time of the 1966 general election the difference between the Conservatives and the National Liberals was merely an historical technicality. That year saw the last two National Liberal candidates elected to parliament: Sir David Renton in Huntingdonshire and John Nott in St Ives, Cornwall. They had labelled themselves 'Conservative and National Liberal'. Two other MPs from the group had been selected by joint associations. Within a year of their election they relinquished their separate organization in the House of Commons and joined the Conservatives for good. The National Liberal Council disbanded in 1968.

The last Northern Ireland government

The Government of Ireland Act of 1920 intended to set up two parliaments, one in Southern Ireland and one in Northern Ireland. In addition, a Council of Ireland was planned to deal with matters of mutual concern, such as an eventual united Ireland. In the event Southern Ireland chose full independence so only Northern Ireland had the parliament as envisaged. The first parliament was opened by King George V on 7 July 1921. In 1932 the Prince of Wales opened the new parliament buildings at Stormont.

In addition to sending MPs to Westminster like any other region of the United Kingdom, Northern Ireland had its own local parliament. It was modelled closely on the Westminster system with 52 MPs in the Commons but with an upper house, the senate, consisting of members elected by the Commons. The government consisted of the prime minister, a small Cabinet and a few other junior ministers. They generally had responsibility for most domestic affairs including law and order.

In 1971 with the increase in violence throughout the province, the British government transferred all security and law and order powers to the Westminster Parliament. This met with outright opposition from the Unionist Northern Ireland government. On 24 March 1972 the British Conservative government suspended the Northern Ireland Parliament. The plans of Home Secretary William Whitelaw for an Advisory Commission failed to satisfy the Northern Ireland Unionists. Brian Faulkner, the last Northern Ireland prime minister, refused to co-operate and resigned with all his Unionist colleagues. The post of prime minister was formally suspended on 30 March 1972.

The position of Governor of Northern Ireland was abolished the following year, on 19 July 1973. Lord Grey of Naunton, a New Zealander from the professional Colonial service, was the last holder of the office. The last general election for Northern Ireland's Stormont government was held on 24 February 1968. The Unionists, led at that time by Prime Minister Captain Terence O'Neill, won as usual (Northern Ireland's Parliament was always Unionist dominated), with 39 of the 54 seats, although badly split by internal divisions.

The last by-elections to take place for Stormont were for the two seats of Bannside and South Antrim on 16 April 1970. They resulted in a shattering defeat for the government, both seats going to the new Protestant Unionist Party candidates, the Reverend Ian Paisley and the Reverend William Beattie.

The last voluntary resignation of a prime minister

1976

Prime ministers in Britain have been notoriously difficult to remove from office. The allure of the ultimate political post has been difficult for all but a few to relinquish voluntarily. Most prime ministers have to be prised out of office by some means or other, usually using the excuse of illness or old age. Of course any good old-fashioned democratic political defeat at the national ballot box will do the trick, sending them hurtling into opposition.

The last prime minister to leave office at a time of his own choosing was Harold Wilson. He became Labour Party leader in 1963, prime minister in 1964 until defeated at the 1970 general election. He returned to 10 Downing Street in 1974 when Labour won the general election in February 1974. He stayed in office until 1976 when a surprise announcement was issued by the Cabinet expressing their 'deep regret' at the prime minister's decision to step down.

For the public at large certainly it was a surprise, a shock even, but for those in the know, Wilson's insiders, it was the announcement they had been expecting for some time. Despite mysterious mutterings of the involvement of the security services, blackmail and other alleged scandals, Wilson's resignation was a genuinely voluntary one. He had planned for it over many years, indeed would have retired even earlier, in office, had the Labour Party won the 1970 general election. His place at the head of the Labour

British Prime Minister Harold Wilson speaking at his last Party conference in Blackpool as Labour leader in September 1975. He had at that time already decided to retire and announced his resignation the following April. He was the last British prime minister to leave office of his own accord. (Hulton)

Party, and in the country's top job at Downing Street, was taken by James Callaghan after a leadership election campaign inside the Labour ranks. Wilson gave up the seals of office on 5 April 1976.

◈ 1981 ◈ *The last independent Members of Parliament*

The political party organizations, the 'party machines', are so all-powerful today that it is difficult for any truly independent candidate to have any hope of besting party candidates. Splits and quarrels within parties have, however, occasionally produced upsets for party managers.

In 1973 Dick Taverne, Labour MP for Lincoln, resigned after fundamental disagreements over policy and re-fought his seat as a 'Democratic Labour' candidate. In the by-election of 1 March 1973 he beat his 'official' Labour opponent. Later that year, with others, he formed a new party grouping, the 'Council for Social Democracy'. At the next general election in February 1974 he retained his seat although in the October 1974 general election Miss Margaret Jackson finally won the seat back for Labour. At the same time, Eddie Milne, another Labour MP, was also having troubles with the Party at Blyth. He fought and won his seat as an 'independent' Labour candidate, against the official Labour candidate, but like Taverne, lost to the official Labour candidate in October of that year.

The last independent of all was first elected during the October 1974 general election. Frank Maguire, an active republican and political internee of the 1950s, was elected as an independent MP for Fermanagh and South Tyrone. His special interest was the welfare of Irish prisoners in English jails. He seldom attended the Westminster Parliament although when there, he did generally vote with the Labour Party, whether in government or in opposition.

Frank Maguire died on 5 March 1981 without ever making a speech in Parliament. His death led to the by-election at which the republican H Block hunger striker, Bobby Sands, won the seat. After his death, Owen Carron took it. Although they were both nominally protest candidates, in retrospect they are now regarded as part of Sinn Fein, or the republican movement of Northern Ireland.

The last £150 deposit

1983

At the end of the First World War a deposit system was devised to deter the more frivolous candidates from standing for Parliament. Before a nomination could be accepted, a deposit of £150 had to be lodged with the returning officer. Any candidate who did not achieve a total 12.5 per cent of the votes cast was required to forfeit the deposit. Saving one's deposit was often a matter of pride among the minor party candidates.

The amount of £150 as a deposit was fixed in 1918. By the 1980s the value of £150 was relatively small. Publicity-seeking independent candidates – especially at by-elections – considered the sum of £150 to be well spent for the coverage one could receive from the media during the campaign. In addition all candidates are entitled to one free delivery, by the Royal Mail, of publicity pamphlets to all electors worth many thousands of pounds. Even without these benefits many independents were happily forking out the money just to see their names in the record books.

The government decided to act. The sum of £1,000 was considered to be more appropriate after nearly a century of inflation. In the end they decided to compromise and settled on a requirement of a £500 deposit and with the proportion of the votes required to avoid forfeiture reduced to 5 per cent of the vote. The last time candidates in a general election had to deposit £150 and secure 12.5 per cent of the vote to retain this money was on 9 June 1983.

The last spring budget

1993

On 16 March 1993, the British Chancellor of the Exchequer, Norman Lamont, presented the last spring budget. The budget is essentially a Finance Bill, stating how money is to be raised. The tradition for spring budgets arose in the 19th century. It was the traditional set piece finance debate of the year for the House of Commons.

In more recent years, the spending review, announced in the latter half of the year, stating where and how the money is to be spent, had gained in importance. The decision to combine the two occasions and present the full budget in the autumn was made by Lamont in 1992. The next budget, combining spending and taxation, was presented by Mr Lamont's successor, Kenneth Clark, less than nine months later on 30 November 1993.

8 PUBLIC LIFE

The last High Constable

The position of High Constable of England was one of the highest offices of state from Norman times through to the Tudor period. One of the High Constable's duties was to control, with the assistance of his deputy, the Earl Marshal, the heraldic and public ceremonial duties of the court. The arrangement of troops and the conduct of war and of tournaments all fell within his sphere of influence. The High Constable was a powerful position and many of the holders of the office were of Royal blood. Before he seized the throne Richard III was the High Constable.

The last holder of the office was Edward Stafford, the Duke of Buckingham. He was executed in 1521 on the orders of Henry VIII. The charge was treason but in reality the High Constable's real crime was for being a Plantagenet with a claim to the throne when Henry was without his own male heir. The vacancy was never filled and the duties of the High Constable were taken over by the Earl Marshal. The holder of the post of Earl Marshal still takes charge of the organization of the great ceremonies of state today.

The last Trial by Battle

William the Conqueror introduced the Trial by Battle as part of the feudal system of justice. Two nobles, or their appointed champions, would fight it out, to the death if necessary, to settle a dispute. To the victor went the argument. It was generally supposed that God would intervene on the side of right and ensure both victory and justice at one stroke. Trial by Battle fell into disuse until the early part of the 19th century. In 1817 the law was used by Abraham Thornton of Warwickshire to defend himself from accusations of murder. He had been tried and found not guilty of murdering Mary Ashford. Her brother, William Ashford, was so incensed by what he saw as a gross miscarriage of justice that he used an ancient law to issue a private writ of appeal. On the strength of this appeal Thornton was imprisoned in Warwick jail to await another trial.

Thornton too, however, was not above using ancient laws and after consultation with a lawyer he was advised to petition for a Trial by Battle. In November 1817 he appeared before the Lord Chief Justice at the Court of the King's Bench in Westminster Hall, London and successfully proved that he had the right to 'trial by battel' against his accuser.

It was clear that in any physical contest Thornton would have the better of it. William Ashford refused to accept the challenge and, to the amazement of the legal profession, at the time, Thornton walked free. There had been no actual battle but, obviously, the law was still valid. As a result of this extraordinary case, Trial by Battle was hastily examined and removed from the statute books by an Act of Parliament in 1819.

The last duel
1852

It is difficult to say precisely when affairs of honour, or duels, actually became illegal in Britain. The last duel in England, however, where the antagonists faced each other at dawn with pistols, was at Egham in Surrey in 1852. The Frenchman Monsieur Cournet was mortally wounded by his compatriot Monsieur Barthélemy while defending his honour.

By the 15th century duelling had become a cult. An argumentative gentleman, entitled to wear a sword, often felt obliged to use it on receipt of an insult, however slight or unintended. An Act of Parliament under Oliver Cromwell in 1654 forbade duelling; and Charles II, not many years later, also had to issue a proclamation against the practice. By the 18th century society was beginning to stir against the futility of young men killing each other over pretended slights. Beau Nash, the famous society host at Bath, forbade not only tobacco in his rooms but swords as well. This did much to change society's view of what was acceptable behaviour.

Pistols at dawn on the continent in the 1880s. Formal duels, 'affairs of honour', continued abroad for many years after the practice was finally eradicated in Britain. (ME)

The wearing of swords in public died with the 18th century but affairs of honour continued. Now it was with pistols, usually specially made for the purpose in matched pairs. Strict rules applied to the duels: seconds, surgeons and independent observers all played a part on the deserted fields and commons to see the ritual through. If a fatality occurred the surviving duellist could be charged with manslaughter, but would usually manage to escape and live quietly for a few months until the fuss had died down. By this time the idea of killing the opponent was often the least of the intentions. 'Honour satisfied' was the aim and the protagonists could safeguard their reputations by firing into the ground or deliberately missing their targets, as long as they did not flinch in the face of the flaring pistols.

Habits died hard, however. 'Satisfaction' was regularly granted to participants in quarrels among army officers. Even dukes fought duels, even well-known ones. Possibly one of the most famous quarrels was between the Duke of Wellington, when prime minister, and Lord Winchilsea in 1829. The affair ended in Battersea Fields when neither of the duellists aimed at each other when discharging their pistols. By the 1840s public opinion had thoroughly turned and the duel was no longer acceptable. The law against it began to be applied with more and more vigour, many duellists ending in prison for manslaughter.

One of the last publicly acknowledged duels in England was fought in July 1843 – predictably between two army officers. Lieutenant Alexander Munroe of the Horse Guards was killed by Colonel Fawcett of the 55th Regiment. The result of this killing was public outcry at such behaviour and the formation of an Anti-duelling Association. Fawcett fled the country but eventually returned to face trial and was convicted of manslaughter. Pressure was brought to bear on the authorities. In the Army an article of war, which had actually obliged officers to 'redeem their honour' in a duel, was repealed in 1844.

A few more duels did take place but because they were conducted in great secrecy gave little cause for 'satisfaction'. At the last recorded death by duelling at Egham in 1852, Monsieur Cournet brought this extraordinary ritual to an end in the British Isles. Duels of course continued abroad. Many an English gentleman, in fact and in fiction, used the ferry to Boulogne to meet his opponent and look at him along the barrel of his pistol. In Britain, however, the affairs of honour were over.

 ## The last duke

In the hierarchy of the aristocracy no-one, apart from royalty, comes higher than a duke. In these days of equality the creation of new peerages in Britain is, with a few notable exceptions, limited to life peers. These are barons, the lowest of the five ranks of 'lord', created only for their lifetime and unable to transfer the honour to their descendants when they die. Not so the hereditary peerages; and certainly not the dukes. Outside the relatively common creations for royal princes, the last creation of a duke was in 1889.

In the creation of dukedoms, however, nothing helps more than a proximity to the royal family. The last creation was no exception. When Her Royal Highness the Princess Louise, 22-year-old daughter of the Prince of Wales and granddaughter of

Queen Victoria, married the 40-year-old Alexander Duff, Marquess of Macduff, from County Banff, Ireland in 1889, a suitable wedding present was not slow in arriving. Lord Macduff was a close friend of the Prince of Wales, and Queen Victoria was persuaded to elevate him to the dukedom.

Two days later, on 29 July 1889, the Marquess became the Duke of Fife and Britain's last dynasty of dukes was created. This creation was, it must be admitted, only an Irish one, so on 24 April 1900 the Duke of Fife was promoted to a Duke of the United Kingdom. His descendant, the current Duke of Fife, remains last in the list of seniority of Dukes of the United Kingdom.

The interesting side to this dukedom did not end there. It descended to the present Duke through the female line. The first Duke had no sons but in honour of his wife (created Princess Royal in 1905) it was decreed that on his death his daughters could succeed. This they duly did. His eldest, Princess Alexandra, became Duchess of Fife in her own right. On her death (to complicate matters even further) her son, already Duke of Connaught from his grandfather (Arthur, Duke of Connaught, Queen Victoria's son), did not become Duke of Fife. That honour passed to her nephew, her younger sister's son. He became known as the third Duke of Fife, his aunt the Duchess being the second Duke.

On his resignation as prime minister in 1955, Sir Winston Churchill was offered a dukedom, probably the very last to have been offered. The 'Duke of London' was the suggested title. He refused as it would have been a 'blight on the prospects' of the political careers of his son Randolph and his grandson Winston. They would have been unable to sit in the House of Commons when they, in turn, inherited the title.

The last Blue Ribboned Victoria Cross ◇ 1918 ◇

When it was first instituted in 1856 the Victoria Cross was awarded with different coloured ribbons, depending on whether the recipient was in the Royal Navy or in the Army. The Army awards were attached to the familiar and now universal maroon ribbons; the Naval Victoria Crosses were supplied with blue ribbons.

On 1 April 1918 the Royal Flying Corps, technically part of the Army, was re-formed to become the Royal Air Force. Without an obvious new colour for the ribbons of RAF Victoria Crosses, King George V suggested that all recipients from whatever branch of the armed services be given maroon ribbons on their VCs. From November the blue ribbon was consigned to history.

The last Royal Naval Victoria Cross to be awarded on a blue ribbon was that for Chief Petty Officer George Prowse, who served in the Royal Naval Division, alongside the Army on the Western Front. Prowse was a coal miner before he joined the Navy in 1915 at the age of 30. He quickly rose to the rank of Chief Petty Officer and, in the Drake Battalion, displayed courageous leadership over many difficult months, fighting in the trenches.

Towards the end of 1918, the 63rd Division, of which Drake Battalion was part, was involved in one of the final pushes of the war, towards the Hindenburg line. In early September Prowse led several attacks against enemy machine-gun positions, either killing or capturing the enemy soldiers. Most of the men he led were killed around him.

In one ferocious assault he cleared two enemy machine-gun nests which were holding up the battalion advance and emerged the only survivor.

He was recommended for the Victoria Cross but was killed at Cambrai on 27 September before the award was confirmed. His VC was gazetted, officially notified, on 30 October 1918. His widow Sarah received the medal, the last VC ever with a blue ribbon, from the hands of King George at Buckingham Palace in July the following year. In 1920 eligibility for the Victoria Cross was extended to all the armed services, the merchant marine and even civilians. At the same time the change to a universal ribbon colour for all recipients was belatedly recognized in the records.

1936   The last Marquessate

The Marquessate is a special honour reserved for someone providing a very special service for the country. The last time it was thought necessary to promote someone to this high rank was in 1936 when the Earl of Willingdon retired from his post as Viceroy of India. The Earl of Willingdon, who had begun his public life as Mr Freeman Freeman-Thomas, had been elected to parliament in 1900 when he was returned as the Liberal member for Hastings. He was the MP for Bodmin from 1906 until his retirement from the House in 1910. On retirement he took his first step on the peerage ladder when he was created the first Baron Willingdon of Ratton.

After the war, in 1924, he went up one rung to become Viscount Ratendone of Willingdon to be followed by the next step, the first Earl of Willingdon, in 1931. By this time he was well advanced in his second career as a top diplomat having been Governor of Bombay, Governor of Madras and Governor-General of Canada. He ended his career as Viceroy of India and came home to very near the top rung when he became the first Marquess of Willingdon on 26 May 1936, the last ever Marquess to be created.

1954   The last Court of Chivalry

The Court of Chivalry, presided over by the Earl Marshal, originated in the 14th century. It was tasked with dealing with many of the military and ceremonial matters which were outside the normal common law of England. Over the years it dealt with many disputes on the precedence within the heraldic fraternity and on the rights to bear and display coats-of-arms.

The last sitting of the Court of Chivalry was in 1954. The Corporation of the City of Manchester was in dispute with a cinema company, Manchester Palace of Varieties, which was displaying the city's coat-of-arms without authority. The Court was petitioned to hear the city's complaint. It convened, under the Lord Chief Justice of the day, Lord Goddard, with the Earl Marshal, the Duke of Norfolk, in attendance. The Court found in favour of the Corporation. Despite the recommendation from Lord Goddard that the Court should be set up on a more regular and formal basis, it has not been in session since 22 December 1954.

The last débutante

The tradition of arranging for the presentation of one's daughter to the reigning king or queen ended in 1958. Part of 'coming out' for every young lady in the upper classes, the débutantes or 'debs', was to be presented at court: formally introduced to the sovereign by a suitable chaperon. The custom was formally abolished in 1958, the practice being declared too élitist for a modern royalty. In London, the last debs were presented at Buckingham Palace in March, and later that year at Holyroodhouse in Edinburgh Miss Fiona Macrae was the last débutante to formally curtsey to the Queen on 3 July 1958.

Young débutante Susan Hampshire, aged 17, photographed outside Buckingham Palace on her way to be presented 'at court' in 1955. She went on to become a leading lady in films and on television. Formal presentations of débutantes were abolished three years later. (Hulton)

The last barony

The last hereditary baron to be created was Baron Margadale, formerly John Granville Morrison, Member of Parliament for Salisbury from 1942 to 1964. He was created the first Baron Margadale on 1 January 1965. For many years after 1965 it was thought that his creation would be the very last hereditary peerage. And so it was until in 1983 prime minister Margaret Thatcher, amidst her triumph of a second general election win, opened up the hereditary peerage box again.

1968   *The last of the royal 'blue pencil'*

The Lord Chamberlain is the head of the Lord Chamberlain's Office, one of the main departments of the royal household. The Lord Chamberlain's Office has a variety of duties including looking after the Queen's swans and arranging the procedures to be followed at Royal weddings. One of the Lord Chamberlain's duties that has now disappeared was to ensure that all theatre productions were suitable for public viewing.

The duty had its origins in the court of Henry VII. The Lord Chamberlain was given the task of making sure that the Court amusements gave no offence to the King. Elizabeth I set up more formal procedures to protect the royal person from public abuse. Over the years this duty, retained within the Royal household, in some measure reflected the ancient convention that all actors were servants of the crown. An Act of Parliament of 1843 reinforced the Lord Chamberlain's role in a formal way.

All publicly performed plays in Britain had to first gain approval, in the form of a licence, from the Lord Chamberlain's Office. The Lord Chamberlain did not actually read many of the plays himself, instead the Office employed a few selected official 'examiners' who read the scripts and made the initial recommendation. This was passed on to the Assistant Comptroller who checked and usually endorsed the proposal and passed it to the Lord Chamberlain who issued the licence. Any plays in which cuts or alterations were recommended before a licence could be issued would be read by the Lord Chamberlain himself, as would any that were to have their licence refused outright. Traditionally the Lord Chamberlain used a 'blue pencil' when making alterations and cuts.

The most obvious reasons for refusing a play a licence were the inclusion of scenes of general depravity, obscenity, obvious sex, nudity and so on. In addition to these, any plays representing God or Jesus Christ were excluded until 1966 – offstage voices or flickering lights were usually all that were allowed. Portrayals of living or recently living members of the Royal Family were also excluded. Queen Victoria could not legally be portrayed on stage until 1937. Even commoners (usually politicians or other public figures) had protection as a licence could be refused if they were represented in an 'invidious' manner.

Clearly such censorship (Lord Cobbold preferred the more positive description of his duties as a 'Licensor' of plays) had become outdated by the 1960s. Cinema, television, radio and, of course, books merely had to comply with the fully accepted laws of libel and defamation. It was high time the world of drama followed suit. The last Lord Chamberlain to have this responsibility was Lord Cobbold who served in the office of Lord Chamberlain from 1963 to 1971. He had himself argued for many years that it was inappropriate for the Queen to be involved in any way in such matters.

After many years of discussion throughout the 1950s and 1960s a Bill was passed in Parliament which abolished the Lord Chamberlain's theatrical duties. It did away with the Lord Chamberlain's 'blue pencil' of censorship on the manuscripts of the nation's plays. His responsibilities for licensing theatres was also removed at the same time and transferred to the local government authorities. The Bill was given its third reading in Parliament on 19 July and became law on 26 July 1968. Normally there is a three months' wait for a Bill to become law but Lord Cobbold, desperate to draw a curtain down on this ambiguous period, asked for one month only. The last play to receive an official licence was *As Long as I Live* by J. C. Gray, which received its recommendation for licence on 17 September 1968.

The last play to be refused a licence by the Lord Chamberlain's Office had been, in the same year, *A Fig for Eloquence* by Alec Coppel. Charles Heriot, the Senior Examiner in the Lord Chamberlain's Office, described it as 'one long snigger at the male genitalia'. The Assistant Comptroller, however, recommended approval of a licence so long as the naked male statue, central to the play, was turned away from the audience. The Lord Chamberlain himself became involved and on taking further advice endorsed the original recommendation for refusal. It was a fittingly preposterous piece of theatre that signalled the end of British public censorship.

The 'Tribal Love Rock Musical' *Hair* had been submitted to the office in May 1968. Alterations to avoid the full frontal nude scenes were suggested but the producer declined. A second milder version was submitted a month later and this too was refused. A third even milder version was submitted in July. Production problems would probably have delayed the opening anyway but fortuitously the Lord Chamberlain's censorship role disappeared officially on 26 September and *Hair* opened at the Shaftesbury Theatre in London's West End on 27 September. Its scenes of nudity, its language and particularly its improvisation were a breath of fresh air in popular British theatre. It was, in the words of the show's most famous song, truly 'the dawning of a new age' of freedom.

The last George Cross

◁ **1979** ▷

The George Cross was instituted in 1940 to be awarded for similar acts of bravery as for the Victoria Cross, but not 'in the face of the enemy'. The last award, to date, of the George Cross was to Captain Robert Nairac of the Grenadier Guards. It was awarded posthumously after he was murdered by the IRA in Eire in May 1977. He was on undercover duty in South Armagh, Northern Ireland and was captured by Republican terrorists and abducted across the border to the south. Despite being brutally beaten and ruthlessly interrogated, Captain Nairac refused to reveal any details of the security forces' covert operations in the Province.

Captain Nairac's body was never recovered but his courage under torture was testified to by those responsible for his death. They were eventually caught and convicted. During their trial they commended him for his bravery, one of the few occasions when such testimony was largely instrumental in the granting of an award which was gazetted on 13 February 1979

The last Victoria Cross

◁ **1982** ▷

The Victoria Cross, probably the most famous of all the bravery medals, was instituted in 1856 at the personal request of Queen Victoria. It was to be awarded for conspicuous bravery in the presence of the enemy. The last award of the VC was for action in the Falklands campaign in 1982. Sergeant Ian McKay of the 3rd Battalion, the Parachute Regiment, was given a posthumous award after showing extraordinary bravery and leadership in the Battle for Mount Longdon on 11 June in the closing days of the campaign.

Two companies from the battalion were assigned to take the Argentine positions on the summit overlooking Port Stanley in a night attack. In the confusion of battle the advance faltered. Sergeant McKay, who had taken command of No. 4 platoon after his platoon commander had been injured, realized that quick action was required to avoid being pinned down by enemy fire. With a group of three other men he led a furious charge at an enemy machine-gun position. One of his men was killed, the other two injured, but he managed to reach the enemy and hurl a grenade into the bunker. He died under a hail of enemy bullets at the moment of his success.

His platoon gained control of the position and the rest of the company soon followed to the summit of the mountain. McKay's action was obviously crucial in the success of the operation and on 14 June 1982, three days after his act of heroism, the Argentine forces surrendered to the British. Sergeant McKay's body was sent back to England and buried with full military honours at Aldershot on 26 October 1982. His widow received the Victoria Cross from the Queen at a special ceremony at Buckingham Palace on 9 November 1982, the last such investiture, to date.

◇ 1984 ◇ *The last hereditary lords*

The elevation of courtiers and politicians to the peerage was long the privilege of sovereigns down the centuries. The royal mistresses of the Stuart kings were often created duchesses as a sign of more lasting appreciation than the temporary occupation of the royal bed. A politician was more likely to be loyal to his king as a belted earl than as a commoner. Hereditary honours were coveted as a way of passing on more than just land and money to your heirs. A title, or 'handle', would ensure the respect due to the family name.

Direct selection by the sovereign of those to be rewarded with peerages and other honours faded throughout the years of the 19th century. The royal fingers were eventually prised from the levers of patronage in Queen Victoria's reign although the creation of a new order, the Royal Victorian Order, has allowed royalty to retain some personal influence on the fringes of the honours system. A small number of awards in the Victorian Order, for personal service to the monarch, are still given each year.

There are five grades of Lords in the British system and all holders are entitled to be addressed as 'Lord'. In the rarefied upper echelon is the highest rank, the duke, next comes the marquess. The third in rank is the earl, followed by the viscount. Last of all is the humble baron. The heir to a title is usually given the courtesy title of the next rank down, for example, a duke's son and heir would be a marquess but an heir to a baron would be simply referred to as an 'honourable'. The courtesy ranks give no privileges and certainly no rights to sit in the House of Lords, although there are exceptions.

'Life' peerages, awards for the duration of the life of the recipient only and not handed down to succeeding generations, have all been in the lowest of the five ranks: the baron for men or, for women, baroness. (The baronetcy, the hereditary knighthood, is in a different class and confers no seat in the House of Lords.)

The real power in the British Honours System now lies firmly with the politicians, in particular with the prime minister of the day. In line with the more egalitarian approach of socialism, the Labour Government that came to power in 1964 announced that non-hereditary 'life' peerages, introduced in 1958, would be enough for their purposes, and it would refrain from creating any more anachronistic hereditary peerages. At the time outright abolition was never a consideration and the possibility of new hereditary awards never tempted another prime minister until Margaret Thatcher came on the scene.

Prime Minister Margaret Thatcher briefly revived the creation of new hereditary peerages after the general election of 1983. She created only three and the last of these was Harold Macmillan, the ex-Conservative prime minister, who was elevated to the peerage as an earl in 1984, the last creation, to date, of any hereditary peerage of any rank.

Harold Macmillan was prime minister in the Conservative government, from June 1957, when he took the reigns of power after the Suez Crisis, until October 1963, when he resigned due to ill health. Born in 1894, he served as a Guards officer in the trenches during the First World War, before entering the House of Commons in 1924. His premiership was his final achievement in a long and significant political career. Macmillan declined the offer of an earldom in 1964 after he had retired from office but twenty years later he did finally accede to the privilege and was created first Earl of Stockton, the name chosen in honour of his parliamentary constituency. Given the hereditary title under the premiership of Margaret Thatcher, he was, ironically one of her fiercest critics. A speech that the 90-year-old peer made in the House of Lords contained some especially stinging rebukes to his successor. Lord Stockton died on 29 December 1986. His son had died two years earlier so his grandson succeeded to the title.

The last hereditary knight

◁ 1990 ▷

In the British system of hereditary titles, the baronet is the lowest in the order of seniority, ranking below a baron. He is not a peer and has no hereditary seat in the House of Lords, but then he has no duties either. His only privilege is that of styling himself 'Sir', calling his wife 'Lady' and passing on his title to his eldest son. The order was created in 1611 by James I as a money-earner, as newly created baronets were expected to make a substantial contribution to the royal coffers to pay for the new protestant settlements in Ulster. The first to be given his hereditary knighthood was one of Queen Elizabeth's retainers, Nicholas Bacon, Francis Bacon's father.

Tradition used to be that the son of a knight could claim the right to be formally knighted, or dubbed, by the sovereign when coming of age or when succeeding to the title. Although under George IV the practice was discontinued, it was briefly revived in Queen Victoria's reign and last performed in 1874.

Before Margaret Thatcher became prime minister, the last creation of a baronetcy, an hereditary knighthood, was on 31 December 1964, when Graeme Finlay became Sir Graeme Finlay, Baronet. However, after 30 barren years, the hereditary knighthood reappeared in Sir Denis. The last creation of a baronetcy took place in 1990 when the husband of Margaret Thatcher was created Sir Denis Thatcher, a just reward, some

Denis Thatcher listening carefully to one of his wife's campaign speeches during the 1987 general election. In 1990 Mrs Thatcher rewarded him with a baronetcy for his loyalty and devotion; he was the last person to receive an hereditary knighthood. (Popperfoto)

would say, for over a decade of dutiful silence. Margaret Thatcher was then officially 'Lady' Thatcher but she let it be known that she wished to be addressed, for the time being at least, as plain 'Mrs'. Should his son survive him, Sir Denis knows that his son will one day be Sir Mark.

The last 'working peer'

The regular awards by the government of life peerages on the basis of 'other than for merit' ceased in 1993. Shirley Williams, the veteran politician of Labour, SDP and Liberal Democrat persuasion, was the last political peer to be created. These so-called 'working peers' were nominated by their political party to carry out their party's work in the House of Lords. Prime Minister John Major declared, in his usual obfuscated language, that elevation to the peerage will henceforth be on 'merit' only.

The last British Empire Medals

The British Empire Medal, or BEM, was the most junior of the five classes of the Order of the British Empire. It was last awarded in the New Year Honours list on 1 January 1993. In March of that year Prime Minister John Major announced measures designed to cut out some of the class distinction in the awards system. The BEM was to be abolished and those deserving people that would have been given the award were now to receive the next class in the Order, the MBE, or Member of the Order.

ROYALTY 9

The last Viking king *954*

The last independent Viking king in Britain was Erik Blood-axe, King of York. Erik Haraldsson inherited the kingdom of Norway in 942 from his father who abdicated at the age of 80. After a series of fierce family quarrels, in which several of his brothers were killed, he was finally deposed in 947 by his youngest brother Haakon. He fled Norway and crossed the North Sea to Scotland.

As his nickname 'Blood-axe' implies, he was a brutal, savage man not averse to a fight. After a series of bloody adventures in Scotland he took over the Northumbrian kingdom of York in 952 with the support of some of the Norse warlords already resident there. He was finally killed at the Battle of Stainmore on the Yorkshire moors in 954, fighting against an army from Wessex. His demise led to the recognition by Northumbria that the Kings of Wessex were to be the dominant Royal House in Britain.

The last coronation not at Westminster Abbey *1042*

The last coronation of an English King not to take place in Westminster Abbey was that of Edward the Confessor in 1042. He was crowned at Winchester. A few years later he established an Abbey on a remote marshy island in the Thames to the west of London; it became known as West Minster and it has been the site of every English coronation since.

The last Anglo-Saxon claimant to the throne *1100*

On the death of King Harold at the Battle of Hastings in 1066, Edgar Atheling, the grandson of Edmund Ironside and great grandson of Ethelred the Unready, was chosen as king by the Witan, the English parliament. He was never crowned and in 1067 he led a delegation of submission to William the Conqueror, forgoing all rights to the English throne. With some of his family he then fled to Scotland where his sister, Margaret, married Malcolm III of Scotland. In 1074 Edgar Atheling made his peace with William. In 1100 the Anglo-Saxon dynasty was joined to that of the Norman kings of England when Malcolm and Margaret's daughter Edith, taking the Norman name of Matilda, became Queen of England by marrying Henry I.

The last native prince of Wales

Wales was ruled by a series of warrior princes until 1282, when Llywelyn ap Gruffydd, the last native prince of Wales, was killed by the English. Five years before his death, Llywelyn had been forced to concede the overlordship of the English King Edward I. However, an uprising led by Llywelyn's brother Dafydd tempted him to make another bid to win control of Wales. Edward by this time was determined to conquer the whole of Wales. Llywelyn died in battle at Builth in mid-Wales and his brother was captured the following year. Dafydd was condemned for treason and cruelly executed by the new method of hanging, drawing and quartering.

In 1301, Edward gave his new-born son, later Edward II, the vacant title of Prince of Wales. Not only did this set the precedent for most male heirs to the English throne, it was also the first time the official title of prince was used among the English royal family.

In the early 15th century Owain Glyndwr was proclaimed as Prince of Wales and led a rebellion against the newly enthroned Henry IV. This war, abetted by the King of France and some of the English nobility, dragged on for many years. Glyndwr's son Maredudd finally conceded a peace with England in 1421.

 ## The last English king to die in battle

The battling contenders for the crown of England over many centuries were testimony to the courage and physical prowess required of the monarchy. Many of the kings of England met their end literally fighting for their crown. The last king to do so provided what was perhaps the most dramatic change of rule in the history of the English monarchy. Richard III was a strong and forceful king, but no more so than most in the violent 15th century which saw the bloody battles of the Wars of the Roses. Henry Tudor also claimed the kingdom and was determined to supplant Richard.

Their armies finally met at Bosworth on 22 August 1485. Richard had superior numbers but decided to stake all on a quick thrust directly at Henry, whom he hoped to kill in single combat. It nearly worked, Richard and his men reached Henry and his retainers and the fighting was fierce. Richard's horse was killed under him and he was forced to fight on foot. His party were cut off and in the ensuing mêlée Richard was felled and hacked to pieces. In a dramatic gesture, Richard's crown, which he had insisted on wearing in the battle, was retrieved from under a nearby hawthorn bush and placed on the head of the victorious Henry Tudor. Although other English kings since have been forced to fight for their throne, or at least to retain it, none since have had to die doing so.

Richard III is slain at Bosworth field by Henry Tudor's soldiers (opposite). He died bravely but suffered a character assassination at the hands of the Tudor dynasty that succeeded him. He was England's last king to risk and lose all by dying in battle. (ME)

The last Scottish king to die in battle

1513

The Battle of Flodden was the scene of a tragic massacre of an army headed by the Scottish King James IV. In September 1513, while Henry VIII of England was in France capturing Tournai, James of Scotland, in a move intended to aid his ally Louis XII of France, invaded England. At Flodden Field in Northumberland on 9 September his army was decisively defeated by the English army commanded by the ageing Earl of Surrey. James was killed and in the rout that followed over 10,000 Scots lost their lives. James IV was the last Scottish king to die in battle. The Scots king's seventeen-month-old son inherited the throne and was crowned James V two weeks later.

The last Plantagenets

1541

Although the last reigning Plantagenet monarch was Richard III, the male Plantagenet line survived until the death of the Earl of Warwick in 1499. He was executed for treason by Henry VII. Alongside him on the scaffold was Perkin Warbeck who had claimed to be 'Richard IV', one of the missing princes in the Tower commonly thought to have been murdered by Richard III.

Had Perkin Warbeck really been Richard, Duke of York, Richard IV of England, as he had once claimed, he and Warwick would have been first cousins. Warwick was the son of the Duke of Clarence, secretly killed for treason against Edward IV in 1478.

Warwick was beheaded and Warbeck, as a commoner, was hanged on 24 November 1499. Many years later, in 1541, Warwick's sister, Margaret, Countess of Salisbury, the last of the House of Plantagenet, was executed for supposed treason against the increasingly paranoid Henry VIII at the ripe old age of 72.

The last English child sovereign

Many of the kings of England were crowned and ruled as children. Edward VI was England's last child sovereign. He acceded to the throne at the age of ten, on 28 January 1547 on the death of his father Henry VIII. A capable scholar and an intelligent follower of the politics of the day he was never to enjoy good health. He died at the age of sixteen on 6 July 1553, probably of tuberculosis. He was succeeded by his elder half sister Mary after his distant cousin Lady Jane Grey had ruled for just nine days.

The last Scottish child sovereign

Mary Queen of Scots gave birth in June 1566 to a son who was to turn out to be the last child sovereign in the British Isles. The following February, Darnley, Queen Mary's husband and her son's father, was killed mysteriously when his house was blown up. She was remarried within months to James Earl of Bothwell. Civil war ensued and Queen Mary was captured by Bothwell's opponents in June 1567.

Within a few weeks she had been forced to abdicate and her son, barely a year old, was proclaimed James VI of Scotland. James VI was the last King of the Scots who was not also the King of England. A law was passed in England to specifically exclude Mary from the English throne and James VI was recognized as the heir to Elizabeth of England. As a young man James (later James I of England) concluded a further treaty with Queen Elizabeth which ruled out any possibility of his sharing the throne of England with his mother.

The last Scottish monarch to die a violent death

Mary Queen of Scots was executed by the English in 1587 after being found guilty of complicity in a plot to assassinate the Queen of England, Elizabeth I. Mary had been deposed twenty years earlier in favour of her young son James VI (later to be also James I of England). After a dramatic escape from her Scottish captors she fled to England. As the mother of the accepted heir to the childless Queen Elizabeth I of England she was a continual threat to the stability to the English regime and she was held in captivity for what turned out to be the rest of her life. Although Elizabeth never met Mary and knowingly signed her death warrant, the 'virgin queen' was distraught when she learnt of the execution.

The last separate monarch of England ◇ 1603 ◇

Elizabeth I, Queen of England, daughter of Henry VIII and Ann Boleyn, was the last sovereign of England who was not also sovereign of Scotland. She died unmarried and childless on 24 March 1603 at the age of 69. On her death, James VI of Scotland became James I of England as well. He was crowned in Westminster Abbey in London on 25 July 1603 uniting the Scottish and English crowns and bringing to an end the separate monarchies. From that date, the thrones of England and Scotland have been combined; the 21 sovereigns who succeeded James VI of Scotland and James I of England have reigned over Scotland as well as England.

The last heir apparent to die without issue ◇ 1612 ◇

The last heir apparent who died without leaving descendants was Henry, Prince of Wales, eldest son of James I of England and VI of Scotland. Henry was born at Stirling in Scotland on 19 February 1594 while his father was still only King of Scotland. On moving to England Henry was created Prince of Wales just before his 16th birthday. He was very accomplished, intellectually and in the martial talents, and had a wide range of interests. Many regarded him as the epitome of a royal prince and even hailed him as another Henry V. His death at the age of 18 from typhoid fever shattered the royal family and the country at large. His younger brother succeeded him as heir apparent and as Prince of Wales, eventually to reign as Charles I.

The last British monarch to die a violent death ◇ 1649 ◇

When Charles I mounted the scaffold in London's Whitehall on a cold January morning in 1649 to be beheaded he became the last British sovereign to die a violent death. He had been beaten in the English Civil War and was tried at Westminster for treason. The Parliamentarians who signed his death warrant expected that he would be Britain's last monarch, but this was not to be. The monarchy was restored eleven years later when his son was crowned Charles II.

The last king to be crowned twice

The last king to be crowned twice was Charles II. In the past some kings had been crowned more than once to reinforce their claim to the throne. Charles II's first coronation was on 1 January 1651 at Scone in Scotland. He had to wait ten years for his second crowning. On his restoration his formal coronation at Westminster Abbey in London took place on 23 April 1661 and was a fuller grander affair, in the ceremonial tradition of the time.

The last pedilavium

In Britain on the Thursday before Easter, Maundy Thursday, the religious service of Royal Maundy is performed. This is usually held in one of the cathedrals and the central figure is the sovereign who presents specially minted Maundy money to a selected group of deserving elderly locals.

    The ceremony has its origins in the Last Supper, when Christ washed his disciples' feet. Until the 17th century the sovereign of the day also carried out this act of contrition by washing and kissing the feet of the recipients of the Maundy money. It was known by the Latin word, pedilavium. The feet of the local pensioners were usually washed thoroughly before the ceremony to save the monarch any unpleasantness, but, as the dignity of the service increased over the years, the practice died out. On Maundy Thursday, in 1685, James II was the last king to perform the pedilavium personally.

The last Catholic king

When Charles II died in 1685 he was succeeded by his younger brother James. This succession was, in many ways, against all the odds, as Parliament had spent much of its time during the preceding eight years in open defiance of King Charles in its efforts to exclude James, an avowed Catholic, from succeeding to the throne.

    James II, King of Great Britain, was an unsettled sovereign, doomed by his espousal of the Roman Catholic faith. He was Britain's last Catholic king, and his second wife, Mary of Modena was the last Catholic queen. He was also the last king to proclaim the divine right of kings, the cause that had brought such grief to his father Charles I, conflict to the country during the Civil War and finally resulted in the execution of a reigning king.

    James II became Britain's last king to be deposed when his wife at last bore him a son in 1688 – a Catholic son who, as king, would be unacceptable to Parliament. His own daughter Mary and her husband, his nephew and son-in-law, William of Orange, were invited by Parliament to replace him. James effectively abdicated on 13 December when he tried to flee the country and threw the Great Seal, the symbol of office, into the Thames. He was humbled by being brought back to London from the coast. When

William reached Windsor he demanded that James leave London. Britain's last reigning Stuart king obliged and left England on 23 December 1688.

In what came to be called the 'Glorious Revolution', William and Mary were crowned jointly King and Queen of Britain in April the following year. Parliament gained important rights and Catholics were debarred forever from succession to the British throne. James unsuccessfully attempted to regain the throne by invading Ireland in 1690, but was decisively defeated at the Battle of the Boyne. No Catholic monarch has sat on the British throne since.

His Royal Highness James, Duke of York in his Garter robes. Despite the fact that he had already converted to the Roman Catholic faith, he succeeded to the throne as James VII of Scotland and II of England. Britain's last Catholic king, he was deposed in 1688 during the 'Glorious Revolution' and died in exile in 1701. (ME)

The last of the 'King's Evil'

Monarchs of many countries have been involved in the ancient practice of 'Touching for the King's Evil'. Diseased subjects would present themselves to the sovereign who would ceremonially touch them, in the belief that they would be cured of their affliction. Scrofula, a disease now known to be bovine tuberculosis, involving glandular swelling, was called the King's Evil and was the affliction most commonly presented to the king or queen for cure. Scrofula often disappears suddenly anyway but its obvious and visible cure soon after a touch from the king was often heralded as part of the miracle.

The practice, reputedly started in Britain by Edward the Confessor, developed over the centuries into a ceremony where alms were also given to the patient, usually a gold coin, a 'touchpiece', which was then supposed to be hung around the patient's neck until the cure was effected. Queen Anne was the last reigning British monarch to indulge in touching. She last performed the ceremony, in private, in 1714. The exiled Stuart pretenders continued with the practice until the death of the 'Cardinal King', Henry, Duke of York, in 1807.

 1743

The last king to lead his army in battle

The reigning British monarch has always been the titular head of the Army, its Commander-in-Chief. The Royal Family have, also, had a very close association with the armed forces which continues to the present day. Although even in very recent times members of the Royal Family have seen active military service, the last occasion to date being Prince Andrew's piloting of naval helicopters in the Falklands campaign, it is over two hundred years ago that the last reigning British monarch participated in fighting and led his troops in battle.

In the middle of the 18th century, George II was not only the British King but also the Elector of Hanover, a powerful position among the small independent German states. He spent much of his time on the continent and regarded Hanover with especial fondness. Europe was embroiled in the War of the Austrian Succession and an army commanded by the British Lord Stair at Aschaffenburg was made up of British, Hessian, Austrian, Dutch and Hanoverian troops. It was confronted by the French Army under the command of Marshal Noailles who was attempting to cut them off from their base and Hanau on the River Main.

King George arrived to take over command of his army in early June 1743. Fully protected from the normal rigours of campaigning, with a huge luggage train which included nearly a hundred carts and wagons for his own personal luxuries, he nonetheless was an enthusiastic commander at the age of 60. He was accompanied by his 22-year-old son, William, Duke of Cumberland, who in the Jacobite rising in Scotland two years later was to become known as 'Butcher' Cumberland. The King visited his troops regularly, showing the keenest interest in the details of daily military life. There were problems, however. They were running desperately short of food and nearly all other supplies. On 15 June it was finally decided to retire to Hanau. The French had a large detachment, some 28,000 men under the command of Count Gramont, waiting for them at the village of Dettingen. As they moved north, the rest of Noailles' French troops moved to cut them off in the rear.

Hemmed in by the river on one side and the forest on the other, King George's army seemed to be making its way inexorably into the trap set for them. The French artillery were placed across the river and on 27 June they opened up on the Allies' cavalry and infantry. The result was dreadful carnage. The Allies' own artillery was at the rear of the column and had to make its way painfully and slowly up the line. King George gave the order for the column to face the river and at that moment Gramont attacked their rear. Unperturbed the King turned his army about to meet and repel the French infantry attack. The French cavalry attacked but were also repelled by the Allied army.

At this time King George was at his finest: leading the counter charges against the enemy cavalry, urging his troops into the fight, guiding the artillery fire and generally displaying the courage and leadership expected from any good Army Commander.

Eventually the enemy cavalry retreated, the French infantry broke and ran, many drowning in the river. The Battle of Dettingen was a lucky win for the Allies but to a certain extent King George made his own luck with his courage and character. The battle decided nothing and today is remembered mainly for being the last occasion when a British reigning monarch led his troops in battle.

The last death of the heir apparent to the throne

1751

The heir apparent to the throne is the eldest male child of the reigning sovereign. No female child can be the heir apparent – even if she had no brother – as, in theory at least, her parents could always yet produce a male heir to supersede her. The last heir apparent to die without succeeding to the throne was Frederick Louis, Prince of Wales and eldest son of George II. Like most of the Hanoverian dynasty he quarrelled furiously with his parents for most of his life. Frederick Louis also seemed to be most unpopular with his brothers and sisters.

Frederick Louis was born in Hanover in 1707, some seven years before his grandfather succeeded to the British throne as George I. He remained there until 1728 when his father, now King George II sent for him. Frederick married in 1736, his wife was the Princess Augustas of Saxe-Gotha. They produced nine children before he died of pleurisy at the age of 44 on 20 March 1751, nine years before his father. His son, the future George III, succeeded him as Prince of Wales.

The last of the House of Stuart

1807

The first sovereign of both England and Scotland, Britain's first member of the House of Stuart, was King James I of England and VI of Scotland. The troubled and autocratic dynasty that succeeded him lasted just over a hundred years on the throne and a further hundred in exile. His son, Charles I, was beheaded by the Parliamentarians after the Civil War and his grandson James II was chased off the throne over the issue of Roman Catholicism. His great-granddaughter, Anne, was the last Stuart sovereign to sit on the British throne. That was not, however, the last of the dynasty. Henry Stuart, Cardinal, Duke of York was the last legitimate male Stuart claimant to the British throne.

The birth of James II's son in 1688, by his second marriage to the Roman Catholic Mary of Modena, was one of the issues which precipitated the 'Glorious Revolution'. The ruling classes would not accept the prospect of James Edward ruling over them as a Catholic and despotic king. Instead they invited the Prince of Orange and his wife (James II's daughter) Mary to rule as joint sovereigns – William III and Mary II.

The last of the troubled Stuart line, Henry Benedict, Cardinal, Duke of York. He was styled 'King Henry IX' on the death of his elder brother 'Bonnie Prince Charlie' and was the last legitimate Stuart to claim the British throne. (Hulton)

James II and his family fled, but the dynastic split precipitated two major 18th-century rebellions. In Scotland in 1715 James Edward, then styled James III, tried to claim his crown. He failed. In 1745 his son, the 'Young Pretender' known as Bonnie Prince Charlie, tried again on his father's behalf. His invasion of England came close to success but he was forced to retreat and his army was finally defeated at Culloden. The Stuarts retired to the Continent where, in the Roman Catholic courts, with varying degrees of social success, they lived out the rest of their days in peace.

Bonnie Prince Charlie married in later life but had no children and died in 1788. His younger brother Henry survived him and 'reigned' over the now dwindling band of Stuart adherents, under the title 'King Henry IX'.

On his birth Henry had been unofficially created Duke of York by his father. He grew up to be a mild-mannered Prince who took to his religion with great fervour. His attempts to help his brother in the '45 rebellion came to nothing; the troops he raised failed to reach Scotland. He was made a cardinal deacon by Pope Benedict XIV in 1747 and took priestly orders the following year. Securing various bishoprics and archbishoprics, Henry followed a routinely successful career within the upper ranks of the Catholic Church in Europe.

Henry proved to be no threat to the ruling Hanoverians back in Britain. Near the end of his life, after he lost all his possessions in Italy to Napoleon's army, George III even granted him a suitable annual pension. The 'Cardinal King' was a pious man. He never set foot in Britain and ended his days quietly in Frascati on 13 July 1807. He was buried in St Peter's, Rome.

◁ 1811 ▷ *The last regency*

S everal times in British history a regent has been appointed to act on behalf of and to carry out the duties of the sovereign. The appointment of a regent is required, under established law, when the monarch is incapacitated, otherwise unavailable or under 18 years of age at the time of succession. The last instance of a regency in Britain was in 1811 when the Prince of Wales, the future George IV, was appointed after his father George III was declared insane.

Custom demands that to recognize a need for a regent at least three people, from among a list of specified high-office holders, must declare the monarch to be incapacitated. It is also now accepted that the next in line to the throne, if over 18 years old, should if possible be appointed the regent. Otherwise it would be expected to be another close relative. This has not always been so. Regents in the past have often been ruthless outsiders, using their real power behind the throne to amass great fortunes and to appoint their own men to important offices.

George III had exhibited signs of insanity for many years before 1811. When a previous serious bout of madness was causing concern in 1788 a Regency Bill, introduced to Parliament by Pitt, was halted by the immediate and very opportune recovery of the King. By 1810, however, the King's insanity was too far gone. The Prince of Wales too was champing at the bit and Parliament had no alternative but to act. After the due process of parliamentary business he was sworn in as Prince Regent on 6 February 1811. His powers at first were slightly restricted, in the creation of peers and appointment of salaries, but these were lifted a year later. This appointment heralded a period of high spending and lavish living for 'Prinny'. When his father died in 1820 he continued his dissolute lifestyle as King. The 'Regency' period, 1811–20, is now regarded as a time of high culture and 'society', with much interest in the arts and architecture.

A more recent regency nearly took place. Queen Victoria succeeded to the throne on 20 June 1837 at the age of 18 years and one month. Had her uncle, William IV, died just a few weeks earlier it is probable that her mother, the Duchess of Kent, would have been regent until Victoria had reached her 18th birthday.

The last royal trial

1820

For many centuries British history has been regularly punctuated with the trials of members of the royalty. They were accused, tried and convicted of serious charges. Female members were particularly vulnerable: King Henry VIII's wives, Anne Boleyn and Catherine Howard, although perhaps the best known, were not the only queens to have affairs that proved fatal. Most of these trials were riddled with hypocrisy; many had elements of farce. The last royal trial – of Queen Caroline, George IV's wife, in 1820 – contained more than its fair share of hypocrisy.

In 1795 the Prince of Wales eventually succumbed to his father's pleadings to marry and produce an heir. Unfortunately he had already been secretly (and illegally) married for ten years to a quiet, devoted Catholic widow, Maria Fitzherbert. A bigamous marriage to the brash and graceless Princess Caroline of Brunswick went ahead. Nine months later their heir, Princess Charlotte, was born. Duty done, the dissolute Prince or 'Prinny' as he was later known took his leave, never to return to the marriage bed.

Princess Caroline, a woman who was as unsuited to chastity and a quiet life as 'Prinny' himself, was soon involved in a series of public scandals with a number of men, many in public life, who visited her court at Blackheath on the outskirts of London. Her husband was predictably furious, despite his own continued affairs with a number of mistresses and reconciliation with his 'other' wife Maria. In 1811, when the Prince of Wales was made Regent, one of his first actions was to remove his daughter from her mother's keeping.

Caroline became increasingly ostracized from society and in 1814 she moved to the Continent where her behaviour became more and more vulgar and flagrant. She left a trail of ex-lovers all over Europe and became a social outcast. In Italy she became involved with a former cavalry quartermaster, Bartolomeo Bergami. She was ignored by society to such an extent that she only learned by accident of her daughter's death in childbirth – she had not even been aware that she had married.

Early in 1820 the old, mad King of England died, the Regency was over and

The trial of Queen Caroline, wife of George IV, in the House of Lords. Standing next to the Queen (seated right of centre) is Lord Brougham who robustly conducted her defence against the charges of adultery. (Hulton)

Caroline's husband became King George IV. She was 52 years old and, at last, the Queen of Great Britain and Ireland. She was determined to have her revenge on the society that had treated her so cruelly and at once set out to return to England. She arrived at Dover and such was the unpopularity of both the King and his government that she was immediately taken up by the crowds and mobs in all the towns and cities on her way to London. Very soon she became the rallying point for all opposition. There were riots in the capital and troops had to be called out to keep order.

Within a month the government had been persuaded to act; they knew that Caroline would have to be legally deprived of her position. They postponed the coronation and presented in the House of Lords a 'Bill of Pains and Penalties' 'to deprive Her Majesty Caroline Amelia Elizabeth of the Title, Prorogations, Rights, Priveleges and Pretensions of Queen Consort of this realm on the grounds of a most degrading intimacy between the Queen when Princess of Wales and Bartolomeo Bergami, a foreigner of low station.' The gloves were off and the stakes, if not the very highest, were at least the most serious that a member of the royalty, the Queen no less, had faced for many years.

The government's attempt to pass this Bill through both Houses of Parliament now became *de facto* the public trial of the Queen for adultery. The Parliament buildings were surrounded by heavy barricades to keep the mobs at bay, cavalry were stationed in the nearby streets and the River Thames was patrolled by armed boats.

At the start of the trial, to applause from the throng outside, the Queen herself arrived at the Houses of Parliament in her new state landau drawn by six chestnut horses. Veiled and dressed in deep mourning, she swept into the House and, much to the government's consternation, took her rightful place as a Peeress of the Realm to watch the proceedings. Not all the noble lords supported the Bill; many were appalled at the entire proceedings. The fact that such a notorious *roué* as the King should have instigated such a harassment of his Queen was unacceptable to many of the more reputable politicians and public figures of the day. Despite strong pressures to attend and support the Bill many stayed away in protest.

The evidence was presented over several days; the Attorney-General put the case for the government. Defending, for the Queen, was her personal attorney Lord Brougham. Witnesses were called; there was no lack of circumstantial evidence of the Queen's affair with Bergami. Servants, cooks and spies all were called to give their stories and be cross-examined. As the weeks passed the country was agog with the details; there was a serious possibility of civil war as the riots and disturbances from the Queen's supporters continued.

The House was convinced that the Queen was guilty yet the Lords knew that the King himself was even more so. Even if the Bill were passed and presented to the House of Commons they would undoubtedly throw it out anyway. There was the additional problem of the reaction of the rioting mobs.

On a vote, the House of Lords did pass the Bill by a slender majority, finding against the Queen. But the prime minister, Lord Liverpool, a realist, had the Bill withdrawn on 10 November. The jubilant mobs took part in celebrating the Queen's 'acquittal' in cities as far apart as Edinburgh, Dublin and Manchester, as well as in London itself for three nights in succession. The King was apoplectic with fury but the constitutional crisis passed.

Poor Queen Caroline was, however, done for. Officially humiliated and ignored despite being the legitimate Queen, she never recovered. The following year, when trying to attend her husband's coronation, she was forcibly turned away from the doors of Westminster Abbey to the derision of the watching crowds. She died at Hammersmith three weeks later, reviled and largely unloved, one of Britain's unhappier queens. Perversely, the ever capricious London mob honoured her by rioting at her funeral. The irony of Queen Caroline's acquittal – everyone in Parliament knew her to be guilty as charged – was matched only by the sheer hypocrisy of King George himself in pressing for the trial. His example of 'royal' behaviour too, it is thought, was the last of its kind.

The last king's champion ◇ 1821 ◇

The kings and queens of Britain have, over the years, exercised a right to nominate a champion to act on their behalf in cases of a challenge to combat. Obviously the sovereign could not engage in combat personally, so the champion was appointed to carry out this task on his or her behalf, although there is no record of a champion having to perform anything other than a ceremonial duty.

The king's champion seems to be unique to England and the idea originates in the feudal laws of the 14th century. The champion's main duty came during the banquet held directly after the coronation – he rode on horseback into the assembled company to defend the new sovereign 'by his body, if necessary' against anyone who dared challenge. The last occasion when this was performed was after the outrageously extravagant and lavish coronation of King George IV on 19 July 1821, when Henry Dymoke was the champion.

The feast was held in Westminster Hall, a stone's throw from Westminster Abbey where the coronation had taken place. A series of wooden galleries had been constructed in the hall for spectators to watch the celebrations. After the first course had been served the champion was called in to do his duty. A flourish of trumpets heralded his arrival on a piebald charger, flanked by the Duke of Wellington as Lord High Constable and Lord Howard as Deputy Earl Marshal. Dymoke read out his challenge at the gates to the hall:

'If any person of what degree soever, high or low, shall deny or gainsay our sovereign lord King George IV, of the United Kingdom of Great Britain and Ireland, defender of the faith, son and next heir of our sovereign lord King George III, the last king deceased, to be right heir to the imperial crown of this United Kingdom, or that he ought not to enjoy the same, here is his champion, who saith that he lieth, and he is a false traitor; being ready in person to combat with him, and in this quarrel will adventure his life against him, on what day soever shall be appointed.'

He flung his gauntlet onto the stone floor. There was no-one to accept his challenge and it was returned to him by his esquire.

The party rode to the middle of the hall and the challenge was repeated. It was finally issued for the third and last time, amidst great applause from the assembled throng, at the steps leading to the royal banqueting table. His Majesty, now presumably relieved that there were no takers for the challenges, drank the health of his champion. He then passed the golden goblet to his champion who drank to His Majesty's health in turn with the cry, 'Long live his Majesty, King George IV!' The cup was passed to his page who bore it away for Dymoke family posterity.

The King soon left the hall to return to the palace. The feast rapidly descended from sublime pomp into embarrassing farce. The guests and serving attendants now approached the deserted royal tables. Cautiously at first but then with increasing boldness, souvenirs of gold cutlery, plates, vases and many other portable items disappeared into the pockets of the surrounding crowd. The Lord High Chamberlain managed to push his way through the crowd and save the more important items.

Even at the time the expense of the coronation was extensively criticized. The King's robes for the occasion cost £25,000 and were worn for only a few hours. The total cost was a quarter of a million pounds. The King's popularity, never high, was soon as low as ever in the country. Nine years later his brother William IV spent only £50,000 on his entire coronation.

Never again was the king's champion required to perform these official duties. The position of champion, however, still exists. It is hereditary, tied to the lordship of the manor of Scrivelsby in Lincolnshire since 1377 and the present incumbent is the direct descendant of the last active champion, Henry Dymoke.

The last British monarch to leave no legitimate issue

1837

The last British monarch to die without leaving a direct descendant as heir to the throne was William IV. William, the Duke of Clarence, was one of several younger sons of George III. He had enjoyed a 20-year relationship with an actress, Mrs Dorothea Jordan, who had borne him ten healthy illegitimate children, the FitzClarences, five boys and five girls.

When Princess Charlotte, the Prince Regent's daughter and second-in-line to the throne, died in childbirth in 1817, all the King's unmarried sons were cajoled to marry and try to produce at least one legitimate heir between them. The Duke of Clarence chose Princess Adelaide of Saxe Meiningen. A joint marriage was arranged; his younger brother, Edward, Duke of Kent married Princess Victoria of Saxe-Coburg at the same ceremony on July 1818. The Duke of Clarence and his wife were surprisingly compatible but, unfortunately, the Princess had a melancholy series of miscarriages and sickly children who died very young. After twin boys were stillborn to the Princess in 1822, the childless couple became resigned to their fate. When the Duke of Clarence was proclaimed King William in 1830, on his brother's death, his acknowledged heir was his niece Princess Victoria, daughter of his late brother, the Duke of Kent.

William IV died in 1837 and although most of his illegitimate children survived him none could succeed to the throne. His sons had quarrelled with him terribly but his daughters were much more amenable and had all married well. Princess Adelaide loved all her husband's illegitimate children and she herself was especially loved and appreciated by her niece, Queen Victoria. She died in 1849 deeply mourned by most of the royal family.

The last change in the Royal coat-of-arms

1837

The coat-of-arms of the British royal family has changed many times since Richard the Lionheart adopted the lions of England as his emblem in the 12th century. The last change occurred when Victoria ascended the throne in 1837 and the shield representing the Kingdom of Hanover was omitted.

Claims to different kingdoms, England, Scotland, Ireland and particularly France, have played an important part in the design of the British royal coat-of-arms through the centuries. In addition, the Hanoverian kings had brought with them to the British throne the lands of German Hanover. An escutcheon (a smaller shield within the larger shield) on the British royal coat-of-arms displayed the Hanoverian coat-of-arms, the two lions of Brunswick, the rampant lion of Luneburg and the famous white horse of Hanover, capped with the crown of Charlemagne. This escutcheon was dropped when Queen Victoria ascended the throne because under Salic law, she could not succeed to the Kingdom of Hanover.

Today the royal coat-of-arms indicates only wholly legitimate claims and is unchanged from Victoria's. The shield consists of four 'quarters' on which are the devices of the different kingdoms of the United Kingdom. 'England' in the first and fourth quarters, 'Scotland' in the second quarter and 'Northern Ireland' in the third quarter. Wales, a principality not a kingdom, is not represented. 'England' in heraldic language is described as: *Gules three Lions passant guardant Or, armed and langed azure* (three golden lions, each with blue claws and tongue, on a red background). 'Scotland' is: *Or a Lion rampant within a double tressure, flory counterflory Gules* (a red lion, standing on its hind legs, on a gold background inside a double border decorated with fleur-de-lys). 'Northern Ireland' is: *Azure a Harp Or stringed Argent* (a golden harp with silver strings on a blue background). In Scotland the royal coat-of-arms gives priority to the Scottish single lion rampant, it being placed in the first and fourth quarters and 'England' taking up only one quarter, the second.

When Queen Victoria married Prince Albert in 1840 she so adored him that she must have forgotten all the normal royal heraldic rules. She requested that the shield of her coat-of-arms should be quartered with those of her beloved Albert. She was very annoyed when reminded that, unlike other coats-of-arms, hers symbolized the realms over which she ruled and not family alliances or other minor dynastic details. A change now in the royal coat-of-arms will occur only if there is a significant change in the status of the United Kingdom of Great Britain and Northern Ireland.

The last birth of an heir apparent to the throne

1841

Not many kings or queens of Great Britain were born directly as heir to the throne. Many were born as second or third in line, with one of the parents already the direct heir. Many others became the heir and succeeded only due to the death of a close relation. As longevity and the survival chances have increased from generation to generation, the likelihood of an heir being born in direct line of succession has receded.

The last truly 'majestic' birth, as far as the British crown is concerned, was that of Albert Edward, the Earl of Chester, heir and second child of Queen Victoria, the future Prince of Wales and King Edward VII. This momentous event took place in the morning of 9 November 1841 at Buckingham Palace. Up to that moment the heir to the throne was his one-year-old sister, Princess Victoria, whom he automatically replaced in the line of succession. Prince Albert Edward was christened in St George's chapel at Windsor Castle the following January. The Queen went on to give birth to another seven children, nine princes and princesses in all, seven of whom survived her and married into many branches of the royal families of Europe.

The last Hanoverian kings

When Queen Anne died in 1714 without living descendants, the Stuart line, so far as it was recognized in Britain, died with her. The British line of succession passed to the descendants of Elizabeth Stuart, daughter of James I. Elizabeth Stuart's daughter Sophia had married the German Ernest Augustus, ruler and Elector of Hanover. Sophia, the Electress of Hanover, had been declared Anne's heir but died just a few months before her. Her son 'German George' succeeded to the throne as George I. Along with his entire German entourage, he brought to the British crown the name and hereditary Electorship of Hanover.

The Hanoverian dynasty ruled Great Britain for over a hundred years. Each Hanoverian monarch was also Elector of Hanover until 1814, when Hanover itself became a kingdom. The British king at the time, the mad King George III, thus became King of Hanover too.

William IV was the last of the kings of Hanover on the British throne. He disliked the place and one of his younger brothers, Adolphus, Duke of Cambridge, had ruled there on behalf of the British kings, since the early part of the century. William, the 'sailor' king, died on 20 June 1837. The British crown passed to his young niece, Victoria, but the Hanoverian crown was governed by Salic law which debarred inheritance through the female line. Thus the next king of Hanover was another of Victoria's uncles, one of William IV's other younger brothers, the eccentric, bombastic and mischievous Ernest Augustus, Duke of Cumberland.

Thus William IV was not only the last of the male Hanoverians on the British throne (Victoria was a Hanoverian too) but he was also the last of the kings of Hanover on the British throne. Ernest died in 1851 and was succeeded as king of Hanover by his son George V. He was blinded in an accident at the age of 13 and was to be the last king of Hanover. He died in 1866 and that same year Hanover was annexed by Prussia.

The last of the Duchy of Lancaster ◄1873►

The Lancaster estate was created by Henry III for his second son Edmund Crouchback. Later, in the 14th century, John of Gaunt, Edward III's son, became Duke of Lancaster through his wife's inheritance. Although John of Gaunt never became king, his son Henry IV, did. The Duchy of Lancaster thereafter became inextricably linked with the British Crown. The Duchy finally lost its real powers in 1873 when the Judicature Act removed the last of its responsibilities in exercising the criminal and civil law within its lands.

The Duchy of Lancaster consists of 21,000 hectares of land in the north of England; ironically most of this land is not in Lancashire but in Yorkshire. Until 1873 the Chancellor of the Duchy of Lancaster was responsible for a number of administrative and legal duties. They included the control of the law courts and the issue of rulings that the Lord Chancellor carried out for the rest of the country. From the appointment of the High Sheriff of Lancaster downwards, the Chancellor of the Duchy exercised his rights and privileges. In 1873 the government decided to abolish this anomaly and incorporate the Duchy, for all practical purposes, into the rest of England. The position of Chancellor to the Duchy, however, was retained.

Today the Duchy of Lancaster still exists, the estate managed by the Crown on behalf of the Queen. The revenues from the Duchy form part of the contribution provided for the upkeep of the sovereign. The Chancellor of the Duchy of Lancaster is a government appointment, strictly political, its holder usually a member of the Cabinet with some special responsibility appropriate to the politics of the day.

◇1892◇ *The last death of an heir*

The last British heir in direct line to the throne to die before succeeding was Prince Albert Victor, the Duke of Clarence. He was the eldest son of the Prince of Wales, Albert Edward, the first in direct line of succession from his mother Queen Victoria. Prince Eddy, an otherwise certain future king, died very suddenly in 1892 when he was 28 years old. His younger brother, Prince George, who had been destined for a career in the Royal Navy, took his place – in more ways than one.

Prince Albert Victor, known to his family as Eddy, managed to inherit all of his father's faults and many of those of his great-great uncles, George IV and William IV. He had the languid, sensuous looks of his father and he indulged in most of the readily available vices of the period. It was widely rumoured that he frequented brothels, in London and elsewhere, and met many ladies of the 'lower classes'. Spells at Cambridge and in the Army failed to produce the desired qualities so necessary for a future king of Great Britain, Ireland and Emperor of India. Much loved by the rest of the royal family he was nevertheless a cause of their despair too.

He was not averse to his own class, however. Naïve and rather flighty, he conducted a number of love affairs, although not quite as publicly as his father, with members of 'society'. He finally did undertake to do his duty, and at the insistence of his parents and his grandmother, the Queen, set out to find himself a suitable wife and settle down.

He responded by falling in love with Princess Alix of Hesse, his cousin. She turned him down and was later to marry the future Tsar of Russia, Nicholas II and to die a bloody death with him at the hands of the Bolsheviks. Eddy rapidly turned to Princess Hélène of Orleans, a Roman Catholic and the daughter of the Comte de Paris, pretender to the French throne. It was an unsuitable match, on both religious and political grounds; the couple were gently persuaded to give each other up. After a brief passion for a well known beauty of the day, the Lady Sybil St Clair Erskine, the Prince at last set his sights on Princess May of Teck. Shy May was from the fringes of the European royal families but a great-granddaughter of George III. It was all agreed: he proposed in December 1891 and she accepted. The royal family were delighted; she was sensible, young and pretty, eminently suitable as the Princess who could love Eddy and keep him in line.

A month after their engagement, the royal couple were at Sandringham when Eddy was struck down with influenza. He grew worse, developed pneumonia and lingered for several days surrounded by anxious members of the family. On 14 January 1892, he died in the arms of his mother, the Princess of Wales. The family and country were deeply shocked. Princess May was grief stricken.

Prince Eddy, the Duke of Clarence and Avondale, is not much remembered today. His ex-fiancée became better known. She married Eddy's younger brother George the following year and eventually became the indomitable Queen Mary. She lived to see her granddaughter 'Lilibet' become Queen Elizabeth II.

Prince Albert Victor, the Duke of Clarence – 'Handsome Eddy' – in full military uniform. Albert Victor died of pneumonia at the age of 28, the last direct heir to die before succeeding to the British throne. (ME)

The last Tsar

The last crowned Russian Emperor, Tsar of all the Russias, was Nicholas II, son of Alexander III. He was a weak, inflexible ruler, unable to cope with the demands for democracy and the disaster of the First World War. In March 1917 the Russian Revolution broke out and the Tsar was forced to abdicate by Prime Minister Kerensky. His son, Alexis, could have succeeded to the throne but as he was young and suffered from haemophilia Nicholas decided to abdicate for him too. The next in line was Nicholas's younger brother, Mikhail Alexandrovich. On 14 March 1917 Nicholas abdicated in favour of the Grand Duke Mikhail Romanov. For a day Mikhail Alexandrovich was, technically, the Tsar, but he wisely decided to refuse the throne. He was the last of the Romanov dynasty to rule, if only in name, any of Russia.

Nicholas and his immediate family, his wife Alexandra, his son and his daughters, were held prisoner until July the following year. By this time, they were under guard at Ekaterinberg. Lenin and the Bolsheviks were in power and the country was in the grip of civil war. With the rebel White Russians threatening to capture the city of Ekaterinberg, the Bolsheviks feared that the Romanov family could be rescued and restored to the throne. To thwart any such plans Bolshevik orders were given for the execution of the entire family. On 16 July 1918 in the basement of the house where they were being held they were bayoneted and shot to death.

Tsar Nicholas II, the last of Russia's autocratic monarchs. His marriage to Princess Alexandra of Hesse was one of the few stabilizing influences on this weak and doomed ruler. After the Russian Revolution even Britain's Royal Family were unwilling to intervene on his behalf; he was murdered with his family in 1918. (AKG)

The last sovereign to abdicate

The last reigning monarch to quit the British throne was Edward VIII, after it became clear that a marriage to his mistress, the twice divorced Mrs Wallis Simpson, would never be accepted by the British public or the overseas dominions. His determination to make her his wife had convinced the prime minister, Stanley Baldwin, that abdication was the only solution.

He had succeeded his father George V on 20 January 1936. Less than a year later, on 10 December he signed the instrument of abdication. On 11 December he broadcast his farewell to the nation on the radio as Edward Windsor and on 12 December he sailed away into exile as the Duke of Windsor. On the date originally planned for the coronation of Edward VIII, 12 May 1937, his brother took centre stage and was crowned as George VI. The Duke of Windsor finally married his beloved Wallis in France the following month.

The last Emperor of India

1947

King George VI was the last of the British sovereigns to hold the additional title of Emperor of India. Queen Victoria had been created the Empress of India in recognition of the importance of India in the government's foreign policy. The title was also a response to the Queen's own aspirations amongst the royal families of Europe. She was determined to maintain her senior position; the German Kaiser and the Russian Tsar both had imperial titles and she was not to be outdone.

In May 1876 the title was steered through parliament by Disraeli and on 1 January 1877 Queen Victoria was first proclaimed Queen and Empress. All her successors took the title 'Rex and Imperator' until 1947, when Indian independence was negotiated. On 15 August 1947, George VI was the last king-emperor, his loss of title heralding the start of the break-up of the British Empire.

The last Sovereigns of Britain's Royal Houses

The House of Denmark: Hardicanute, 1040–42.

The House of Cerdic: Edward, *the Confessor*, 1042–66.

The House of Godwin: Harold II, 1066.

The House of Normandy: Henry I, *Beauclerk*, 1100–35. Henry's daughter, Matilda, *Empress Maud*, reigned briefly in 1141 and died 1167.

The House of Blois: Stephen, 1135–54.

The House of Anjou (Plantagenets): Richard II, 1377–99, deposed, died 1400.

The House of Lancaster (Plantagenets): Henry VI, 1422–61 and 1470–71, deposed, died 1471.

The House of York (Plantagenets): Richard III, 1483–85, killed at Battle of Bosworth.

The House of Tudor: Elizabeth I, 1558–1603.

The House of Orange: William III, 1689–1702, reigned jointly with his wife and cousin Mary II, 1689–94.

The House of Stuart: Anne, 1702–14.

The House of Hanover: Victoria, 1837–1901.

The House of Saxe-Coburg and Gotha: George V, 1910–36.
George V became the first sovereign of the House of Windsor in 1917, when he changed his name because of anti-German feeling during the First World War.

ARTS, SPORT
10   AND LEISURE

 The last of the original Olympic Games

It was the Ancient Greeks who instituted the tradition of competitive games for their young men. The games were held on the Greek Peloponnese peninsula at Olympia, a place that had origins that went back to the beginning of Greek civilization as a place of ancient sacrifice and worship.

The games were usually held every four years and developed into a regular national Greek festival. This reflected the Greeks' deep commitment to an all-round education including a harmonious training of mind and body. At first, somewhere around 776 BC, there was simply one race. As the festival developed, however, more races were added and other events such as throwing, boxing and wrestling were included. The prizes for victory remained simple, wreaths of laurel leaves and the acclamation of the spectators.

Over the many centuries of the ancient Olympic Games, about a thousand years in all, the successful games were interspersed with long periods of poor organization and sparse attendance. By the time the Romans finally conquered the Greeks and occupied Greece, the games were past their peak. They continued, however, approved, preserved and adapted by the Roman authorities. All the competitors in the 175th games in 80 BC were taken to Rome to participate in a duplicate set of games for the Roman citizens to see for themselves. Roman nobles took a strong interest in the traditions. Later, even the Emperor Tiberius participated.

At the Olympic site the temples and statues to the Greek gods were supplanted by those for the Roman gods, and many of the newer statues were of the Roman emperors and minor deities. This connection with the ancient gods was to prove the undoing of the games. By the time of the Emperor Theodosius, the Roman Empire was avowedly Christian. The pagan nature of the Olympic Games was offensive to him and the Church authorities. The last Olympic Games were held in the year 393. A year later Theodosius declared them anti-Christian and banned them forever. The records of the later games were sparse and, even in their day, were incomplete. The last victor to have his name recorded for posterity was an Armenian prince, Varazdates, in 385.

The Olympic site suffered tragic depredations over the succeeding years. Theodosius had the gods' statues destroyed and those made of iron were melted down for good measure. Within a year of Theodosius' banning of the games, Alaric and his Gothic hordes overran and badly damaged the whole area of Olympia. In 426 the Eastern Emperor Theodosius II ordered the Temples of Zeus and Olympia to be razed. However, some of the gods at least were still angry and a century later severe earthquakes in 522 and 551 wreaked further destruction. Today the ancient site of Olympia is visited by thousands of tourists. It is here every four years that the modern Olympic flame is kindled, using sunlight, to light the Olympic torch for the Modern Olympic Games.

The last Thames frost fair

1814

One of the more reliable sources of information on past weather patterns has been the recorded occasions when major rivers have frozen over. Making a detailed analysis on what the weather was like in the past, before scientific meteorological records were kept, from about the middle of the 19th century, is extremely difficult. One of the firmest indications of exceptionally cold winters has been the dates when London's River Thames has been frozen over.

The freezing of the Thames was certainly quite regular throughout most of the 17th and 18th centuries, occurring perhaps a couple of times in a generation, perhaps as much as once every decade. It was still obviously an exceptionally notable event and when it occurred large markets, fairs and entertainment of all kinds were held on the ice. These sometimes went on for many days and weeks. The festivities were known as 'frost fairs' and the last occasion when the Thames was frozen hard enough for this to happen was in the winter of 1813–14. Sheep were roasted in the middle of the river and skittles and other games were played with great gusto.

Early in 1814 an elephant was actually led onto the ice. To the amazement and astonishment of the thousands of assembled Londoners, the animal made a crossing

The frozen River Thames brought out revellers determined to enjoy the experience of walking on London's river. Early 1814 was the last occasion when the ice was strong enough to support a Thames Frost Fair. (ME)

of the Thames downstream of Blackfriars Bridge. This is certainly the first and last recorded instance. On 6 February 1814, the ice gave way and the Thames had seen its last frost fair.

The early years of the 19th century proved to be the last years of what is now referred to as a 'mini' ice age. The River Thames has, however, been frozen since. In February 1895 it was cold enough for the ice upstream of the City to support skating for several weeks. Unfortunately the ice was too lumpy and not strong enough for a regular fair to be held.

◁1823▷ Beethoven's ninth and last

In 1817 Ludwig van Beethoven, probably the greatest composer ever to have lived, began writing what was to be his last symphony. By that time almost totally deaf, Beethoven composed his symphony in D minor, known as the 'Choral' symphony, finishing it at Baden in 1823. It was first performed on 7 May 1824 and published two years later in Mainz in 1826, dedicated to Friedrich Wilhelm III of Prussia. It was highly acclaimed, then and now, and many critics consider it a triumph that has yet to be surpassed. The symphony contains the famous setting of Schiller's 'Ode to Joy' which is instantly recognizable to all music lovers.

Beethoven spent the remaining two and a half years of his life composing music for string quartets. Although he accepted a commission and the sum of £100 from the London Philharmonic Society to compose a symphony for them, he never wrote another major opus. On his way to Vienna in 1826 Beethoven fell ill and never recovered. He died on 26 March 1827.

◁1834▷ The last of the Royal Menagerie

In the 18th century, as today, the Tower of London was one of London's top attractions for visits from the public. Along with the Royal Mint, the crown jewels and the very impressive collection of weapons and armour on display there was a fascinating menagerie, the Royal Menagerie no less, housing one of the finest collections of wild animals in Europe. As standards and expectations improved, the animals at the Tower were moved to the newly opened Zoological Gardens in Regent's Park and the Royal Menagerie finally closed in 1834.

The first record of a Royal Menagerie is in the reign of Henry III (1216–72) when the gift of three leopards from Germany's Frederick II first established the collection of wild animals in the Tower. Soon there were other noble wild animals: lions and elephants drew amazed crowds from all over London and beyond. The animal collection grew with newer and more exotic creatures for the royal court's amusement. Many of the animals were used in entertainment, in particular the bears for bear-baiting. The big wild cats intrigued the courtiers and they tested their ferocity by pitting tigers and lions against each other or by arranging for packs of dogs to be mauled by them.

But fashions and fashionable entertainments change and by the early part of the 19th century the royal collection at the Tower had dwindled to a few flea-bitten creatures hardly worthy of the name. A new royal keeper, Alfred Copps, was appointed in 1822 and he set about restoring the menagerie's reputation. Within a few years there were more than fifty different species of wild animal including an Indian elephant, an alligator and many snakes from all over the world. The collection exceeded its former glory.

On the other side of London, however, in Regent's Park, a new kind of animal collection was rapidly being gathered together. The Zoological Society of London was founded in 1826 by Sir Stamford Raffles. Within two years it was opened to the public and became a great success. There had been another royal animal collection at Windsor Castle and this was transferred to the Regent's Park 'Zoo' around 1830. By then the park appeared the most logical place to keep wild animals. The process of transferring the animals from the Tower started in 1832. A lion attacked and badly injured one of the garrison in the Tower and the process was hurriedly completed. In 1834 the Royal Menagerie closed forever.

In Regent's Park the tradition of keeping wild animals for amusement, for fascinating the public and even for scientific study continued. In Britain the tradition, started by royalty many years before, was now firmly in the hands of 19th-century scientists and philanthropists.

The last legal bear-baiting ◁ 1835 ▷

Of all the sports involving animals, bear-baiting was certainly one the crueller spectacles indulged in by the British public. A tethered bear would be set upon by a pack of dogs for the amusement of the crowd and bets were taken as to the fates of selected animals in the contest. It was an extremely popular sport throughout Europe from the middle ages onwards. In the early part of the 19th century the public conscience was at last pricked and in 1835 the sport was declared illegal.

Bear-baiting was one of those sports which attracted huge crowds whether at custom-built bear-baiting rings ('bear gardens') or at travelling fairs. A bear would first be chained to a post and goaded into anger by being whipped and taunted. A number of dogs would then be set on it and the crowd would watch the fun. During the fight bets were taken on which dogs would be the first – or the last – to die. In later years the bears were muzzled to prolong the spectacle and give the dogs more of a chance. Sometimes the bear would be killed, sometimes it would survive. Both the bears and the dogs were specially bred for the purpose. The sport had a long, almost reputable history. Henry VIII for instance had a special bear-baiting ring built at Southwark in south London. His daughter Elizabeth I also enjoyed the contests.

Banning the sport was tried many times by various groups. The puritans abhorred the sport, 'not', it was said, 'because it gave pain to the bear, but because it gave pleasure to the spectators.' Nonetheless public opinion did at last swing against such bloody affairs. In 1835 a law was passed which made bear-baiting, and all similar sports such as bull-baiting, illegal.

Bear-baiting continued illegally for some years, but in public the practice was over. Very few fights took place after the 1850s. The British public gradually became ashamed of their amusement in watching pain being inflicted on other creatures. They submitted to the civilizing influence of the regulation and the eventual ban of the sport. Today, blood sports of various kinds still continue although no fighting against tethered animals is permitted.

1839   *The last tournament*

Tournaments of mounted armoured knights jousting against each other alongside supporting foot soldiers began, probably in France, in the latter part of the 11th century. Over the centuries it developed into a highly organized sport with a complex set of rules governing the conduct and honour of the events and the participants. It also became a useful, if not vital, part of the training and preparation for war, for both horseback and infantry tactics.

In Britain tournaments were last held regularly in King James I's time at the beginning of the 17th century. They had, however, by this time become occasions for the demonstration of prowess at highly stylised jousting skills, rather than genuine preparation and practice for war. The development of firearms had ensured that individual hand-to-hand combat was now only part of the set piece battle in future wars. The last tournament to be held in Britain was a Victorian revival. It was the carefully stage-managed Eglinton Tournament held in Scotland in 1839.

After the modest coronation ceremonies of both William IV in 1830 and Victoria in 1838, the traditionalists among the aristocracy felt slighted and insulted by the dumping of centuries-old traditions. With a young queen on the throne, few of them could expect another chance to participate in a 'proper' coronation. Their memories went back to the extravagant affair when George IV was crowned and they yearned for its splendour.

Among the disaffected lords of the land was one Archibald William Montgomerie, 26-years-old, and the 13th earl of Eglinton. He was too young to remember George IV's lavish coronation feast but he was steeped in the myths and magic of the High Ceremonial of the land – his stepfather was deputy to the Earl Marshal – and felt utterly deprived by the government's parsimony. Young Lord Eglinton was ardent, impetuous and above all rich. Within months he had been persuaded to finance a proper celebration of the past, A grand tournament was decided and the venue was to be his fake Gothic Scottish castle at Eglinton in Ayrshire.

Planning was vigorous and enthusiastic if not exactly thorough. 'Knights' were invited from all over Britain to participate, impersonating real valiant knights from history. Many bankrupted themselves to obtain the correct equipment for the modern tourney. A knight's battlefield accoutrements were never cheap, even in medieval times; in the 19th century prices of bespoke armour were cruelly ruinous.

Planning, however, could not pre-arrange the weather. On the great day, 28 August 1839, a severe rainstorm washed out most of the events, leaving the participants extremely bedraggled and looking ridiculous. The estimated 100,000 spectators, some of whom had travelled for days and many miles to be present, were bored and very disappointed. Myth and reality did not mix well at this the last British tournament. Jousting of a highly stylized sort of course continues today. A revived interest has ensured that skilled and highly trained riders can demonstrate some of the ancient skills to their paying audiences at several sites throughout the country during the tourist summer months.

The last cockfighting

1849

In its heyday, in the 17th and 18th centuries, cockfighting was the most popular sport in the British Isles. It appealed to all classes of society from royalty downwards and one of its main attractions was as an excuse for betting. Two cocks would be placed in a ring, or 'cockpit'. Bets were placed and huge sums of money could change hands at the end of the fight. The last legal cockfight in Britain took place in 1849, after which the practice was outlawed.

The natural aggression of cocks towards each other has been used throughout history to enable the staging of fights to the death. Betting on the outcome of such fights – on which bird would die and which would live – was the major incentive for the development of the sport. Specially bred fighting cocks were very valuable. Their owners often gave them as much care and attention as racehorses might receive today. The assets essential to a fighting gamecock – strength and aggression – were developed by careful

An early 19th-century cockpit surrounded by 'sporting' men from all classes of society who socialized and placed bets. Cockfighting was made illegal in Britain in 1849. (BAL)

breeding. To their natural abilities was added the practice of artificially sharpening their claws and beaks and, in many cases, attaching lethal metal spurs to their legs.

The cockpits were often inside specially constructed buildings. In the towns and villages, fairs would bring a crop of cockfights and many smaller outdoor cockpits were to be found all over the country, often surrounded by a fence, next to a public house. Some fights were arranged with more than two birds, the winner was the last bird on its feet. But the cockpits were turned to other uses after 1849 when legislation outlawing cockfighting was enforced by a £5 fine.

Cockfighting is still permitted in many parts of the world. To this day there is no doubt that secret fights are still staged illegally in various parts of Britain. The crueller side to the human character will ensure that the sport will continue for many more years to come.

The last of the Vauxhall Gardens

Vauxhall Gardens in south London were once the exciting playgrounds for Londoners of all classes. They were at their peak in the early 19th century, the regency period, when thousands of London's 'society' spent their summer evenings in the gardens, strolling and eating, watching the dancing and singing. The popularity of the pleasure gardens faded in the 1830s and 1840s and in 1855 the gardens were closed forever, the land being sold for building. Vauxhall Gardens were on the site of the Manor of Fauxe Hall, on the south bank of the River Thames. Samuel Pepys records visiting the 'Spring Gardens', as they were first known, 'at Fox Hall'. However, it was not until the early part of the 18th century that they became really popular, when the owner put on open air entertainment *ridotto al fresco*. Musical evenings with dancing girls, fireworks and circus acts drew the crowds.

Dr Johnson was a frequent visitor, commenting 'it is peculiarly adapted to the taste of the English nation; there being a mixture of curious show, gay exhibition, music, vocal and instrumental, not too refined for the general ear, for all of which only a shilling is paid; and, though last not least, good eating and drinking for those who choose to purchase that regale'. Visitors were free to walk along eleven acres of winding paths, past follies and colonnaded ruins, fountains and statues, lit by thousands of lamps. Balloon ascents and even some attempted parachute jumps were performed. The numerous bandstands, coffee rooms and eating places were highly popular. The more secretive parts of the gardens were widely acknowledged as the rendezvous for lovers.

The gardens, however, did not last. As they became more popular and the entrance fee was reduced, the type of visitor changed. Visits from royalty became fewer and the Duke of Wellington, once a common stroller at Vauxhall, now shunned the place. The place grew more seedy and, it was said, the very trees and shrubs looked worn out. Every year, Londoners were told, was going to be the last year of the gardens. But they lasted until the autumn of 1855 when the last paying visitors were ushered from the gates.

But Londoners did not lose out completely. Nearby Battersea Fields were bought by the government. They were landscaped and planted and opened to the public in 1858 to become one of London's most popular parks. In 1859 the public were allowed into

Vauxhall Gardens for the last time – for the auction of effects. Paintings, lamps, statues, fountains and furniture were all disposed of at knock-down prices. Buildings were soon built on the gardens. Times had changed and more demure, austere, outdoor pursuits were the order of day.

The last 'handling' in football 1863

Football, as an organized game, began in the English public schools in the early years of the 19th century. It was very quickly adopted by northern working-class clubs, most notably in the Sheffield and Nottingham areas. The rules of the game, played by different teams, varied widely but many allowed handling of the ball. Each club had its own set of rules; whenever different teams met an agreement had to be reached before kick-off on which rules were to be used. 'Handling' of the ball was last permitted in 1863.

The early rules of football, the so-called 'Cambridge Rules' of 1848, now seem not very different to those of rugby. In particular, handling the ball was permitted, usually to enable the player to make a free kick or to catch the ball and then either kick it immediately or make a 'mark', as in rugby. This was called the 'fair catch'. The player had to catch the ball cleanly and was not allowed to run with it or throw it, these distinctions being the main differences between football and rugby.

The rules, as they are known today, finally came together in the mid-1860s shortly after the formation of the Football Association in 1863. Initially the FA consisted of eleven clubs, mainly southern English amateur sides. The long awaited big clash between the Football Association and the northern clubs, the gentlemanly south and the working-class north, came on 31 March 1866 with a game between Sheffield and London. It was at this time that the fair catch was abolished and the handling of the ball by the players, apart from the goalkeeper, banned. Sheffield Football Club joined the Football Association a year later. The rules have changed gradually ever since. In 1870 the last important variation between different clubs was removed when it was universally agreed that the regular number of players per team would be eleven.

The last Dickens novel   1869

Charles Dickens, possibly Britain's greatest novelist, was a flamboyant man who loved public admiration. In 1869, with failing health, he began to write his last book, *The Mystery of Edwin Drood*. Although publication in monthly parts had already begun, the book was unfinished when Dickens died in June 1870.

For his huge breadth of social vision Dickens was unrivalled in the 19th century. Full of comedy, romance and adventure, his stories were taken to the nation's heart, and the world beyond Britain has come to appreciate his translated work. He was a campaigning writer; his stories always involved causes which the burgeoning middle classes wanted to know about. The public identified with his stories, and his books had a considerable influence on the social reforms of the time.

As well as being a superbly gifted writer he was an extremely able actor himself and he loved giving readings of his own work to large public audiences. The audiences loved him for it. His gruesomely realistic readings of Sykes murdering Nancy in *Oliver Twist* had the ladies swooning with fright. On tours throughout Britain and the USA his adherents flocked in their thousands, devotedly queuing for tickets to his performances. Financially these readings provided him with an important part of his income – his tour of America made him a clear profit of £20,000. But the punishing schedule of public reading did nothing to help his poor health.

Dickens began *The Mystery of Edwin Drood* in 1869 after a gap of four years after his previous novel. He received £7,500 for the copyright, with a half share of the profits. The story is one of murder and mystery, and has caused much discussion and controversy ever since it was published. Its unfinished nature adds to its own mystery; whether Drood is dead or alive remains unsolved as no plans for the completion were found.

Dickens gave his last reading in March 1870 in London just as the book's publication began in the usual monthly parts. Its sales exceeded those of all his other books. On 8 June he was busily writing, trying to add to the 23 chapters so far completed when he collapsed with a stroke. The following day he was dead. Opinions on *The Mystery of Edwin Drood* at the time were varied. Some thought it was 'a last laboured effort, the melancholy work of a worn out brain'. Others thought it his masterpiece. It was certainly the last of what is arguably the most famous list of fiction in the English language.

The last all amateur FA Cup Final

In football circles the Football Association Cup Final is the highlight of the season. The two best clubs meet to battle it out for the sport's most coveted prize, the FA Cup. The Football Association was formed in 1863, the teams and players on the whole being ex-public school and amateur. An annual competition for the FA Cup was established in 1871. As more and more northern, semi-professional working-class clubs joined the FA the drift to professionalism accelerated. As far as the top teams were concerned, the amateur player gradually disappeared and the last FA Cup Final with two wholly amateur teams was played in 1881.

The final took place at the Kennington Oval, in London, on 9 April. The Old Etonians played the Old Carthusians. Some 4,500 people watched the match which was won 3-0 by the Old Carthusians. Page, Wynard and Parry scored the goals. The Old Etonians again played in the final of 1882, against the professional Blackburn Rovers. They won 1-0 to become the last amateur team to win the FA Cup. Again in 1883 they appeared in the final, this time against Blackburn Olympic; they lost but had the further distinction of being the last amateur side to reach the final. The FA Cup Final was played at the Oval until 1892. It then was played at various sites, mainly Crystal Palace, until 1923 when it was moved to today's famous venue, Wembley.

The last formal bare-knuckle championship fight taking place in the USA in 1889 (opposite). John Sullivan took 75 rounds to beat Jack Kilrain. He won $10,000 and the title of world heavyweight bare-knuckle champion. (Bettman)

The last bare-knuckle prizefighting

1889

Prizefighting was a sport with its origins in the mists of time. In Britain it developed into a popular racy spectator sport, with heavy side betting, in the 18th century. By the Regency period it had achieved a certain respectability with patronage from the highest echelons of royalty downwards. Bare-knuckle fights were beginning to be considered dangerous by the 1870s and were gradually replaced by more formal fights, with padded gloves, under the Marquess of Queensberry's rules. The last recognized bare-knuckle fight in Britain was for the heavyweight championship in 1885. By 1889, the year of the last recognized international bare-knuckle contest ever, in Belgium, the days of rough prizefighting were over.

Regulations for conducting these bloody battles, which went on for as long as the contestants could stand up unaided, were stipulated in the so-called London Prize Ring Rules. By 1838 these were accepted in the USA and on the continent of Europe. The longest fight on record was in Cheshire, where a 276-round contest lasted a gruelling four and a half hours before the victor was decided. Short fights occurred too, one fight lasted for a mere seven seconds. By the time of the first recognized 'World Title' fight in 1860 (in England between local boy Tom Sayers and John C. Heenan of the USA), which was declared a draw after 37 rounds, the new rules were beginning to spread. In

1867 the sporting aristocrat, the Marquess of Queensberry, had devised a formal set of rules, initially for amateurs but soon adopted by professionals.

The main stipulation of the new rules was that the fighters would wear gloves, the count of ten was introduced for a knock down and behaviour in the ring was more rigorously controlled. For some years these rules were used as well as the London Prize Ring Rules; indeed many fighters fought under both rules at different times in different fights.

The authorities were beginning to clamp down on bare-knuckle fighting, however. In America it was quite common for the police to step in to stop a fight, if the referee refused to do so. Several fighters were prosecuted for assault. The last British bare-knuckle prizefight took place in London on 17 December 1885. Jem Smith beat Jack Davies to a bloody pulp to retain his heavyweight title. Smith later went on to fight and beat Frank Slavin at Bruges in Belgium in 1889 – in the very last internationally recognized glove-less prizefight ever staged.

The closing stages of the bare-knuckle world championship were, appropriately enough, fought out in the USA. Jem Smith of England had fought Jake Kilrain for the world championship in France in 1887. The result, after a brisk 106 rounds, was declared a draw as the light began to fade. In the States 'Boston Strong Boy', John L. Sullivan, was the recognized number one contender and, tempted by a $10,000 purse offered by the proprietor of the *Police Gazette*, agreed to fight Kilrain. Because Kilrain had already fought England's Jem Smith, admittedly resulting in a draw, the winner of the contest was to be declared the undisputed world champion.

The fight was held on 8 July 1889, at Richburg in Mississippi. It attracted great crowds. Spectators travelled from miles around by special trains. It lasted a mere two hours and sixteen minutes. Kilrain's seconds threw in the sponge after 75 rounds and John L. Sullivan was declared the winner and world heavyweight bare-knuckle champion.

Sullivan went on to make many appearances at demonstration fights all over the USA. When the more organized boxing matches began, Sullivan was defeated in the very first championship fight on 7 September 1892 by 'Gentleman' Jim Corbett who became the first undisputed champion of the world.

◁ 1889 ▷ *The last of the crinoline and the bustle*

Ladies' fashions of the 19th century were epitomized by the awesome sight of the huge bell-shape of the crinoline dress. The skirts, laid over several layers of petticoats supported by a cage, came right down to the ground, covering even the lady's footwear. The crinoline was later replaced by the bustle, a strategically positioned bulge at the rear of the waist. These extraordinary devices finally disappeared from the fashionable scene in 1889.

From Queen Victoria downwards, all ladies of means wore hugely supported dresses, almost completely concealing their figures. A stranger to the scene might have wondered whether these Victorian ladies had any legs at all. A framework of hoops underneath the dresses was the secret. Originally they were made of horsehair and linen but was soon replaced by whalebone or steel. The style was first dome-shaped and then in the 1860s became more pyramidal. In this period, when crinoline dresses were at their largest, it would have been difficult to find anything less practical for women to wear for everyday use. But wear them they did, and today they remind us that blind devotion to the heights of fashion is nothing new. Some of the particular varieties of crinoline shapes had peculiar names such as 'cage américaine', 'ondina' and 'sansflectum'.

Gradually some kind of practical sense began to prevail in the late 1860s: the front of the crinoline dress became flatter, the rear pushed out even more. The rearwards movement of the crinoline over several years resulted in the recall of the bustle, a cage attached to the back of the petticoat to push out the dress. This modified crinoline was referred to as a crinolette. Later the bustle proper, a separate wad of padding tied around the waist with tapes, held the dress out to the required shape. Sometimes the skirt at the back was made to stand out at a right angle, forming a small platform. The last year when the bustle itself could be worn fashionably was 1889. A more practical approach began to creep into ladies' fashions as women – even wealthy women – needed to move about a lot more, to do more things. Slimmer, sleeker dresses – displaying the figure more fully – were the rage by the end of the century.

The last Gilbert and Sullivan operetta $\diamondsuit$ 1896 $\diamondsuit$

In the late 19th century Gilbert and Sullivan created a successful partnership that produced a glittering list of comic operettas. The productions that they wrote together, William Gilbert the librettist, Arthur Sullivan the composer, have become classics. Most of them were originally staged by the impresario Richard D'Oyly Carte and were the talk of the town in the 1870s and 1880s. They have enjoyed considerable worldwide success ever since with stage productions by amateurs and professionals. After a stormy relationship, worthy of a melodrama set to music in its own right, the last operetta that Gilbert and Sullivan wrote together was *The Grand Duke*, staged at the Savoy Theatre in 1896.

Near the beginning of their exceptionally successful partnership Gilbert had declared, with typical Victorian aplomb, that 'Sullivan and I intend to produce comic operas to which any man may bring his mother and his aunts.' After a long collaboration stretching from their first success, *Trial by Jury* in 1875, to *The Yeomen of the Guard* in 1889, they fell out bitterly during the writing of *The Gondoliers*. Sullivan had tired of the light operatic touch and was looking for fresh musical fields in which to graze. Gilbert was quite happy to continue as before. Eventually they quarrelled over expenses, most ignobly over £500 spent on carpets at the new Savoy Theatre.

After a long and, it now seems, extremely childish argument, conducted mainly by letter, the two were reconciled in 1893 to write *Utopia Limited*. At the first performance they shook hands publicly to great applause. The opera itself was not a success and the two friends drifted apart again. Finally in 1895 Gilbert came to Sullivan with his outline plot for the last of their joint operas, *The Grand Duke*.

Sullivan, by now Sir Arthur Sullivan, agreed to write the score and *The Grand Duke*, or *The Statutory Duel*, opened at the Savoy the following year in March 1896 to very mixed reviews. It suffered greatly in comparison with their earlier production *The Mikado* which, after a very successful revival at the same theatre, had closed three days earlier. Everyone knew then that it was to be their last joint production. Although some thought it magnificent ('It may claim to stand in the front row of Comic Operas') others thought differently. One critic summed up the production and the partnership when he said, 'The last curtain had fallen on the greatest collaboration in the history of the modern stage.' *The Grand Duke* closed after 123 performances. Although it has not been performed on the London stage since, Gilbert and Sullivan's temperamental partnership is still unsurpassed, their legacy of operettas very much revered. Sullivan died in 1900, Gilbert in 1911.

 ## The last Olympic Live Pigeon Shooting

The weirdest event of all Olympic events must have been the Live Pigeon Shooting. This was held for the only time in 1900 in Paris. Leon de Lunden from Belgium sneaked the gold, killing 21 birds in the process. Frenchman Maurice Faure could only manage to down 20 birds and took the silver. Two Americans, Donald Mackintosh and Crittenden Robinson, tied for third place with 18 plump pigeons each. The event was not repeated.

 ## The last Olympic Standing Jumps

In addition to the more familiar jumping with running starts in high, long and triple jumps there were standing jump versions as well. The star of these events during the early games was Ray Ewry of the USA. He won the gold in all three standing jump events in 1900 in Paris and also in 1904 in St Louis. After the 1904 Olympics the standing triple jump was abandoned so in the 1908 London Games he had only the two events to attempt – he achieved the gold double.

The 1912 the Stockholm Games were the last to have the standing high jump and standing long jump. In the high jump Platt Evans from the USA came first with a jump of 1.63 metres (5 feet 4¼ inches). His brother Ben was second and Constantin Tsiklitiras from Greece came third. In the long jump, Tsiklitiras won the gold with a jump of 3.37 metres (11 feet ¾ inches), the Evans brothers the silver and bronze. These three jumpers together claimed the last ever Olympic standing jump medals.

 ## The last Olympic Men's Cross Country event

The Men's Cross Country event was last run in 1924 at the Paris Games. The course was so ill-prepared and the event run on such a hot day that most of the competitors succumbed to severe heat exhaustion before the race finished. In some parts the track was so overgrown with thistles that it was almost impassable. Those runners that survived the high temperatures and the thorns had to submit to noxious fumes from a nearby chemical factory. The hero of the race and the eventual winner was Paavo Nurmi of Finland. Hours after the race was declared finished Olympic officials, aided by the Red Cross, were still searching the course for missing runners. It was decided that this Olympic cross country race was to be the last.

Some more Olympic Lasts

	Last competed	Venue		Last competed	Venue
Equestrian Jumping (high jump and long jump)	1900	Paris	Men's Golf	1904	St Louis, USA
Swimming Obstacle Race	1900	Paris	Lacrosse	1908	London
Underwater Swimming	1900	Paris	Rackets	1908	London
Rope Climbing	1932	Los Angeles	Polo	1936	Berlin
Club Swinging	1932	Los Angeles	Rugby	1924	Paris
Cricket	1900	Paris	Tug-of-war	1920	Antwerp
Individual Croquet.	1900	Paris	Motor Boat Racing	1908	London
Women's Golf	1900	Paris			

The last of the experimental television   ⟨1937⟩

The invention of television is quite correctly ascribed to the Scottish electrical engineer John Logie Baird. Living at Hastings in England in the 1920s he devised a mechanical system capable of producing pictures for radio transmission. It was, very definitely, a low-definition system, producing a 30-line picture. However, using this system the BBC transmitted a daily service to the public, whereby sight and sound alternated every 2 minutes. This service lasted only a few months, it was last broadcast on 29 March 1930. A second transmitter was then installed so that full sight and sound could be broadcast simultaneously. This service, still 30-line low-definition, was an expensive luxury, receiver sets cost 25 guineas each. It ran for several years until its last transmission on 11 September 1935.

Big technical improvements were on the way. Baird now had an improved television; the picture definition had been increased to 240 lines, scanning at 25 pictures per second. But real competition had arrived. A new electronic television system had been devised by the Marconi-EMI company under the technical leadership of Isaac Schoenberg. It used electronic means rather than mechanical, it had 405 lines, scanning at 50 pictures per second, in alternate directions, to avoid flicker. The Marconi-EMI system was vastly superior to Baird's but the BBC agreed to give both systems a fair deal.

A trial period of both high-definition television systems now started, on 2 November 1936. The transmitter at Alexandra Palace in north London had an official range of 25 miles but 'viewers' were able to receive their flickering, foggy pictures as far away as Ipswich in Suffolk.

The trial consisted of each system being broadcast at different times. A week of Baird's 240 lines would be followed by a week of Marconi-EMI's 405 lines. It was no contest. On Saturday evening, 13 February 1937, 'viewers' were treated to 'A half hour of Variety' on their 240-line Baird television receivers, and then, no more. It was the last public broadcast of the Baird mechanical system. The Marconi-EMI television was declared superior and adopted for general use.

1939 The last of the pre-war television

The BBC's high-definition pre-war TV service lasted less than three years. On 1 September 1939, with war about to engulf Europe, the BBC pulled the plugs in mid-broadcast without explanation. A Mickey Mouse cartoon was on air, he was mimicking Greta Garbo and was cut off in mid-sentence. A new service was started in 1946, after the war. Those viewers who had survived, with their television sets, were treated to the missing half of their Mickey Mouse film.

1969 The last Le Mans sprint start

The Le Mans 24-hour road race for high performance sports cars is one of the most famous motor races in the world. The *Le Mans Grand Prix d'Endurance*, to give its full name, was first run in 1923 on a circuit around the roads near the French village of Le Mans. The race lasted 24 hours and the format became a favourite with motor racing enthusiasts. Apart from the duration of the race, which requires more than one driver for each car, swapping over at regular pit stops, the Le Mans race was famous for its start. The cars were lined up, in echelon, on one side of the track, the drivers were lined up on the other. At the starting signal, a dropped flag, the drivers ran across the road, scrambled into their cars, started their engines and roared off down the track. It was a spectacular if dangerous way to begin the most competitive 24-hour endurance race in the world.

As cars became faster over the years, safety became an increasingly important consideration. One of the new safety measures was to abandon the running start, too many drivers were ignoring basic safety rules to save a few seconds and heading off into the race with their safety harnesses unfastened. The last Le Mans race to start in the traditional manner was in 1969. The start of the race had been brought forward two hours from the normal 4 pm, so that the French motor sport enthusiasts could return home early enough the following day to vote in the final round of the presidential elections.

So at 2 pm on 14 June 1969, the 45 drivers in the Le Mans race dashed across the track for the last time. The sensible drivers took those extra seconds to fasten their safety harnesses before heading out into the traffic stream. It was an eventful race. John Woolfe, driving a Porsche, was killed in a crash on the first lap. The remaining Porsches, led by two of the big 4½-litre, 12-cylinder, type 917 cars soon dominated the race.

By the following morning, however, things had changed, and at 11 am the leading Porsches dropped out leaving the Ford GT 40 driven by the Belgian Jacky Ickx (co-driver Jacky Oliver) in the lead. But close behind was a Porsche 908 which soon overtook the Ford. In a thrilling last lap Ickx regained the lead and raced across the line the winner.

Ickx went on to win the Le Mans race a record six times to add to his eight Formula One Grands Prix victories. The Ford GT 40 became a motor racing legend and the French crowds left Le Mans that day returning home to vote for Georges Pompidou to be their leader to replace the ageing Charles De Gaulle.

Quickly off their marks, the drivers in the 1969 Le Mans 24-hour road race dash across the tracks to their cars. It was the last Le Mans race to be started this way as the following year drivers were seated and firmly strapped in before the starting signal. (Hulton)

The last 15 rounds in professional boxing

During the days of bare-knuckle boxing, the duration of the fights was unlimited. They lasted for as long as both of the contestants could stand up. Despite the bare fists, this meant that many fights lasted for several hours, with many, many rounds. With the acceptance of the Marquess of Queensberry rules, the number of rounds was restricted, usually to 15. This was the normal number of rounds until well into the second half of the 20th century. As safety came to be accepted as a prime consideration, the number of rounds was usually reduced, by agreement before the match, to 12.

The last official professional world championship to be scheduled to last for 15 rounds was that for the Strawweight title, under the International Boxing Federation's control, in 1988. Strawweight is the lightest of professional boxing's seventeen different weight divisions, for boxers weighing under 48 kg, 105 pounds. This last 15-rounder was fought in Bangkok on 29 August 1988 between Mahasamuth Sithnaruepol of Thailand and the South Korean Inkyu Hwang. The fight went the full distance and the 29-year-old Thai, Sithnaruepol, won on points. No professional world championship fight since has lasted for more than 12 rounds.

INDEX

The page numbers in italics
indicate illustrations.

Acland, Sir Richard 133
Admiralty 137, 138
Air Ministry 137, 138
aircraft carrier 83
airships 114
Albania 74
Albert Edward, Prince of Wales
  168
Albert Victor, Duke of Clarence
  170, *171*
Albert, Prince 18, 168
Aldrin, Edwin 'Buzz' 97
Ali Maow Maalin 98
Allen, Peter Anthony 55
almanacs tax 5
Anjou, House of 173
Anne, Queen 118, 160, 173
Apollo 97
Apollo-Soyuz 97
Arabian ostrich, 'na-ama' 104
Ark Royal 83
Armstrong, C. W. 135
Armstrong, Neil 96
Ashford, William 142
Asia (flagship) 76
Asquith, Herbert 130, 138
aurochs, *Bos primigenius* 99
Austen, John 34
Australia 35, 44, 45, 99
Automaton 106, 108

Baird, John Logie 187
Baker, Peter 135
Balaclava 87
Baldwin, Stanley 172
Balfour, Arthur 129
Ballot Act 127
baron 147, 150
baronetcy 150, 151
Barrett, Michael 45
Barthélemy 143
Bayezit 63
Bazalgette 17
BBC 187
bear-baiting 177
Beattie, Rev William 139
Beethoven 176
beheading 36
Bellingham, John 35
Belyayev, Pavel 97
Benn, Tony 137
Berlin Wall 73, *73*
Berry, James 49
Big Foot, Chief 90
birch 56
Birmingham 13, 121
Birmingham and Liverpool
  Junction Canal 106
Black Death 100
Blackburn Olympic 182
Blackburn Rovers 182
Blakely, David 54
block *33*
Blois, House of 173
body snatchers 38
Boots 21
Bosworth, Battle of 154, *154*

Botany Bay 44
Boulsover, Thomas 13
Bow Street Runners 36, 40
Boyd-Orr, John 134
Brand, Vance 97
Bright, John 12, 15, 126
British Empire Medal 152
broad gauge 109, *110*
Brougham, Lord Henry *164*, 165
Brunel, Isambard Kingdom 109
Brunskill, William 34
Burke, William *38*, 39
bustle 184
Bykovsky, Valeri 97
Byzantium 59

Cadmus 82
Calcraft, William 47
Calendar New Style Act 71
canals 106
Cardigan, Lord 87, 88
Cardwell 48, 88
Carmichael, J. 133
Caroline, Queen 163, *164*
Carr, Gerald 97
Carron, Owen 141
castle siege 84
cat-o'-nine-tails 48
Catholics, discrimination against
  120
Catholic emancipation 4
Catholic king 158
cavalry charge 87, 91
Cerdic, House of 173
Cernan, Eugene 96, *96*
Challenger 96
Channel Islands 71
Charles Edward, Bonnie Prince
  Charlie 85, 86, 162
Charles I 25, 157
Charles II 25, 85, 157, 158
Chief Secretary for Ireland 137
Children's Employment Act 17
Children's Newspaper, The 23
Chillianwallah 70
chimney sweep boys 16
Churchill, Winston 72, 91, 129,
  134, 145
cigarette commercials 21
Clarkson, Thomas 6
Clean Air Act 105
Clement V 63
Clerk, Jane 32
climbing boys *16*
Cobbett, J. M. 127
Cobbold, Lord 148
Cobden, Richard 12, 15
cockfighting 179, *179*
Codrington, Edward 76, 78
Colchester 84
Cold War 54, 57, 73
Collier, George 76
Colonial Office 137
Common Wealth Party 133
Commonwealth Affairs 137
Constantine I, Emperor 59
Constantine XI, Emperor 59, 64
Constantinople 59, 61, 64, *64*
Cook, James 40
Cooper, Gordon 97

Corbett, 'Gentleman' Jim 184
Corn Laws 11, 126
corporal punishment 56
Coryell, C. D. 96
Costello, John 72
Cotton, H. E. A. 129
Cournet 143
Court of Chivalry 146
Court of Exchequer 125
Crimean War 87, 88
crinoline 184
crown coin 29
crusade 62
Crusader battle 63
Crystal Palace 13, 18, 182
Culloden 32, 86, *86*, 162
Cumberland, Ernest Augustus,
  Duke of 169
Cumberland, William, Duke of
  85, 160
Custer, General George
  Armstrong 89
Cutterman, George 37

D'Oyly Carte 185
D-day, decimalization day 28, *29*
Daily Chronicle 23
Daily Herald 23
Daily Mail 23
Daily News 23
Daily Sketch 23
Daily Telegraph 15, 23
Dallinger 81
Dance, Charles 107
Davies, Jack 184
de Lunden, Leon 186
de Molay, Jacques 63
de Valera, Éamon 72
death sentence 57
débutante 147
Denmark, House of 173
Derby, Lord 126
Dettingen, Battle of 160
Dickens, Charles 35, 181
Diocletian, Emperor 61
Disraeli, Benjamin 12, 125, 173
dodo 101
dodo tree, *Calvaria major* 101
Douglas-Home, Sir Alec 129
Downshire, Marquess of 119,
  120
Duchy of Lancaster 169
ducking stool 34
duel 143, *143*
Duff, Marquess of 145
duke 144, 150
Dymoke, Henry 166

Earl Marshall 142, 146
earl 150
East India Company 15, 70
Edgar Atheling 153
Edward I 154
Edward II 154
Edward IV 155
Edward VI 156
Edward VII 168
Edward VIII 172
Edward 'the Confessor' 153,
  160, 173

Edwards, Susannah 32
Egham 144
Eglinton 178
Eglinton, Archibald Montgomerie,
  Earl of 178
election deposit 141
Elizabeth I 65, 156, 157, 173
Elizabeth II 78
Elliot, Walter 134
Ellis, Ruth 54
elm trees 105
Emperor of India 173
Erik 'Blood-axe' 153
Eugenius 60
European Court of Human
  Rights 57
Evans, Ben 186
Evans, Gwynne Owen 55
Evans, Platt 186
Evans, Ronald 96
Evening News 23
Evening Standard 23
Evening Star 117
Ewart, William 40, 46
Ewry, Ray 186
Examiner, The 14
execution 55

FA Cup Final 182
farthing 28, 30
Faulkner, Brian 139
Fawcett, Colonel 144
Ferrers, Lord 32
Feversham, Lord 85
Fielding, Henry 40
Fife, Duke of 145
Finlay, Sir Graeme 151
'fir' frigates 75
First Division (in prison) 54
First Lord of the Treasury 129
FitzAlan, Lord 137
Fitzgerald, Vesey 121
Flodden, Battle of 155
flogging 47
florin 27, 28, 30
football 181
footpads 40
Ford GT 189
Ford, Gerald 127
Foreign Office 119
Forsyth, James 90
Fox, Charles James 4, 119
Francis I, of Austria 66
Fraser, H. 137
Frederick Louis, Prince of Wales
  161
Fremantle 45

gallows 58
Gemini 97
George Cross 149
George I 169
George II 160
George III 162
George IV 162, 166
George V 138, 173
George V, of Hanover 169
George VI 173
gibbeting 39
Gibson, Edward 97

Gilbert, William 185
ginger beer 7
Gladstone, William 10, 12, 15, 51, 88, 126, 134
Glasgow 117
Glendenin, L. E. 96
'Glorious Revolution' 159, 161
Goddard, Lord 146
Godwin, House of 173
Gorbachev, Mikhail 74
Gough, Hugh 69
Gow, Sir Michael 93
Gowlatt 40
Graf Zeppelin 115
Graham, A. J. 133
Granada 66
Great Central Railway 113
Great Exhibition 13, 18
Great Reform Bill 123
Great Western Railway 109
great auk, *Alca impennis* 102
Greece 71, 174
Greenwood, H. 137
Gregorian calendar 71
Grenville, Lord 4
Grey, Lord 123, 124, 139
groat 30
grog 83
Guardian, The 23, *24*
Guernsey 72
guinea 26
Gujarat 69
Gurney, Sir Goldworth 107
Guy, King of Jerusalem 63

Hair 149
half-crown 27, 28
halfpenny 28, 30
Halley's Comet 98
Hampshire, Susan *147*
Hancock, Walter 108
Hanover, House of 173
Hanseatic League 66
Hardicanute 173
Hardie, Keir 133
Hare, William 38, 39
Harold II 153, 173
Harris, L. 92
Hattin, Horns of 63
Hawaii 73
Heavy Brigade 87
Heenan, John C. 183
Henry I 153, 173
Henry II of Cyprus, King of Jerusalem 63
Henry III 169
Henry IV 154, 169
Henry IX 162
Henry VI 173
Henry VII 154, 155
Henry VIII 142, 155, 156
Henry Stuart, 'IX', Duke of York 160, 161, *162*
Henry, Prince of Wales 157
hereditary knight 151
hereditary lord 150
Hess, Rudolf 52, *53*
Hetherington 14
Hibbert 46
High Constable, Lord 142
highwayman 37
Hillsborough, Earl of 119
Hindenburg 115
Hobart 104
Holy Roman Emperor 66
Holyroodhouse 147
Homan, Cornelius 136

Hong Kong Auxiliary Air Force 93
Honorius, Emperor 59, 61
Hospitallers, Knights 63
House of Commons 4, 35, 125, 128, 135, 141
House of Lords 4, 15, 52, 89, 128, 150, 152, 164, *164*
House of Representatives 127
Hoxha, Enver 74
Huj 91
hulks (prison) 42, *42*

Ibrahim Pasha 76
Ickx, Jacky 189
impeachment 127
Impress Service 80
income tax 10
Independent Labour Party 133
Independent Servicemen' candidates 136
independent Members of Parliament 140
India 16, 69
Indian Mutiny 15, 70
Inkyu Hwang 189
inland waterways 106
Ireland 8, 72
Irish Office 137
Irish Parliament 119
Irish tithes 7
Isle of Man 56, 57

Jack the Ripper 49
James I of England and VI of Scotland 156, 161
James II 85, 158, *159*
James III, the 'Old Pretender' 162
James IV, of Scotland 155
James V, of Scotland 155
Jeffreys, Judge 85
Jellicoe, Earl 137
Jenner, Edward 98
Jersey 72, 87
Jews 124
Johnson, Andrew 126
Johnson, Lyndon 137
Jones, Morgan 10
Jones, Thomas Isaac Mardy 131
Jordan, Dorothea 167
Jovian, Emperor 60
Joyce, William 54
Julian calendar 70
Julian, Emperor 59
Julius Caesar 61, 70

Kelly, Marie Jeanette 50
Kennedy, John F. 96, 136
Ketch, Jack 31, 47, 85
Kilrain, Jake *182,* 184
King's Evil 159
king's champion 165
Kubasov, Valeri 97

Lamont, Norman 141
Lancaster, Avro 94
Lancaster, House of 173
larboard 78
Lawson, Harry 113
Le Havre 11
Le Mans 188, *189*
Leach, Charles 136
Leander 75
Lee, F. 137
Lee, John 48
Leech 19

Leeke, Sarah 34
Leominster 34
Leonov, Alexei 97
Lewis, Thomas 131
Liberal Party 12, 130, 138
Liberals 125, 130
libraries, private 21
Life peerages 150
Light Brigade 87
lighthouse 8
Lijwiji Trucannini, Queen 102
Listowel, Earl of 137
Little Big Horn, Battle of 89
Liverpool 4, 10, 55, 117, 165
Liverpool, Earl of 36, 165
Lloyd George, David 130
Lloyd, Mary 32
Llywelyn ap Gruffydd 154
London 4, 17, 18, 105, 116, 153
London Philharmonic Society 176
London Star 23
Long Kesh Prison 55, *56*
Lord Chamberlain 148
Lord High Admiral 78
Lord High Chamberlain 166
Lord Lieutenant of Ireland 137
Louis XII, of France 155
Louis, 'the Pious' 62
Louise, Princess 144
Lovat, Simon Fraser, Lord 32
Lovell, Jim 97
Lucan, Lord 87

MacDonald, Ramsay 131, 133, 134
McKay, Ian 149
Mackintosh, Donald 186
Macmillan, Harold 129, 151
Macrae, Fiona 147
MacRobert, Alexander Munro 130
Maguire, Frank 140
Mahasamuth Sithnaruepol 189
mail coaches 21
Malcolm III, of Scotland 153
Mallalieu, J. 137
mammoth 99, *100*
Manchester 24, 55, 116, 146
Manchester Guardian, The 15, 23, 24
mantraps 37
Marconi-EMI 187
Margadale, Lord 147
Margaret, Countess of Salisbury 156
Marinsky, J. A. 96
marquess 146, 150
Martello tower 86
Mary II 159, 161, 173
Mary Queen of Scots 156
Mary I, Queen 65
Marylebone Station 113
Matilda, (Empress Maud) 173
Maundy money 30, 158
Maxentius 59
Maxim, Sir Hiram 111
Maximian, Emperor 61
Maximus 60
Maxton, James 133
Mehmed, Sultan 64
Melbourne, Lord 8, 124, 125
Mercury 97
Metropolitan Board of Works 17
Metropolitan Police 40
Mikhail Alexandrovich, Grand Duke 172

'Military' guinea 26
Millington, E. R. 133
Milne, Eddie 140
Minister of Post and Telecommunications 137
Monmouth, Duke of 31, 85
Moon 96
Moors 65
Morning Chronicle 23
Morning Herald 23
Morning Post 23
Morrison, Hugh 129
Morse, Samuel 79
Mudie, Charles 21
Muhammad Abu-Abdullah 66
Munroe, Alexander 144
Munroe, J. M. 131, 144

Nairac, Robert 149
Napier, Sir Charles 70
Napoleon 66, 87
National Liberals 138
Navarino, Battle of 76, *77*
New Evening Standard 23
New Orleans, Battle of 67, *67*
New South Wales 44
new penny 29
Newgate 37, 45
News Chronicle 23
newspaper tax 14
Nicholas II, Tsar 172, *172*
Nixon, Richard M. 127, *127*
Norfolk, Duke of 146
Normandy, House of 173
North, Lord 119
Northern Department 119
Northern Ireland 55, 72, 132, 134, 138
Northern Ireland Parliament 138, 139
Nott, John 138
Nurmi, Paavo 187

O'Connell, Daniel 8, 120
O'Neill, Terence 139
Old Bailey 47, 52, 57
Old Carthusians 182
Old Etonians 182
Oliver, Jacky 189
Olympic Games 71, 174
Orange, House of 173
Oregon 68
Orkney and Shetland 102, 132
Osborn, Ruth 32
Outer Hebrides 21
Owain Glyndwr 154

Pakenham, Edward 67
Palmerston, Henry 43, 45, 126, 134
Parker, Janet 98
passenger pigeon, *Ectopistes migatorius* 103
'pea-souper' 105
pedilavium 158
Peel, Sir Robert 10, 12, 37, 40, 121, 124, 126, 134
Peelites 12, 126
penal colonies 35
penny 28
penny post 12, 18
Perceval, Spencer 35, *35,* 136
Philip IV, 'the Fair' 63
pigeon shooting 186
pillbox 92
pillory 44
Pipes, Jenny 34

Pitt, William, 'the younger' 10, 134
Pius II, Pope 62
Plantagenets 155
Pluto 95
Pogue, William 97
political prisoners 55
Polk, James 69
Pontefract Castle 84
Poor Man's Guardian, The 14
Post Office 18, 22
post boys 21
Postmaster General 137
Prempeh, King 91
press gang 80
Prince of Wales 154
Prince Regent 36, 163
prizefighting, bare-knuckle 183, 183
Promethium 95
proportional representation 132
Prowse, George 145
public ballot 127
public hanging 45
public hangman 47
purchase of commissions 88

quagga, Equus quagga 102
Queen's Own Mercian Yeomanry 92

R 101 115
radio licences 22
Ramsden, J. 137
rationing 19, 20
Red Flag Act 112
redcoats 90
Rees, Merlyn 56
regency 162
rendezvous 11
Reynolds Weekly Newspaper 23
Reynolds, G. 137
Richard II 173
Richard III 142, 154, 154, 155, 173
Robinson, Crittenden 186
Rockingham, Marquess of 119
Romulus Augustulus, Emperor 59, 62
Roosevelt, Franklin D. 131, 131
Ross, Eliza 39
rotten boroughs 121
Royal Assent 118
Royal coat-of-arms 167
Royal Mail 109
Royal Menagerie 176
Royal Mint 25, 28
Royal Naval Division 145
Royal Victorian Order 150
royal trial 163
royal veto 118
Russell, John Francis Stanley, Earl 52
Russell, Lord John 122, 123, 125, 126
Rutlandshire 43

Salisbury, Robert Cecil, Marquess of 128, 128
Samuel, Sir Herbert 130
Sands, Bobby 141
Saturn 97
Saxe-Coburg and Gotha, House of 173
Sayers, Tom 183
Scarlett, James 87

Schmitt, Harrison 96
Schoenberg, Isaac 187
Schwägel, Anna Maria 32
Scottish Parliament 118
Scottish Universities 132, 134
scrofula 159
Secretary of State for Commonwealth Relations 137
Secretary of State for India and Burma 137
Secretary of State for War 137
Secretary of State 118
Sedgemoor, Battle of 31, 85
semaphore 79
Shackleton, Lord 137
Shaftesbury, Lord 17
Sheffield Plate 13
Shelburne, Lord 119
shilling 27, 28
Shore, Peter 137
Sidmouth, Lord 36
Sigismund, King of Hungary 63
Sikh War 69
silver threepenny piece 27
Simpson, Wallis 172
single-tier post 22
Sitting Bull, Chief 89, 89, 90
sixpenny piece 28
Skerries Lighthouse 8, 9
Skylab 97
slaves 4, 6, 6
Slavin, Frank 184
Slayton, Donald 'Deke' 97
Slovik, Private 93
smallpox 97
Smith, Jem 184
Smith, Michael 184
Sophia, Electress of Hanover 169
South Africa 7, 102
South America 115
South Antrim 139
Southern Department 119
sovereign 26
Soviet Union 57, 74
Special Powers Act 55
Spencer, H. 129
spies 57
Spitfire, Supermarine 93
spring budget 141
square riggers 114
Stafford, Thomas 97
stage coaches 108
Standard, The 23
standing jumps 186
Stanley, E. L. 127
Stanley, Lord 12
Stanton, Edwin 127
steam omnibuses 107
steam trains 117
steam underground 116
Stephen, King 173
Stephens, Edward 114
Stephenson, George 108
Stewart, Michael 137
stocks 44
stone bottle tax 7
Stonehouse, John 135, 135, 137
Stormont 119, 139
Straits Settlements 16
Stuart, House of 161, 173
Sullivan, John L. 182, 184
Sullivan, Sir Arthur 185
Sun, The 23
Sunday Citizen 23
Sunday Dispatch 23

Sunday Graphic 23
Sunday Herald 23

Tasmanian Aborigines 102
Tasmanian wolf, (thylacine) 103, 104
Taverne, Dick 140
taxes on knowledge 14
Teare, Tony 57
television 187
Telford, Thomas 106, 108
Templars, Knights 63
Tenure of Office Act 127
Test and Corporation Acts 120
Thames, River 17, 42, 175, 175
Thames steamboat 116
Thatcher, Margaret 151
Thatcher, Sir Denis 151, 152
The Times 14
Theodosius I, 'the Great', Emperor 59, 60, 61, 61, 174
Theodosius II, Emperor 174
Thistlewood, Arthur 36
Thompson, G. 137
Thompson, M. 136
Thornton, Abraham 141
threepenny bit 27, 28
Tiberius, Emperor 174
tithe wars 8
Tombaugh, Clyde 95
tournament 178
Tower Mint 25
Tower of London 25, 32, 52, 176
Trafalgar, Battle of 87
traitor 54
tram 116
transportation 35, 37, 44
treadwheel 50, 51
treaty ports 72
Trevithick, Richard 107
Trial by Battle 142
Trinity House 8, 9
Tsar 172
Tsiklitiras, Constantin 186
Tudor, House of 173
Turnpike Trusts 107, 112
two-shilling piece 28, 30
Tyburn 33, 34

Union, Act of 118, 119
university Members of Parliament 134
US Army 89
US President 131
USA 4, 11, 44, 67, 68, 73, 76, 79, 93, 115, 132

Valentinian, Emperor 60
Vauxhall Gardens 180
Vernon, Edward 83
Victoria 81, 82
Victoria Cross 145, 149
Victoria, Queen 18, 82, 90, 124, 163, 173
viscount 150
Vortigern 61
Voskhod 97
Vostok 97
Voyager 95
Vulcan, Avro 94, 94

W. H. Smith 21
Walton, David 94
Wandsworth Prison 58
War Office 137, 138

Warren, Sir Charles 50
Warrior 81
Warwick, Ambrose Dudley, Earl of 65
Warwick, Edward, Earl of 155
Warwickshire Yeomanry 91
Watergate scandal 127
Waterwitch 114
Watkin, Sir Edward 113
Weekly Dispatch 23
Weidman, Eugene 46
Wellington, Duke of 70, 88, 120, 122, 124, 125, 128, 144, 166
Wembley 182
Wenham, Jane 32
West Yorkshire Regiment 91
Westminster 35, 119, 153
Westminster Abbey 153, 158, 166
Westminster Hall 142, 166
Wheatstone, Sir Charles 79
Whigs 124, 125
Whitaker's Almanac 5
Wilberforce, William 4, 6, 41
William I, 'the Conqueror' 65, 153
William III 158, 159, 161, 173
William IV 78, 123, 124, 163, 166, 167, 169
Williams, Shirley 152
Willingdon, Marquess of 146
Wilson, Harold 139, 140
window tax 12
Windsor, House of 173
witches 31
wooden walls 75, 81
Worcestershire Yeomanry Cavalry 91
Wounded Knee, Battle of 90
Wrangel Island 99
wreckers 41

Yalta Conference 132
yard arm 81
York 34, 37, 153
York, House of 173
Yorkshire Post 15

Zanzibar 5
zeppelin 115
Zeppelin, Count von 115

PICTURE ACKNOWLEDGEMENTS
The publishers would like to thank the following for permission to reproduce the pictures in this book, which are individually credited by the abbreviations listed below:
Ann Ronan Picture Library (AR); Archiv für Kunst and Geschichte (AKG); Bridgeman Art Library (BAL); The Bettman Archive (Bettman); British Library; Gamma; Hulton-Deutsch Collection Limited (Hulton); Image Select (IS); Mary Evans (ME); Popperfoto; Rex Features (Rex); Science Photo Library (SPL); Topham Picture Source (Topham).